Far From Perfect

Insights into Living with Anxiety and Panic Disorders

By: Kristina Horton
With Foreword by: Jeanette Revay, Psychiatric ARNP

Copyright © 2021 Kristina Horton.

All rights reserved. No part of this publication may be reproduced, distributed, or transmitted in any form or by any means, including photocopying, recording, or other electronic or mechanical methods, without the prior written permission of the publisher, except in the case of brief quotations embodied in critical reviews and certain other noncommercial uses permitted by copyright law.

ISBN: 978-1-7360488-0-1 (Paperback)

Cover Design by Karen Baltimore

Printed in the United States of America.

First printing edition 2021.

Kristina Horton
PO Box 1123
Rochester, WA 98579
kristinahortonauthor@gmail.com

www.KristinaHorton.com

Dedicated to Ty.

*If I knew then what I know now,
you might still be with us.*

*This book is written so that no one else
suffering with anxiety feels alone.*

---

*And the light shines in the darkness,
And the darkness did not comprehend it.
John 1:5 (NKJV)*

DISCLAIMER

This book does not purport to cure you of an anxiety or panic disorder. Instead, it offers clear, first-hand knowledgeable experience and points of view on living with these disorders. This book is helpful to the person that struggles with such disorders and to the person who wants to better understand those that do.

TABLE OF CONTENTS

Foreword by Jeanette Revay, Psychiatric ARNP vi
Acknowledgements ix
Introduction 2
Prologue: Anxiety and Panic 4

PART I – MY STORY 13

Chapter One: And so, it begins (Childhood) 15
Chapter Two: Unsure (Teen Years) 28
Chapter Three: Confusion (Ages 18-28) 34
Chapter Four: Avoidance (Ages 28-37) 57
Chapter Five: Zenith (Ages 38-43) 118
Chapter Six: Reconstruction (Ages 44-50) 160
Chapter Seven: Conclusion 201

PART II – THE TOOLBOX 213

Chapter Eight: Am I broken? 214
Chapter Nine: Why am I this way? 219
Chapter Ten: Don't tell me to RELAX! 224
Chapter Eleven: Down the rabbit hole 232
Chapter Twelve: Practicing self-care 246
Chapter Thirteen: I love me 252
Chapter Fourteen: Recognizing Anxiety 261
Chapter Fifteen: The Positive Aspects 266
Helpful Scriptures 269

FOREWORD

The fact that you picked up this book and are reading this page suggests that you have, or currently are, experiencing anxiety. Maybe you suspect it is anxiety yet seek information to diagnose and put a name to your experience. I'm glad you're here. This book walks through Kristina's journey as she came first to recognize and understand what she felt made her "weird" and different from everyone around her. Once Kristina gave a name to her affliction, she found ways to conquer and deal with it. Maybe this is the first time you have sought help, or maybe you've tried numerous ways to get relief.

Anxiety is painful, not only emotionally but physically as well. Another symptom that describes this painful experience is excessive worry. A worry that is troubled, uneasy, and comes with a foreboding feeling of doom. You find yourself anticipating and fearing that you will faint, lose control, have a heart attack, stroke out, choke, stop breathing, or die and ultimately embarrass yourself.

People who suffer from chronic anxiety often have some or all the following symptoms: trembling, nausea, dizziness, shaking, racing heart, heart palpitations, chest tightness or discomfort, muscle tension, headache, numbness, shortness of breath, hot and cold flashes, fear, feeling helpless, panic, and at the base of it all, fear, and that need to get to the safe person or safe place that will "save" you.

You may feel that the only way you can survive your anxiety situation is to leave wherever you are. You have to get to the reassurance that you will be okay and survive. You may have a list of things you can't do. You didn't have a list, but as time has gone on, you have developed one and realize the list is growing. It may include things like; not being able to be in crowds, not being able to go shopping, uneasiness with being alone, unable to drive on the freeway or not being able to drive at all, and not socialize, not being able to make decisions. Perhaps, the size of your world has gotten quite a bit smaller.

The thing is, about this time, you aren't the only one realizing it. Your close family and friends are noticing it too. You have no explanation that makes any sense, and people start questioning if you are okay. You have been wondering if you are going insane or losing control of yourself. As you read this book, you will see Kristina's anxiety further progress as the list of things she can't do gets longer and longer, while her dependence on her husband increases. She will talk about her experience in a way that you can relate to.

Anxiety disorders often come from childhood experiences or backgrounds that have the following in common: addiction in the family, strict upbringing, control through guilt and fear, parents with high expectations, negative emotional environment, feelings not talked about, lack of praise and approval, feeling that you never quite measure up, feeling that you are always being evaluated or judged, feeling that you must prove yourself and parents that are emotionally absent. Due to these experiences, you've adopted certain personality traits such as nervousness, feelings of guilt, being emotionally sensitive, being overly concerned with other's opinions of you, a need to please, low self-esteem, and a need to feel in control. These are just a few. You can see how therapy is an important part of mastering your anxiety.

I cannot emphasize enough the importance of cognitive therapy in the process of overcoming anxiety. One of the hardest things you can ever do in your life is to take an honest look at yourself. This is why many people don't like therapy. It's not uncommon for people to fear that looking too closely at their lives and experiences will make them vulnerable and may make them experience feelings they cannot recover from. Just as going through labor and delivery is the only way you can come out of pregnancy; therapy is the surest way of coming out of your anxiety. We experience things in our young lives that we take messages from, either which is told to us or inferred, as truth. Frequently, we take those messages about ourselves into our adult lives and never question them. Sadly, we allow them to influence how we feel about ourselves. Often they are lies. Sometimes, these experiences are statements that are made to us, or again, actions that inferred messages about ourselves. Still, being a child, we took it the wrong way and had been living it as a truth and a reflection of our value when it was never the original message intended.

You will read about Kristina "emptying her garbage can." We take our negative experiences, messages, and thoughts about ourselves and put them into our "garbage can," which is a metaphorical place where we put negative "garbage" that we don't know how to deal with. What happens with garbage, especially after you have carried it around all your life? It starts to decay and stink and then leaks out of us in negative behaviors like irritability, worry, poor self-esteem, self-doubt, fear, to name only a few of the symptoms of depression and anxiety. Garbage doesn't just go away. It must be emptied and cleaned up.

You will see Kristina take on her anxiety, and she will walk you through her experience of learning about not only her anxiety but about herself. This is all part of the journey out of the anxiety that controls you. This is the therapist's purpose of guiding and reassuring you as you take your journey. I always feel it a great honor to take this journey with anyone. I admire Kristina for sharing, all in the interest of using what she saw as a weakness in herself that she is now using as a strength to help others.

— *Jeanette Revay, Psychiatric ARNP*

ACKNOWLEDGEMENTS

This book would not have been written without support and help from:

Ray, my sweetheart of more than 34 years. His longsuffering patience, unlimited confidence in my abilities, and shining heart has helped me through many tough times. I am forever grateful that you give me a push when I need it.

Stan, Lynn, Katie, and Aaron, for being gracious and excited when I surprised you with the news that I was writing this book – after I had already finished the second draft. I love you.

Jeanette Revay, Psychiatric ARNP for helping me process my feelings and thoughts as I went through this writing process, and for taking the time out of your busy schedule to write the foreword.

Brian Worden, LMP who helped me "see" my vision of this book.

Laurie Owen, who, asked if it wasn't that I hadn't been anointed to write the book, like I thought, but rather that I wasn't allowing myself to be anointed to write this book.

Jan Bill, my dear friend, who has always been a good listener and tells me the truth even when I don't want to hear it. She is a true gift from God.

Olivia Salazar De Breaux, a fellow author who has been an inspiration and source of motivation for me. She also connected me to …

Sage Adderly-Knox, my AMAZING author coach who has gifted me with her knowledge, shared in my tears and laughter, and is superb at keeping me on track, encouraged, and accountable.

All the other people in my life who encouraged and inspired me without even knowing it.

THANK YOU!

Far From Perfect

INTRODUCTION

This book isn't about how to fix yourself. I can't tell you a surefire cure for anxiety. There are plenty of books and programs out there that already offer that kind of help. Instead, this is a story about my life experiences dealing with anxiety and panic from a very young age, and the knowledge and experiences I've had that might help you. This book is divided into two parts. Part I is my story. Part II is helpful information (and so much more!).

Even admitting that I am frequently attacked by panic and anxiety was hard for me. I certainly didn't want to put voice to it. My story, however, just might give hope to someone else that deals with anxiety and panic, as well as an understanding to those that need it. That is why I am writing this book, to tell my story and pray that it helps someone else. Plus, God has put it in my heart to do this. I know that all my struggles are for a reason, and this book is one of those reasons.

If you too are struggling with anxiety and panic, then I hope this gives you comfort in knowing you are not alone. Having anxiety or panic attacks does not mean you are bad, broken, or unlovable. Others know what you are going through and understand. God knows and understands and He is ALWAYS with you. I am a Christian, but I'm not writing this book only for other Christians, or to try and convert anyone, even though I do have hope that my story will bring others closer to God. My story is so connected to my relationship with God, that He must be a part of my telling of it.

Some may wonder why the cover of the book shows a cracked pot with light beaming out of it. For a long time, I felt cracked, broken, and unusable, but I discovered that I could be repurposed to shed light. The cracks allow the light inside to shine out and guide those nearby. If you put a candle inside a pot that is not cracked, and put the lid on, the flame extinguishes. It's our imperfections that draw others to us, and that allows us to shed light into the darkness of life.

I saw a demonstration of this years ago during an episode of Joyce Meyer's television show "Enjoying Everyday Life" (joycemeyerministries.com). That image, and the teaching that she did about it, impacted me. It has helped change my perception of "broken", and I hope it changes yours too.

If you don't struggle with anxiety and panic then hopefully my story will help you better understand those of us that do. Believe me when I say, we know how it affects those around us, and God bless those that choose to love us anyway.

So, let's begin.

PROLOGUE
ANXIETY AND PANIC
WHAT DOES THAT MEAN?

Before you go any further, I want to make one thing very clear. Anxiety and panic disorders are not due to normal, everyday stressors that most of us experience; it goes much deeper than that. There is nothing more frustrating to me than, when I share with someone that I'm experiencing anxiety or having a panic attack and they ask "Why?" or "What happened?" If you haven't experienced daily or random anxiety or panic attacks, then you don't realize that they can happen for no apparent reason. I've woken up in the middle of the night because I was having a panic attack. It makes no sense at all. I'm sleeping and nothing scary is happening, nothing stressful is going on, yet I have a panic attack. I've been at home watching television and suddenly, I get a fearful thought and start to get the early body symptoms of a panic attack which can include rapid heart rate, dizziness, an overwhelming need to escape where I'm at, irritability, and a plethora of other symptoms. One minute, I'm totally engrossed in the show and the next I'm dealing with anxiety symptoms. On the other hand, something might happen that would make you think, *That would definitely cause a panic attack for someone with anxiety or panic disorder, let alone someone that doesn't!* but then I don't have a panic attack.

I often think there's a glitch in my "flight or fight" response because I never know if it's going to get triggered by my thoughts, outside influences, or not at all. It's no wonder I avoid so much of life since I might end up wondering from day to day if my glitch will kick in or if I'll be perfectly fine while being handcuffed and put in the back of a police car (more of that story later). Hopefully, you can see the humor in that.

I use the terms *anxiety attack* and *panic attack* like they are two separate things because they are. The Mayo Clinic[1], Healthline[2], and Merriam-Webster Dictionary[3], provided these definitions:

Anxiety: Intense, excessive, and persistent worry and fear about everyday situations. Fast heart rate, rapid breathing, sweating, and feeling tired may occur.

Anxiety Attack: A sudden episode of intense fear or anxiety and physical symptoms, based on a perceived threat rather than imminent danger.

Anxiety Disorder: A mental health disorder characterized by feeling of worry, anxiety, or fear that are strong enough to interfere with one's daily activities.

Health Anxiety: An obsessive and irrational worry about having a serious medical condition. It's also called illness anxiety, and was formerly called hypochondria. This condition is marked by a person's imagination of physical symptoms or illness.

Psychosomatic: of, relating to, involving, or concerned with bodily symptoms caused by mental or emotional disturbance

Post-Traumatic Stress Disorder (PTSD): A disorder in which a person has difficulty recovering after experiencing or witnessing a terrifying event. The condition may last months or years, with triggers that can bring back memories of the trauma accompanied by intense emotional and physical reactions.

Generalized Anxiety Disorder: Severe, ongoing anxiety that interferes with daily activities (can occur at any age).

Agoraphobia: Fear of places and situations that might cause feelings of panic, entrapment, helplessness, or embarrassment. It usually develops after one or more panic attacks.

Obsessive-Compulsive Disorder (OCD): Excessive thoughts (obsessions) that lead to repetitive behaviors (compulsions). Is

---

1   Mayoclinic.org
2   Healthline.com
3   Merriam-webster.com

characterized by unreasonable thoughts and fears that lead to compulsive behaviors. E.g.: Thinking "If I don't have all of the pens on my desk lined up a certain way, then something bad is going to happen."

Panic Attack: A sudden episode of intense fear that triggers severe physical reactions when there is no real or imminent danger.

Panic Disorder: Having recurrent, unexpected panic attacks and spend long periods in constant fear of another panic attack.

Social Anxiety Disorder: A chronic mental health condition in which social interactions cause irrational anxiety. For people with social anxiety disorder, everyday social interactions cause irrational anxiety, fear, self-consciousness, and embarrassment.

Stress: An automatic physical, mental, and emotional response to a challenging event. There are internal stressors (feelings, expectations) and external stressors (arising from the environment and events around us).

I suffer (or have suffered) from all the disorders listed above, except PTSD. As you can see from these definitions, anxiety and panic attacks are not just stress. Everyone deals with stress, pretty much every day, to some degree. Stress can be positive (motivating), or it can be negative (harmful). Anxiety and panic disorders go beyond normal, everyday stress. I've experienced massive panic attacks at times when I'm not going through high levels of stress in my life. Sometimes too much negative stress in a person's life can lead to anxiety and panic attacks, but they don't necessarily go hand in hand.

Sometimes I'll have what I call a Panic Sandwich. It's my definition of the panic cycle. An example of this is if I wake up in the morning and immediately have a nervous stomach thinking about what I need to do that day. That's the first sign of anxiety creeping in. As the day progresses, the anxiety gets worse until at some point I have a panic attack. The fear of having another panic attack that day causes more anxiety and possibly even another panic attack. Thus, the loop of anxiety leading to panic, then more anxiety and more panic, etc. Think of anxiety as the bread and the panic attack as the meat. By the end of the day it could be a full-on multi-layer sandwich, like a club sandwich. It's alright to have one once in a while, but they're not very good for you to have on a regular basis.

I'm going to try and describe what it's like to have an anxiety and panic attack, but I'm not sure I can do it in a way that will truly allow you to feel it too. Think about a time when you've been extremely nervous about doing something. Perhaps it's public speaking, or taking off in an airplane. Focus on that fearful anticipation. Feel that clenching and the butterflies in your stomach. Wipe away the clammy sweat on your palms. Shift from foot to foot in an effort to free some of the excess energy in your body. Your heart is pounding and you feel like you might pass out. The one thought getting you through this feeling and moment is that you know it will end. As soon as the situation is over, or starts, all those feelings of anxiety go away.

If you are experiencing an anxiety attack, all those thoughts and body symptoms stay with you, at some level, for hours or days – and sometimes, even longer. You're exhausted, I mean that bone deep weariness that comes from never getting any rest or peace. I'm not a parent myself, but I think anyone who has had sleep deprivation and high levels of stress for an extended period of time, such as new parents, nurses/doctors, soldiers, etc. can relate to what I mean about the type of exhaustion that just doesn't quit. I have days where I wake up with the nervous, clenched, butterfly stomach and it doesn't go away all day. I tend to do things faster. All my movements are hurried and seem to match the chaotic frenzy of my thoughts, because along with the body symptoms comes the scattered thinking. It's hard to focus and my thoughts shift from one thing to another as fast as they can. I get impatient and just want to move and escape, or crash into bed and never leave it. Sometimes, if the anxiety attack goes on for too long or is too intense, it can lead to a panic attack.

There is one overall word to described a panic attack and that word is "terrifying!". You really do think you are dying.

Your death is imminent and there is nothing anyone can do to stop it. I've heard that there are hundreds of known body symptoms that can happen during a panic attack. I think it's probably closer to thousands – or at least it feels that way. For me, each panic attack brings about different symptoms. Some are the same, such as hyperventilating, increased heart rate, feeling of light headedness, and shaking. Depending on the episode, I can also throw in: upset stomach, numb arms and hands, black edges or spots in my vision, muscle spasms in my back, tingly scalp, trouble swallowing, sinus pressure, loss of coordination, and the list goes on. Plus, I just want to hide. I don't want anyone to see me like that, to the point that I've suffered in silence during many panic episodes. It's just SO embarrassing.

Having dealt with this for most of my life, I am now generally astute at recognizing the early sign of an oncoming panic attack, but many times it just comes out of nowhere and escalates very quickly. Imagine standing in the produce area of the grocery store trying to pick out a head of lettuce. Suddenly you can't breathe right, you have trouble swallowing, you feel nauseated, and your heart is beating so fast that you think it's going to come out of your chest. What do you do? What is the thought that comes into your head? Is it *Holy crap! I'm having a heart attack!* or *Oh no! Something is wrong with me and I need to get to a hospital!*? Those would be normal reactions if your body felt that way. I don't think there is one of us that experience panic attacks that hasn't gone to an emergency room thinking that we were having a heart attack or dying. I've done it. Twice. Funny thing is that no one at the hospital ever said, "You check out fine, it was probably a panic attack." I really thought something was seriously wrong with me; they just didn't know it, and the next time I would certainly die.

One clue that you're having a panic attack and are not in the middle of dying while standing in the produce aisle at the supermarket, is that your thought process is something like this *I'm dying! I have to get out of here before anyone sees me and I embarrass myself.* Even though I've had hundreds of panic attacks and know that I'm not dying and that I'll be fine, the immense pressure of need to get somewhere alone where people can't see me, because this time might actually be the "real deal," is still a thought that comes into my head. I've said to my husband many times that I can't give him an explanation about the thoughts that happen during a panic attack because they're irrational. When he says, "You know you're not dying. I don't understand why you still think that you are," my response is, "We both know that anxiety and panic do not produce rational, realistic thoughts." My conscious, the in-touch with reality part of my brain, is not in control at that moment. My subconscious "lizard" brain is in control. I often picture my thoughts during a panic attack as a squiggly line drawn inside my head, like when a two-year-old tries to color inside the lines but it ends up going all over the place and looks chaotic. The worst thing is that I feel so out of control, and control is something I think I need to have in order to survive. Of course, I never really have control over anything except myself – and even then, that's a hit and miss – instead, I have the illusion of being in control.

Even though I've dealt with some degree of anxiety or panic almost my whole life, it's just now getting talked about. Sadly, one of the reasons it seems to be getting more attention is that it's become much more prevalent in the world. Some people have lifelong issues with it, while others experience just one or two panic attacks in their life that are usually due to a specific temporary circumstance. There are also some people who experience anxiety and panic due to a horrific incident or series of incidents such as those dealing with Post Traumatic Stress Disorder (PTSD). It doesn't matter how you have come to have anxiety or panic attacks because the effect it has on you follows a commonality. The duration or severity may differ, but the suffering is the same. I want you to know that if you are suffering because of anxiety and/or panic that you are not alone. I understand what you are going through and so do many others. Please, do not give up hope. You many never be "cured," but you can still live life. Perhaps your life will be different from those that don't have these issues, but it can be a good life just the same.

Once I come out of an anxiety or panic episode, I usually start with the negative self-talk which can go something like this:

Once again, I've let the anxiety win. I'm such a loser. I should have been able to get it under control.

I am so unlovable. Why would anyone want to be around me and put up with all this crap?

You get the idea. I beat myself up over the fact that I "let" myself have an anxiety or panic attack. I think it somehow makes me "less than" and "not enough". Not good enough, not strong enough, disciplined enough, optimistic enough, and not worthy of being loved. After a prolonged bout of anxiety or after a particularly bad panic attack I sink into a funk. And it's no wonder with all that degrading self-talk! I also have what I call an "anxiety hangover". This is when it takes me days to recover from the effects of a period of heightened anxiety, or a particularly brutal panic attack. I continue to feel drained and tired. It takes great effort for me to even get out of bed and function. The aftermath is almost as bad as the cause.

What I've come to realize is that I am more than strong enough. The strength of character and inner fortitude that it takes to pull myself out of that "funk" in order to go to work, clean my house, interact with people, and just keep living, is more than most people will ever have to reach down into their soul and extract. My one saving grace is that I know the strength I have is not just mine, but God's strength that I can tap into through the Holy Spirit which dwells within me. If I didn't have that, I'm not sure I would be here to write this book. There have been so many days where the struggles are so debilitating that it would be sweet relief to not have to deal with it anymore. I know there are so many that have chosen to take matters into their own hands and end their suffering on this earth. I pray that if you are reading this and feel like that is a way out of the pain, please do not do it. You are so much more than what you are dealing with and you are precious to someone in this world that needs you in it. Stop reading right now and reach out to someone and talk to them. Get help. I care and so do many more people who may not even know you. They want to help. You are not weak for reaching out and sharing your struggles. You are beyond strong enough for doing that. If you don't want to talk to someone else because it's just too scary, then talk to God. He is always listening and loves you more deeply than you could ever comprehend. Even if you currently don't have a relationship with God, you can reach out to Him, and He will be there. Maybe once you pour out your troubles to Him, you'll feel more comfortable talking to a trusted friend, family member, therapist, or even a stranger on the other end of a hotline call.

For me, it's extremely difficult to talk to someone about the anxiety. I always think they're judging me or will think badly of me for being so weak. It's a vulnerable position to put myself into, and I don't know anyone who is comfortable having their soft underbelly exposed.

I recently attended a leadership class at work. The subject of the class was "Healthy Conflict" and part of it focused on having empathy for the other person. We talked about the difference between sympathy and empathy. That really hit home for me, because often, when I'm having a panic attack or really struggling with feelings of anxiety, I get sympathy from the people around me. What I really need is empathy. Sympathy makes me feel even more alone in the struggle I'm having. Empathy is someone giving me a hug and saying "This really sucks. I'm here for you." Empathy makes me feel like someone is sharing this experience with me and is there to support me in any way I need. Often when people are confronted with my struggles, such as anxiety and panic attacks, they appear to feel very uncomfortable and say something they think is helpful (but isn't). Then they walk away or ignore what I'm going through. If you've been in that situation, you know how painful it is and how it can leave you feeling so much more scared and isolated.

Very few people that have been with me when I'm going through a panic attack have expressed empathy. Most ignore it, downplay it, leave me alone to deal with it, or try to distract me as a way to get it to end. None of these methods are helpful. Please do not behave this way towards someone you see is struggling with anxiety or having a panic attack - it only makes it worse. I'll talk more about this in Part II of the book.

PART I

My Story

ANXIETY

My legs feel heavy
And my stomach is clenched
I'm in the world
But do not see it
My visions are on the future
Thoughts are unfriendly to myself
Gasping to slow my breath
Waiting is torture
Giving the anxiety free reign
Carry me through Lord!
With you I can feel lighter
Otherwise the weight of this
Pushes down my joy
Rescue me, oh Lord, from
The torrent of raining thoughts
Infuse me with your strength
I am yours.

— Kristina Horton

Chapter One
And So, It Begins
(Childhood)

I was a very imaginative child. This probably comes from my love of books. Even before I could read, my mother would take my older sister and me to the library every week or two. We would check out the maximum number of books and I would look at the pictures and make up stories. Then when the book was read to me, it was like a bonus story. Two stories, one book. For a kid like me it didn't get much better than that. My imagination didn't stop at stories in a book though. From a young age, four as best as I can recollect, my imagination had a scary side to it. I would imagine all kinds of terrible scenarios to any given situation; this made me very fearful. This fear made me very anxious, and that anxiety would eventually cause me to have severe panic attacks.

Now, I'm not saying that my overactive imagination is what caused the anxiety. I'm saying that my deeper issues coupled with negative thinking and the ability to let my imagination wander is not a good combination. Many of us that struggle with anxiety have a constant feeling of impending doom which causes us to react differently to situations in life. Throughout my life, and especially when I was young, I could never enjoy or be in the moment because I always visualized something bad was going to happen. I think the quote from Mark Twain says it best "I've had a lot of worries in my life, most of which never happened."

Think of a child during recess at school. Most children would be excited to get out of the classroom, play on the equipment outside, and hang out with their friends. They laugh and don't have a care in the world. They live in the moment. When I was a child, I hated recess most of the time. The classroom was structured and everyone behaved because the teacher was right there. Recess was chaos. For a kid with anxiety, chaos is terrifying. I was sure that if I played on the jungle gym I would fall and break my arm. And I was sure that no one would like me and other kids would be mean to me, so I didn't have many friends.

To be truthful, other kids scared me. They were unpredictable and I didn't like to deal with the unknown. I've jokingly said that even when I was a kid, I didn't like kids. I know now that it was really me that I didn't like. On top of the usual issues and insecurities that we all go through growing up, I knew I wasn't like everyone else. I knew I didn't behave and react to things like the other kids. I knew there was something wrong with me and that I had to work hard to keep it hidden and to make up for it. That's a lot of pressure for a child to put on themselves. No wonder my anxiety just kept escalating.

I think that before I get into the nitty gritty of my dealings with anxiety and panic disorder, I should probably let you get to know me a little, which will give some context to the stories and experiences I describe in this book. I would call myself a pretty boring person, really. I don't have many hobbies or a big social life. I'm not famous, rich in money, or as beautiful as a model. I'm like you, a person just living life the best I know how. I've been described by friends and family as funny, intelligent, thoughtful, clumsy, and loving. It's humorous to me that we often see ourselves a bit differently than others do.

I was born in the fall of 1970 in a small town in the southwest part of the State of Washington. My father worked as a carpenter, and my mother was already a stay-at-home mom to my older sister. Even though she's only two years, one month, and 20 days older than me, my sister has always been my bossy second mother and a fierce protector. My very lovely brother came along seven years after me. I have always felt sorry for him, having two older sisters which pretty much equals three mothers. It's a miracle he survived all the love, tears, and controlling we heaped on him. He turned out quite well, and that's either because of, or despite, his two older sisters. He'll have to decide which. My guess is that it's a little bit of both.

We were a typical middle-class family for the 1970s and 1980s. My parents are both hard workers that instilled that in their children. I was fortunate that my mom was able to be a stay-at-home mother until my brother was around five years old. She was involved in helping in our classrooms and was always home when we got back from school. We attended church every Sunday, the same church my paternal grandparents attended. I hated getting up early on Sundays, but enjoyed Sunday School and the church services once I was there. One of my fondest childhood memories is of standing next to my grandfather in church as we sang hymns. He had a wonderful singing voice, but much to my disappointment, I couldn't hold a tune if it was handed to me in a steel box. To this day, I tear up when I hear some of those old hymns, even though my grandfather went home to God over 20 years ago.

From the age of five to sixteen, we lived on a 15-acre piece of property in the country in a house that my dad built. We had horses – my sister's - and cows, chickens, cats, and a dog. I played outside a lot and would probably have considered myself a tomboy. For my eleventh birthday, my parents bought me a beautiful little pocket knife with pearl type inlay. I can't tell you how much I loved that knife. It's probably my favorite birthday present from my childhood. I would bury baggies of pennies and small random items that only a child would find fascinating, all over the property and then draw maps to my buried treasures. I would use my pocket knife to carve symbols in the trees that would help lead to my treasures. Even though I didn't know it at the time, this was an early indicator of my career path as a Professional Land Surveyor. Who knew?!

As a child, I spent a lot of time by myself, reading, doing art stuff, or I was hanging out with the animals. I was always particularly close to our dogs. They would be my companions as I galivanted around the property. We had a creek that ran through the lower acreage, but I didn't play in it much because the cows would get in there and if you know cattle then you know they tend to poop wherever they want, even in a creek as they cross it. Gross! I have to say, the cows were my least favorite and sometimes a bit scary, especially when we had to herd them into a different section of the property or into the corral or barn. They could get downright ornery! The chickens were bad about pooping everywhere too, but they were cute when they were chicks and were funny to watch and chase around. One of my chores was to get the eggs and close the coop door in the evenings. They would peck at me sometimes when I would try and get the eggs, but I imagine I would too if someone was trying to steal my eggs. When we butchered the chickens, I had to help in the process. The plucking wasn't too bad, but when I stepped on a hay covered dead carcass a few days after the butchering behind the barn and it made a "squeeee" noise as the gasses left its headless neck, I couldn't eat chicken for about two years afterwards. I think we can all agree that was the only thing a self-respecting 10-year-old could do.

When I was around 11 years old, I would wake up every night with a stomach ache. I would sleepily stumble into my parent's bedroom and try to wake up Mom and let her know. My mom is a very deep sleeper. One time when I came in and told her I wasn't feeling well, she told me to take the denominator and divide it by 97 and then it'll all be better. She was taking classes at the local community college at the time. You can imagine me standing there in my flower print flannel nightgown, upset that I even had to bother her, and then getting that as my answer. Dad, who is a light sleeper, was laughing and trying to shake Mom awake. It's a funny story now, but I felt bad for interrupting their much-needed sleep. That was something I put on myself and not due to anything they said or did. In fact, I ended up going into their room with a stomach ache every night for months. I would crawl in bed with them for a few hours and then wander back to my bed when I realized my tummy felt better. During the day, I was fine. Mom ended up taking me to a naturopath and it was discovered that I had a blockage in my colon. I did several colonics over the next few weeks to get my digestive system working better. I know now that the cause was my constant nervous stomach which messed up my digestion. To this day, when I get bad anxiety it always comes with a tightly clenched stomach. Anxiety has greatly affected my digestive system over the years. I always know when I'm dealing with too much anxiety, because it comes to a standstill. Some people get the opposite; their digestive system speeds up and empties out.

Having excessive feelings of anxiety at a young age, but not knowing what it was, created a lot of confusion for me. I grew up in the 1970s and 1980s and these things just weren't talked about. I never knew growing up that I was dealing with anxiety. I did hear the words "nervous breakdown," usually whispered amongst gossiping women, or shown dramatically on TV or in the movies. There was a stigma attached to having a "nervous condition". This was especially true for children, as anxiety or depression were more associated with middle- and upper-class housewives, with Valium being the most prescribed anti-anxiety medication of the 1970s. According to an article[4] titled "How an Age of Anxiety Became an Age of Depression" by Allan V Horowitz, anxiety was the emblematic mental health problem of the 1950s and 1960s, but that various factors in the 1970s through the 1990s transformed conditions that had been viewed as "anxiety" into "depression". I find it interesting that even though historically, both conditions have had societal stigmas attached to them, the focus of diagnosis and prescription of drugs for the treatment of the similar symptoms of both conditions has changed back and forth between "anxiety" and "depression" over the decades.

My parents would say things like, "Oh, she's just a nervous child," or "She's so shy. I don't know what we're going to do

---

4   Mci.nlm.nih.gov

about her." Many children with anxiety are labeled as emotional, nervous, timid, etc.

On and off from about the age of 8 to my early 30s I had a nervous facial tic – and it still pops up from time to time. I didn't even know I was doing it. I have a vivid memory of standing next to my dad when he was talking to someone after church; I was maybe 9 or 10 years old, and dad was putting his hand on my shoulder and saying "Stop doing that." It wasn't in a mean tone, but he was just bringing it to my attention. I was an extremely shy child to begin with and that was so embarrassing to me. It just cemented the thought I often had that people were talking about me and making fun of me behind my back. For a time during my adult years, I was angry at my parents for not recognizing or knowing what I was going through as a child and for not getting me help. I realize now that they were doing the best that they could with what they had available to them. Plus, I wasn't exactly the type of kid to be a squeaky wheel and say, "I have a problem and I need help." I certainly didn't want to cause a kerfuffle or be a problem to anyone. God forbid!

When I was in middle school, I was talked into joining the track team. The coach said that with my long legs I would do well at the sport. I think he was being a good teacher and just trying to get me out of my shell. Like most shy and anxious children, I did not like to do sports. I lacked the confidence and didn't want people watching me. Due to the anxiety, I just wanted to hide and not let anyone know the "crazy" thoughts I had. The best way to do that was to not be in the spotlight and to fly under the radar, so to speak. I went to the practices, and I did okay. I wasn't competitive, so didn't really have that drive to push myself, but I participated and tried my best. I was thinking that this might actually be something I could enjoy and be accepted by my peers for doing it.

When the first track meet rolled around, I was super nervous but in an excited kind of way. As I waited for my event to start, my nerves got worse and worse. I was sitting quietly and not talking to anyone. My stomach was in knots and I found it hard to breathe. There was so much noise and motion going on around me and all I wanted to do was run away (I know....kind of ironic). My dad was in the stands and I kept looking over to him as a way to reassure myself that I would be okay. I got to the starting line, ready to go, and when the gun went off, I started running. I didn't realize it at the time, because I didn't know I was having anxiety, but it's difficult to run when your body is trying to have a panic attack and you're hyperventilating. I just couldn't get enough air in my lungs.

Meet after meet, I would have to quit in the middle of the race because I just couldn't go any further. I didn't know what was wrong with me. *I was a quitter! I was an embarrassment to my family and teammates! I will NEVER put myself through something like that again!* I finished the season but dreaded every moment of it. The worst part was that my dad came to every meet and witnessed my failures. Even though he never said a derogatory word to me about it, and was kind to me, I couldn't help but feel how much of a disappointment I was to him. My teammates pretty much avoided me and acted like I wasn't even there. They weren't mean to me, but I was not part of the team. I was a loser, and no one wants that to rub off on them.

Of course, I avoided sports like the plague after that and gym class was torture because of the anxiety it caused me. Yes, I was one of those girls that ran away when a ball was thrown at her. I felt so bad for the super athletic guy I was teamed up with in high school gym class for badminton tournaments. I looked like a drunk farmer trying to get a bat out of the barn, arms swinging wildly as I ducked every time the birdie came over the net at me. It's a miracle I didn't accidentally maim my partner. Poor guy!

I know that some of my behaviors when I was a child must have pushed the limits of my parents' patience, or made them think, "What is going on with this kid?!" I was so terrified of going to the dentist or doctor that I would make myself sick for weeks before the appointment just thinking about what horrible things would be done to me and the pain I may have to endure. The fear of the unknown is a strong motivator for anxiety and panic attacks. I even knew our family dentist because my grandmother worked for him. He wasn't scary or mean. He even had a treasure chest of toys and would let you pick one out to keep after your appointment. One time, when I knew I was going to have some teeth extracted, I stood up in the dental chair when he tried to give me the shot of anesthetic. It got to the point where my parents wouldn't tell me about the appointments until the morning of.

Another thing I did that was out of the ordinary was get up hours before I had to, get ready, lay back down on my bed – fully dressed – and wait for everyone else to get up. I was so worried I would miss the school bus that I was depriving myself of much needed sleep. I think I was around 9 or 10 years old when I was doing this, and it went on for a couple years. It got worse when everyone left the house before me, and I was fully responsible for making sure I didn't miss the bus. If I did, how would I get to school? I truly thought the sky would fall and my world would end if I didn't make it to the bus and ended up missing school. My parents would be upset, and I would be a bad child. Good grief! I wish I could go back in time and tell my child self not to take life so seriously. I didn't have the ability at that time to just be a kid and enjoy myself. I worried about everything. No exaggeration. If my imagination could conjure up a terrible outcome about a situation, it would.

I also slept fully dressed, shoes and all, for months after we had an assembly at school about house fires. Firefighters came in and gave a talk about having an escape plan and instructed us on what to do if there was a house fire. I especially fixated on the house fire that might happen at night while we were sleeping. I was so worried about it happening, that I kept a "go bag" next to my bed. I thought that if I was fully clothed and on top of the covers when it happened (because I was so sure it would!), then I would be ready to get everyone out of the house. I never mentioned my fears to anyone else. I don't think my parents even knew that I did that.

Once time in middle school, I had to stay after to work on a project. I can't really remember the circumstances, but my mom was supposed to pick me up on her way home from work. I sat on the curb outside the school and waited. And waited. And waited. When she didn't show up after 20 minutes, I started to imagine that she had gotten into a terrible car accident. I even imagined the accident; her getting t-boned at an intersection, and the car door trapped her inside. She was unconscious and bleeding. I could picture the whole scenario of other people trying to get her out of the car, the ambulance showing up and her being carted off to the hospital. I figured that it would take hours for them to reach Dad and in the confusion, he would forget that I needed to be picked up.

I worked myself up and was so scared by the time a teacher saw me on the curb and asked me if someone was coming to get me. Instead of sharing my fears with her, I just said "Yes, my mom will be here soon." The teacher wandered away. There I sat for about an hour or so, totally convinced that my mom was lying in the hospital dying and I wasn't there to say goodbye to her. By the time my mom did show up, I was quiet, stiff, and exhausted. Mom was extremely apologetic and terrified that she forgot to pick me up. It turns out that she had a hellish day, and since it wasn't the norm for her to pick me up – I usually rode the school bus – she just forgot. She had gone home as usual and after a few minutes Dad said "Where's Kristie?" Of course, Mom freaked out and drove way over the speed limit to go the 10 miles along a curvy country road to get to the school in record time. My guess is that I conjured up the scary scenario in order to distract my mind from thinking that I was insignificant and not a priority. Children often think things are their fault. This is especially true for children with anxiety issues. It was one more instance where the message in my head was *You are unlovable.* Now, as an adult, I can forgive my mom, but when I think about it, I can feel the fear, uncertainty, and invisibility that that little girl felt as she sat on that curb alone waiting to be remembered.

I was extremely terrified of doing anything I thought would be dangerous. For instance, I wouldn't play on the monkey bars because I was convinced that I would fall off and break my arm. I wouldn't run with scissors because it just takes that one time for someone to accidentally get stabbed. Okay, that might actually be a good thing to be terrified of, but come on! In grade school we had the round tipped scissors. The likelihood of that happening was basically nonexistent.

I asked my husband the other day if he remembered in grade school when we had a day of competitive games outside. There was the three-legged race, burlap bag races, tug of war, and other group and individual games and sports. I think they gave out placement ribbons for each event. It was complete chaos on the field or so it seemed to me at the time. I absolutely dreaded and hated those days. My husband's reaction was "Oh yeah! Those were so much fun!" He then went on to tell me some good memories he had of those days. Same event and we had two very different reactions to it. That is the difference between a non-anxiety driven mind and an anxiety driven mind. What seems fun, exciting, and normal to most people is scary, terrifying and anxiety-inducing for those of us that struggle with these issues. I remember not wanting to put myself out there and maybe fall or make a fool of myself. People were watching and all I wanted was to fade into the background. I was forced to participate in those games, but I loathed every minute of it.

Growing up, I never wanted attention placed on me. I was afraid that if people really observed me, they would see that something was wrong or different about me. I knew I reacted in a different way to life than most of the kids around me. I just didn't want anyone to focus on that because then I would for sure be labeled a weirdo, insane, or worse. I desperately wanted someone to tell me there was nothing wrong with me, that I was loved, and okay as I was. Not that I would probably have believed them anyway. At least, not at first.

There was this constant struggle in me to try and be like the other kids, to not cause any trouble, to fit in, versus what was going on in my mind. I knew it wasn't right for a kid to not want to be around other kids, to want to be alone most of the time, to feel things as deeply as I did, and to have the scary thoughts about life that I did. I just didn't know what to do about it, so I tried to bury it and hide it as much as I could. That is probably why the facial tic developed. I'm here to tell you that no matter how much you try to suppress your emotions, they will come out in one way or another.

When I was around 11 years old, I was sent off for a week to Vacation Bible Camp. It was at a beautiful lake with lots of activities planned. Most kids look forward to a week full of fun activities, hanging out with friends, meeting new people, and getting way from their families. Not me. New places and people were sure to hit my high anxiety buttons. Sure enough, I only knew one other kid at the camp, and the room I slept in had four other girls I didn't know. My stomach was clenched as tight as a fist days before I even got there. The anxious feeling and body symptoms got worse after the first day. By the second day, I just wanted a quiet place to lay down and be alone. Yeah...that's not going to happen at a summer camp. I remember having some fun weaving a basket, but I refused to go swimming off the dock, get into a canoe, or play baseball with the other kids. I was way too distracted by the chaotic frenzy going on in my mind to have a good time. Then, IT happened.

On day three the nervousness had become too much, and I got diarrhea. I was walking back to the dorms, and it happened. I pooped, just a tiny bit, in my pants. I was mortified. I didn't know what to do. All I could think was to hurry up, get changed, and hide it. I was so ashamed. The one girl I did know found me crying in the bathroom, and I told her what happened. Thankfully, she didn't make fun of me, but did find a counselor and told her. I was then taken to someone who gave me Kaopectate. It was so awkward. No one likes a poopy pants kid. Naturally, I was so afraid of that happening again and so intent on having a good plan in case it did, that I certainly didn't enjoy myself the rest of the week. Needless to say, I never went to summer camp again.

Every time my parents tried to push me out of my comfort zone, which they probably thought would get me over my shyness, something happened to just cement my belief that the world was an awful and scary place; it wasn't worth it to try anything new. I was a very stubborn child, but that was based in fear and the motivation to avoid places and things that made me anxious. I now know that these were early indicators of agoraphobia. I always thought that agoraphobia was someone who wouldn't leave their house, but I came to find out that it includes avoiding all places, events, and people that make you anxious or that you feel you can't escape from. Even the typical things people learn during their childhood years were horribly anxiety-inducing for me. My fear of failure, and of looking like an idiot, made me want to run away and hide.

Prime examples of this are when my dad taught me how to swim on my back and to ride a bicycle. I have to say that my dad is an extremely patient man. He was trying to teach me how to swim on my back, and it took hours. There was this constant back and forth of him holding me up in the water, giving me instructions, and me saying over and over "Don't let me go! I'll drown!" This is funny because we were in three feet of water, and my dad was right there and certainly wouldn't have let me drown. Being on my back felt very vulnerable to me because I couldn't see what was ahead of me or around me. How would I protect myself from the creepy vegetation that floated around in the lake?! My adult rational mind can't fathom why, as a child, I was so fearful of that. From my perspective now, I see it was perfectly safe and should have been a fun experience. The child in me can still feel that sense of being scared and unsure of herself. Thank God that my dad didn't give up, and by the end of the afternoon, I was swimming on my back.

Considering how paralyzing anxiety can be, it really is a miracle that I ever: played the piano at recitals, made childhood friends, and later in life rode four-wheelers, traveled, and did all the other things that always seem so impossible to me in the moment. I truly believe that all the hard parts of my struggles have fortified me and strengthened me in ways that never would have happened otherwise; they have enabled me to accomplish things I never thought possible. I can't say I always enjoyed the journey. In fact, most of the time I did all these things with high anxiety levels and an overwhelming want to run, hide and never do anything that would cause people to depend on me.

I think it's incredibly easy for childhood anxiety go unnoticed. For so long, certain behaviors that indicate anxiety are passed off as just "kids being kids". When you look at the ridiculously long list of anxiety and panic attack disorder symptoms, and throw it together with the limited communication skills that children have, it's no wonder that many children suffering from these disorders are overlooked. I realize all of this now, but as a child I felt abandoned and helpless. Children with anxiety are often afraid of labeling themselves as "different," so they learn early on to try and hide the feelings and body symptoms of anxiety. To talk about it seems horrifying, and they don't even know why. At a time when you're meant to live vivaciously and carefree, a child with anxiety lives fearfully and sees the world around them as a place full of uncertainty and dangers. I was such an overtly cautious person because of all my "worst case scenario thoughts" that I didn't have much fun, especially as a child.

If you recognize a child dealing with anxiety, please be patient with them. Give them a soft place to land and a stable world around them. Build up their self-esteem so that they can gain confidence in themselves and what they do. Let them know that making a mistake is not the end of the world and that not trying at all makes you feel worse. Always let them know that they are loved as they are.

CHAPTER TWO

Unsure

(Teen Years)

I entered my teen years under a cloud of shyness, uncertainty, big hair, and a few pimples. You know, the usual foray into the hormonal hell that is being a teenager. It was during this time, at the age of 14 years and 6 months to be exact, that I met my future husband, Ray. He was a grade ahead of me and had just turned 15. I was in the eighth grade and had just started having boyfriends that year. Ray was a freshman and my total opposite. While I was shy, he was outrageous and outgoing. I was a "good girl" and never broke curfew or behaved badly; he didn't have a curfew and pretty much behaved however he wanted to. I cared all the time about what people thought of me, and he didn't give a rat's ass. I love that about him, to this day.

Ray has been my most consistent "safe" person, someone I would run to when needing to be reassured that I was okay. His calm and carefree attitude in juxtaposition to my panic and worrisome attitude works for us. God definitely knew what he was doing when he put us together, that's for sure. When Ray moved in with his older brother and went to school his senior year in Oregon, I felt very alone. I was a Junior at the time and missed him terribly even though he came to visit every other weekend. That was some serious devotion for him to drive 3-4 hours one way just to spend time with me. My insecurities and anxiety at school ratcheted up during that time since my "safe" person wasn't there for me to see in between classes. I was very lonely, and by then, everyone was already in their set group of friends. I lost my friend group when Ray left.

While in high school, I was dealing with the usual teenage angst of thinking that my parents didn't understand me, that I was ugly (Why, oh why, couldn't I look like Christie Brinkley?!), that school sucked, and all the other drama that comes with trying to figure out who we are and how we fit into this world. Since you feel like you're under a microscope by everyone around you, just waiting to talk crap about you or find fault, I did what any anxiety-ridden teenager does: I tried to hide it. People thought I was stuck up because I didn't join in because I would ignore everyone as I was walking from class to class, or because I didn't go to parties. The truth is that I was just trying to hold it together and not freak out in the middle of class. I had to stay focused and concentrate on just getting from Point A to Point B. Plus, I didn't like the pandemonium of the crowded hallway. I would even walk by Ray and not even acknowledge him. Once he figured out that I was just operating in "tunnel vision," he would tease me about it and try to find a way to get my attention. I was so insecure. I thought that, if anyone did get to really know me, they wouldn't like me once they found out about all the crazy thoughts in my head. At that point, Ray barely even knew the extent of my anxiety issues.

One time we went out for the afternoon on a small lake in a rubber raft he had. We floated around and just relaxed. It was great, up until the point he talked me into jumping into the lake to swim and cool off, then rowed away from me. I completely panicked and started crying and yelling at him. I think I scared him by my reaction. It certainly wasn't rational. I knew how to swim and he was only 10 feet away. I got back into the boat, and he was asking me why I freaked out. I just acted mad because I didn't know what to tell him. I couldn't say "Oh, that's just how I am. I have extreme fear reactions to normal things." Nope. Not going to admit that. That wasn't even the worst part of the day. I had burnt the bottom of my feet by having them propped over the edge of the raft while we floated around. OUCH! Bit of advice, don't ever do that.

As a teenager, it's common to have friends, a social life, and to want to spend time in groups of your peers. In my mind, I conjured up scenarios of what a certain party or get together would be like. I would put such high expectations on the event and people around me that of course I was always disappointed once I was in the reality of the moment. I *thought* that I wanted to be around my peers, but truthfully, I was petrified of being in social situations. I was the kid at the party that would be so uncomfortable, that it would make everyone else uncomfortable. I was labeled as "square". I didn't know how to have fun. I couldn't just relax and do all the stupid stuff that teenagers do. I attended maybe three parties throughout my teen years. I didn't know that I had social anxiety.

I don't know any girl in the 1980s that didn't have a certain type of John Hughes image of how a school dance was supposed to go. Of course that never happens because, well…because teenage boys are riding high on hormones and can't be bothered to appreciate the nuances of a teenage girl's dreams of romance. I wanted to be at the dance, and have a fun time, and interact with my peers, but on the other hand the anxiety voice in my head was saying, *What in the heck are you doing here!? Your dress isn't good enough, your hair looks weird, and oh my goodness girl, what clown put makeup on you!?* Next thing you know, all I wanted to do was run far, far away. I was always so disappointed in myself for not having a "normal" reaction to a common teenage experience. I knew that I was supposed to be the girl that laughed and acted crazy with her friends and got the most out of her high school experience, but I didn't. I was too worried. Not just the typical worry of a teenager, but worried all the time about everything. I would be at school observing most everyone else going about as if the next great catastrophe wasn't right around the corner. I didn't understand why I was so afraid of things that seemed to be no big deal to anyone else.

I tried so hard to be "perfect". I rarely engaged with others in a way that would clue then into the fact that something about me was weird or different. I mostly spent time with Ray.

Obviously, we were in the throes of young love and wanted to spend tons of time with each other, but it was more than that for me. I didn't plan much time to hang out with girlfriends and by the time I graduated, I had a few friends but no close friends. I had pushed them all away. In my desperation to be "perfect" and hide my anxieties, I let people assume I was someone I wasn't just to keep them at arm's length. I don't know how I was perceived at that time, but I'm guessing it wasn't very flattering. I've heard the terms "stuck up," "boring," "mean," and "loner" applied to myself during my teenage years. Hurtful, yes, but I can easily see how I would seem that way through someone else's eyes.

When I was in 9th grade, I was a Junior Varsity basketball cheerleader. Back then, you got on a squad by trying out in front of the whole school and then everyone voted on who would be on the squad. I went to a small school with just under 100 people in my class and maybe a total of 500, or so, in grades 8-12. I think I was voted onto the squad less out of my fantastic cheerleading abilities than the fact that my sister, a 12th grader at the time, had been a Varsity cheerleader the last few years for basketball and football. I really didn't even want to try out, but I felt it's what I was supposed to do. It was me and two other girls on the JV squad. Anyone knows that you should never put a group of three teenage girls together because one is always bound to be left out. I was that one, through no one's fault but my own. I went into the whole thing with an attitude of avoidance and used my relationship with Ray to only do the minimum required of me. I'm not proud of it, but how else was I going to get out of spending a few nights a week in a loud gym full of people? It was hard enough for me to get out there and perform in front of everyone. I hated going to the practices because I didn't feel like I was good enough and pretty much left it up to the other two girls to put together our cheers. I was upset when they would tell me they got together without me and came up with the cheers, and then I would get resentful and not give good effort to try and learn them. At the time, I saw myself as the victim of their hurtful behavior, but I know that it was an easy way for me not to deal with my issues.

I regret not being able to take that opportunity to have fun, make some friends, and learn new things about myself. Instead, because of the anxiety, I half-assed it and gave people the illusion that I was too good to bother with something as lowly as being a JV cheerleader. I never tried out again, and my short stint as a high school junior varsity cheerleader was a crash and burn. Sadly, I don't even have my cheerleading uniform. I loaned it out to a guy doing a skit at a pep rally a few years later and never got it back. I sometimes wonder what ever happened to that cheerleading uniform, but obviously I didn't want it hanging around reminding me of my failure because I never put much effort into getting it back or tracking it down.

That whole scenario was sort of a soundtrack to the effects that the anxiety issues had on my life. I would try to please other people by attempting to do something that I didn't want to do, then I would only put enough effort into it to keep people off my back. I would feel severely disappointed in myself when it was all over, and thought I should have done better. Since I did not know what the anxiety was, I kept blaming myself for not following through, not being able to just be "normal," and for disappointing myself and everyone else. For those of us who grew up in a time when the terms *anxiety* and *panic disorder* weren't heard of, we were especially hard on ourselves for struggling through life.

Part of having an anxiety or panic disorder is the feeling that you are alone in it. That no one understands; if you told someone, they would judge you and can't possibly know what you experience. Actually, that is all true. Even I cannot fully know what anxiety and panic feels like for someone else. One person's manifestations of anxiety and panic are not the same as another's. We all have different triggers, or non-triggers. We all have different tools that help us in our daily lives. Some of us have deep rooted issues that contribute to the cause of the anxiety and panic, and some of us do not. For some, the causes based in emotional trauma and others are based in physical imbalances, diseases, or wounds; and for some, it's a combination of both. One thing I do know is that, for those of us that have had to pull around the heavy boulder of anxiety and panic since a very young age, we seem to share certain traits. We have an odd contrast of needing certain people close by and constantly at our disposal while also needing to have our space or be alone.

A common behavior of mine through my childhood, and most of my adult life, was to hide my feelings of anxiety and panic. If I couldn't understand it, how was I supposed to explain it to anyone else? Dealing with the brain and feelings, which is essentially thoughts and behaviors, is not so cut and dried.

CHAPTER THREE

Confusion

(Ages 18-28)

I turned 18 just a few weeks into my senior year of high school. At the time, I had been living with my paternal grandparents for almost a year. My dad's job at the time required him to travel all over California, Nevada, and sometimes Oregon and Washington. After Dad did that on his own for a year or so, my mom went to be with Dad. My brother, and I went to stay with Grandpa and Grandma. My brother finished up his year of school, then joined my parents and was home schooled. I continued to stay with my grandparents so I could finish up my schooling since I only had a year left.

I'm so thankful my grandparents agreed to let me stay with them, as I'm sure it was an adjustment to suddenly have a teenage girl living in their midst. Growing up, we spent a lot of time with my grandparents, so I was very close to them. Even though I was comfortable with them and with being in their home, living with them was a huge change for me. My curfew time got changed, I wasn't living with my parents and brother anymore, and I really had to step up my personal responsibility. Things were a bit strained with my parents at this time because of the usual conflicts that kids have with their parents as they grow into adulthood. It was almost a relief not having to deal with all that stress, but on the other hand I also felt abandoned. For someone who already felt unimportant and not good enough, it was a bit of a blow. Of course, I never realized all these feelings at the time; I was a pro at burying them and not dealing with them. It certainly made it easier at the time, but I would pay for that practice later in life.

Ray finished high school and moved back home. Shortly thereafter, I turned 18, and we decided to get married after I graduated. We kept that planning to ourselves until a few months before I graduated, since my parents weren't too keen on us being together for so long. They thought I should have dated more people and had more of a life outside of being a couple. What I didn't know how to convey at that time was that I didn't want to be without Ray, date other people, or experience life on my own. I didn't want to be social and adventurous; I wanted to feel safe and loved. I wanted to experience life with someone I had a deep connection with. It was not my fault I found that at such a young age. As an adult, I can see why my parents were concerned. The problem is that they didn't really know what was going on inside my brain or about all the emotions I was dealing with. I never talked about it. I know it was frustrating for them because they had a picture of how they wanted me to be, or how they thought I should be, as a "normal" teenager. The problem is that wasn't me, but I didn't know how to tell them that at the time.

As an 18-year-old senior, I could have written myself permission slips to leave school. I think I did it a couple of times for doctor or dentist appointments and that was it. I didn't skip school or take advantage of it. Yes, I was super "square". Breaking the rules made me extremely anxious, and it just wasn't worth it. Plus, it was a small town and one of the teachers knew my grandparents. I'm sure word would have gotten back to them and it would have been a whole conversation I didn't want to have. I did everything I could to make sure I wasn't a burden on my grandparents. Most Friday and Saturday nights I would hang out and play board games or watch Matlock with them and their friends. I was so not the cut loose and party hard type of senior. I was the "hang out with the elderly seniors" type of senior, but that's what was comfortable for me. I had a lot of fun with them, and now that they're both gone, I'm so thankful I had that time and those experiences with them.

My anxiety at this time was manageable and only came up in a way that affected my day to day functioning when I had to deal with a highly stressful or emotional situation. One of these situations was when I had to tell my parents, over the phone, that I was getting married. When I told them, I swear there was a full minute of complete silence. It was so nerve wracking! The original plan Ray and I had was for us to leave for Alaska (Ray's aunt had promised us jobs in her business), and then get married while we were there. My parents did not like the idea of us going off and living together without being married and for us to get married with no family attending. They proposed that since they would be in town for my graduation anyway, that we should just get married during that week. So, we got married the day after I graduated from high school. Knowing that my parents were coming home and that I would have to deal with the tension in our relationship, along with all that comes with graduating and getting married, I went into hyper-anxiety mode. I put on a mask of, "I'm okay, and everything is just great!" but that was far from the truth.

To say that the weeks surrounding my graduation and our wedding were extremely anxiety-inducing is an astronomical understatement. There are large portions of time during my graduation and wedding days that I don't even remember. I was so busy trying to please everybody else and to keep the peace between everyone, that I forgot to take care of myself. I didn't enjoy or have fun those few days. I didn't even go to a post-graduation party with my classmates or do any of the senior activities. I feel that I skipped over an important milestone in my life because my focus was on the wedding instead of the fact that I was graduating. I always felt bad for Ray's sister, who graduated with me. Instead of being out having fun and spending time with her friends, the day after graduation, she had to be at the wedding. Plus, the focus of that week for her family should have been her graduating, but instead it was the wedding, because it was held at Ray's mom's backyard. I was so wrapped up in my own fears and thoughts that I never got to apologize to her for that.

I almost think Ray's mom was more nervous about the wedding than I was. She was so concerned about having the house and grounds look perfect, and the food she and Ray's aunt prepared be enough, that she was running around the morning of the wedding like a chicken with its head cut off. I remember being at the house and getting ready; I walked into her bathroom and she was frantically wiping down her armpits with a wet washcloth, even though she had just gotten out of the shower. When I asked what was going on, she said that her mind was so distracted that she sprayed hairspray in her armpits instead of her deodorant. It was so out of character for her that it gave me a good laugh. I still remember the annoyed look she gave me when I was laughing, which of course made me laugh even more. Funny, the things I do remember. That whole exchange is very vivid in my mind, but I can't recall most everything else about that day. Just a few snippets of it come back to me. It makes me sad that because of the stress and anxiety, I didn't get to enjoy and really be in the moment. I always thought my wedding day would be joyous and something I would always remember with fondness. I do cherish the fact that I got to marry my best friend, and that is all that really matters.

The day after our wedding was spent loading up my 1981 Ford Escort in preparation of our drive to Alaska. We were headed to the Kenai Peninsula, new and unknown territory. Since I'm not too keen on change, especially in my environment, the thought of leaving was exciting but also scary. It was quite the adventure. During the five-day drive, I was consistently having the "impending doom" thoughts. I worried that we would break down in the middle of nowhere in Canada and deal with that unexpected situation. It's not like there's a pay phone or town every 30 miles. There are long stretches of distance and time where you don't see another vehicle, person, or house. I worried that one of us would get sick or that something or someone would attack us…. or that we'd simply just disappear. I was more worn out by the worry and anxious thoughts at the end of the trip than I was from driving for five days straight. I have to say that only being able to rely on each other in a foreign place cemented our bond and probably helped create the true partner relationship that we've enjoyed.

During this portion of our time in Alaska, we lived for a few weeks in a travel trailer with no electricity or plumbing. We also lived a few months in a tiny shed that was up on spools and again with no electricity or plumbing. After that, we spent a few months in a one-bedroom small apartment above the auto repair shop Ray worked at. The jobs that Ray's aunt said she had for us didn't work out since she ended up giving the jobs to two of Ray's cousins. The first two weeks we were there, we were waiting for his aunt to come and get us for the job. When she did show up, she told us "Sorry. You're on your own." It was a fantastically horrible thing to do to us. It was a scary feeling to have our plan suddenly changed for us.

We scrambled to find jobs since our meager savings were running out. I got a job as a housekeeper for a family that ran a business out of their home. They were nice people, but I was so exhausted most of the time due to not eating well and being stressed out, that I probably didn't do the best job ever. I hated that. I believe that I was probably dealing with some mild depression. Having too many changes and uncertainties in such a short period of time was more than I could handle well.

We did have some fun times and of course, some interesting adventures, but it was all very stressful. The storage shed we lived in didn't have any windows which was nice since it stays bright out for so long there during the summer months. We had adopted a dog at the local animal shelter, a shepherd mix of some kind. She was a sweet dog and was great company for us. One evening we hadn't yet let her in the shed for the night and we heard a weird commotion outside. When we opened the door all we saw was the dog streaking towards us at lightning speed with wolves chasing her. We got her in the shed, slammed the door and just looked at each other like "Holy Smokes!!!".

We also had some encounters with bears coming into our area. I probably would have handled those with less anxiety if I hadn't recently read all three volumes of *Alaska Bear Tales*. Horrifying! I stood there in awe the first time a moose walked into our camp. They are huge and very interesting to watch but can quickly become very aggressive. We spent all our free time outdoors since there was so much to see, do, and explore. I felt the best when we were in nature. My stomach would unclench and my muscles would relax a little. The rest of the time, I felt on edge and ready for the next calamity to befall us. We headed home before winter set in, since we didn't have jobs we really liked or even a good place to live. Having the jobs fall through with Ray's aunt really changed the trajectory of the plans we had for that first year of marriage. We would have been making good wages, saved up and started on something long term. Without that in place, we had to reevaluate and make some major decisions.

After we got back home, we lived with Ray's mom for a few weeks but that was a bit of an inhospitable environment; plus, it's difficult to stay with your parents once you've been on your own. Not an ideal situation. We ended up finding a place to rent in a nearby town. I first got a job as a housekeeper at a nearby hotel, and then a job at an independent fast-food restaurant. Ray worked at a gas station/service garage. We were getting by, but not getting ahead in life. It was good, honest work but were "dead end jobs".

Anxiety was still affecting me, but mostly just that uneasy background feeling I'd always had. I was starting to get mini panic attacks when I felt unsure about myself (i.e. when my lack of self-confidence kicked in), but I didn't know what they were. I thought that I was just overreacting and being an overly nervous person because I was just weird.

At the time, we had a 1980 Chevy Luv, a small pickup truck, with a manual shift transmission. We had sold the Ford Escort when we were in Alaska and had bought this truck. I had only driven a stick shift a few times and wasn't good at it. Once we got home and moved into the rental, we decided to buy an automatic shift vehicle for me. Unfortunately, the vehicle we bought had lots of issues, so I had to learn to drive the truck. Every time I left the driveway, I was terrified that I would break the truck or get stalled somewhere with traffic around me, and I wouldn't get the truck started again. I was sure that I would end up being laughed at and embarrassed because I didn't know how to do something so simple.

Where I worked was only a few miles away, so I did okay with that since it was flat at all the stop signs; there were three of them between home and work, and I dreaded each one of them. The grocery store we went to, which was also where I went to cash my paycheck, was on a busy street and to get there I had to stop at a T-intersection which was on a steep incline. I remember praying furiously as I would approach the stop light, for it to turn green or that I would be stopped behind enough cars that I wouldn't be on such an incline. When I got a green light and didn't have to stop, I was elated. If I got stopped on the incline, then I would be in tears worrying about stalling the truck by not getting the right ratio between the clutch and the gas. There were more than a few times that I pulled into the grocery store parking lot crying and shaking and wondering how I was going to go in the store, do what I needed to do, and then drive back home. A 45-minute errand would occupy my worry thoughts starting the day before. I knew it wasn't a healthy way to react to something that most people wouldn't even give a second thought to. I believed that I was just broken and somehow less of a person than those who didn't react this way.

I'm sure the stress of trying to be an adult and figure out what that looked like, and what marriage was all about, didn't help my mental and emotional state. Ray and I were both struggling in many ways. We had gained a lot of weight; me for the first time in my life. It made me feel bad about myself, but I was totally unmotivated to change it since food was one thing I looked forward to at that time, and it gave me pleasure and comfort. I liked cooking dinner and sitting down to eat together. It was one of the highlights of my day. I'm sure that working at a fast-food restaurant where they provided one meal per shift didn't help either. Oh my gosh! The burgers there were so good! We were both eating way too many of them, plus eating full three course dinners with dessert almost every night. It was a time of more uncertainty as we tried to figure out what we were going to do next. Not having structure and a plan in life is extremely anxiety inducing for me. We were headed down a horribly rutted road, and we needed to change course immediately.

Ray made a bold decision to go into the National Guard. I would stay with my grandparents while he was away at boot camp and training. After being married for just over 9 months, he was gone for 4 months. I think the reality of the burden of having to be responsible for the care of another person really weighed on him, and he felt this was a good option for helping us as we moved forward in life.

It was tough being apart. I couldn't even talk to him or get letters from him for the first two months. I wrote a letter to him every night and mailed it the next morning. I did that for the duration of his time away. I knew that if it was hard on me, it had to be ten times worse for him. He was apart from me and in a strange environment where he was being pushed to his physical and mental limits. As difficult as it was, I think it was good for him. He grew as a person and learned what he is truly capable of doing.

I got a job at a fish processing plant de-boning farm raised fish. It was long hours of standing on my feet, up to my elbows in fish slime, in a cold and noisy environment. The smell isn't too great either, but the pay was decent, and I felt I was doing my part to help us get ahead in life. A couple of the older women, one of them being the mother of a girl I went to school with, took me under their wings. I carpooled with them to work, and they helped support me emotionally though the difficult time of being apart from my husband. I will forever be grateful for their kindness and caring.

Before Ray left, we parked the truck, sold the other vehicle that we'd had so many problems with, and bought a cheap but reliable Ford LTD from Ray's brother. It was older and nothing fancy, but I didn't need to drive long distances and just needed a run-around car. It did have one issue that Ray didn't have a chance to fix before he left; there was a hole in the fuel tank so I could only fill it to about halfway. I was so terrified of running out of gas that I never did test to see how far I could go before getting to empty. I worried all the time that I would be abducted if the car broke down on the side of the road. Once again, my anxious imagination was putting in some overtime. At least the car wasn't a stick-shift!

Since I was living with my grandparents, and they were babysitting my sister's kids almost daily, I ended up watching them quite a lot when I wasn't working. She had two of her three sons by this time, and they were very young. All that time spent with my nephews was a good learning experience for me but made me very anxious. I would worry the whole time they were left in my care that I wouldn't know what to do if something happened to them. I think parents just become numb to it at some point in order to get on with life. Kudos to all you parents out there, but especially parents dealing with anxiety and panic issues! I never had children, partly because I couldn't fathom raising a child while dealing with anxiety struggles.

The first year of our marriage was challenging, and even though my anxiety was present, it wasn't something I had to consciously deal with daily. I was able to function quite well, probably because I was so good at burying my feeling and fears and not dealing with them. Plus, the feelings of anxiety were normal for me and I thought that's just how I was. It was also a growth period for me since I did have to rely on myself more and make decisions on my own that would affect the both of us.

I struggled for a long time with making decisions. I couldn't make them because I was always so worried about making the wrong one. It would freeze me up, so I just wouldn't make them. Doing so would either cause Ray to make all the important decisions or would leave me stuck with not moving in any direction other than the one I was currently in. When Ray was gone, I was so concerned about spending any money, other than what I gave to my grandparents, for food, or necessities. This wasn't because Ray would be upset at me, but because I was so afraid of making a wrong decision about what to spend money on. Without Ray to do things with, I didn't venture out or do many social or other activities. I pretty much went to work, babysat my nephews, and hung out at home with my grandparents. I would go see my mother-in-law, Jessica, every few weeks or so. That was the extent of my life's boundaries. To step outside of those limits caused me anxiety.

When Ray was gone, Jessica invited me to go to a music concert with her. We would have to drive over an hour on the freeway to get to the venue location in a large building. She drove because even then it was hard for me to drive in very busy traffic. We got there a little late, so the concert had already started. We got to our seats, and I was so disturbed by the trapped feelings I was having while being in an enclosed space with so many other people, that I told her we should leave early to beat all the traffic leaving the concert. I just could not relax and enjoy the music. I kept worrying about getting out of there as fast as we could, so I wouldn't have to be part of the crush of people trying to leave. I felt so bad about it later, pushing her to leave early, but I couldn't explain why I felt like I did. I thought I was just an anti-social weirdo.

I was 19 at the time of this incident and should have been able to explore the world around me without being worried and fearful all the time. Obviously, that was not the case. My memories of the time that Ray was away are full of images and impressions of standing for long hours with cold fish slime sticking to my forearms, playing games with my grandparents and their friends, and getting to know the wonders of my nephews. Even though I wrote to Ray each night, I felt adrift inside without my husband there. It's like we got married, rushed to start a big adventure as we began our life together, then everything stopped and time stood still. I felt like I didn't belong anywhere, and it was very disquieting.

Ray finally came home. His mom and I met him at the airport. This was pre 9/11 so you could meet someone at the gate. I cried so hard when I saw him. He looked different and felt different when I hugged him, but he was mine, and he was home. My grandparents were considerate enough to be gone for a few nights camping so we could have some alone time. I hope they knew how much their support and kindness during that time kept me going. They were always a constant and steadfast base of comfort and wisdom. I am eternally grateful that I was able to have spent quality time with my grandparents from my birth until their deaths.

We temporarily moved in with Ray's mom a week later. That change was hard for me. I never felt fully comfortable there. She was always good to me, but her house was so immaculate. I was terrified to mess anything up. I tried to clean and help when I could but generally tried to stay out of her way. I certainly don't like to feel like I'm a burden or imposition on someone.

While Ray was gone, my parents gave us a single wide mobile that had been trashed by renters. I organized getting it moved to a mobile home park. All those first-time adult things I had to do on my own were terrifying to me. I really struggled talking to people I didn't know and going into situations and environments I wasn't familiar with. I did it though. I thought "If Ray can do what he is doing, then I can do this."

We spent the month after Ray got home repairing and remodeling the mobile to make it livable again. It was our first real home together. It wasn't fancy, but it was ours and it was home. My great aunt lived in the same mobile home park, so I would walk down and visit her occasionally and mow her lawn for her. She was an awesome lady that kept me interested in all things art and craft related. I really enjoyed those visits with her and being able to help when I could.

I think it's important to note that, by this time in my life I wasn't going to church, reading my Bible, or forging ahead with any kind of relationship with God. This felt odd to me since I had been raised going to church and continued to attend with my grandparents when Ray had gone to boot camp and training. I didn't realize that I had lost that close connection with God years earlier.

As a child, I got very excited about God and felt very close to Him.

The older I got, the less I felt that connection. I still considered myself a strong Christian, but I really wasn't putting any effort into it. It wasn't until much later in my life that He brought me back to Him. I mention all of this because this loss of a personal relationship with God was a pivotal point in my life. I would feel the ramifications of it for a very long time and in so many ways, that I never realized until I was able to look back and see how that disconnection had affected me. Ray didn't grow up going to church and never expressed the need to go. I didn't want to be one of those sad women that I used to see growing up that were married but their husbands never went with them. I saw the looks of pity and how those women always seemed to be on the fringes of the women whose husbands attended church. I was odd enough; I didn't need to add all of that into the mix of experiences that would just make me feel even more odd. Believe me, I never needed help in that department.

We lived in the mobile home park (or as my husband likes to say "It was a trailer park!") for about two years. During that time, I continued to work at the fish processing place; after working there, I worked as an office assistant and then, in the parts department of a diesel repair shop. Ray worked running heavy equipment, such as backhoes and bulldozers. He also tried his hand at logging but decided it really wasn't all that great (or safe!). My anxiety was generally at a low level, but would escalate to a high level when I was pushed out of my comfort zone or when I had to deal with confrontational situations.

When I worked for the diesel repair shop, I was the parts runner. I had to go to different supply places or junk yards to get parts or deliver parts to a site one of the mechanics was working at. This was way before the time of Google Maps, and I had to rely on verbal or hand written directions. Many of the parts suppliers were in areas around a big city about an hour or more away. I got lost many times and would panic and be afraid to stop and ask for directions, but I had to. I couldn't go back empty handed, that's a sure way to get fired, plus it would have been beyond embarrassing. It was nerve-wracking but each time I got through it successfully it built my confidence a little. It was the early 1990s, and no one gave a second thought to sending a young woman (around age 21) into sketchy parts of industrial areas by herself, sometimes after dark. I think that, on some of those occasions, my fear and anxiety were justified.

Ray never really settled into a job or profession, and was getting restless and frustrated. He is an extremely driven and hard-working person but found it difficult to work at jobs that had no real reward or future. Ray's aunt, that owned the construction company in Alaska was trying to get us to come back up to Alaska and offered us jobs. Understandably, we were not too keen on getting burned by her again. Been there. Done that. It was a bad experience that we did not want to repeat. She called a few more times and said she really needed flaggers and that Ray could probably get hired by the main contractor running a dozer or as a laborer. We decided to sell everything and make the move. We were cautiously optimistic about taking this leap and planned accordingly.

We bought a 1977 Ford truck, an old truck camper (sans a restroom), and made an enclosed trailer using an existing frame and some plywood. We loaded up and away we went to Skagway, Alaska. As I'm writing this, I'm thinking *This sounds like a haphazard plan to me now. What were we thinking!?* I know our families and friends thought we were crazy. It's a miracle that truck made it to Skagway, and we weren't left stranded in Canada somewhere. I really think God must have a sense of humor. He paired me, little miss anxiety, with Ray who is all about major changes and adventures. I'm glad the anxiety was manageable during my early twenties so that I could experience those adventures and even enjoy them to the extent that I could.

Ray got a job with the main contractor the day after we arrived in Skagway, and Ray's aunt helped me get my flagger training card since she was a certified instructor. She worked me part time, giving breaks to the other flaggers. The road we were working on was the only road to a historic site, the Chilkoot Trailhead. There were also many homes along the road, so the traffic wasn't heavy but a consistent line of cars all day long. This was especially true when the cruise ships docked and there was a steady stream of small tour buses coming and going to the historic site. The first few times I had to stop a car; it was hilarious. I was so timid and non-assertive at that time in my life. As uncomfortable as that job was for me, I believe it was also good for me. It caused me to come out of my shell a bit and become somewhat immune to being on display. I would say that was the hardest thing for me to get used to, always being stared at, and having people look at me. I had spent my whole life trying to be invisible and blend in. What the heck was I doing making people pay attention to me! I eventually got the hang of it, but the anxiety and panic would rise in my belly each time a car approached me and I had to stop them or direct them. It's probably a good thing that the first month or so I was on call for 12 hours during the day and would just work a half hour to two hours at a time. It gave me a chance to chill out and get the anxiety calmed down in between shifts. The downside was that I had to be nearby and ready to go during that whole 12 hours but only got paid for the actual time I worked. Truthfully, it was very boring to be on standby.

We spent the whole season, spring to fall of 1992, in Skagway, then came back to Washington for the winter to regroup. Our camper had become infested with ants, so we had to sell it. We ended up going back to Alaska the next spring. I continued to work for Ray's aunt's company, and Ray worked for the main contractor when he could or otherwise would work for his aunt's company too. Sometimes we were on the same jobsite and got to be together, mostly all day, every day. I know that to some people that would have been awful, but for us it was great. We both got certified as Worksite Traffic Supervisors and a few times ended up managing the traffic control on two separate jobs. The few times that happened, we were fortunate enough to be in the same area so that we didn't have to be apart for weeks or months. Ray was still my only "safe" person, so being away from him was an added source of anxiety for me.

We were in our 20s, traveling around Alaska for work, living in campers, travel trailers, 5th-wheel RVs, and saving our money. We had a goal to save enough in our second year of working there to pay for a down payment on a house and property. We took as many work shifts as possible, didn't spend money on anything but the essentials, bought our clothes at second-hand stores, and got teased about being "tight" and "cheap". It was all worth it though because we met our goal. We were exhausted and looked like we lived on the streets, but we were able to buy a single-wide mobile home on 15 acres not far from where I lived as a child. We saved more money the next year and used it to remodel the mobile home and fix up the property. For seven years, we worked in Alaska for 9 to 10 months of the year and then came home to Washington during the hard winter months when little to no road construction was happening. We spent the months in Washington working on our property, fixing up off-road motorcycles and ATVs, and recovering from working 6 or 7 days a week for 12-16 hours a day. As interesting and fun as it was to work and live that way, it was taking a toll on my physical and mental health.

Doing the job of flagging and implementing traffic control plans means that you're often either standing for long periods of time with no breaks or walking for miles a day. The job also required me to lift and carry heavy cumbersome signs and sign stands, along with picking and placing cones and candles (the tall, skinny cones). Holding a stop/slow paddle for 10 hours and often fighting the wind to keep them upright and visible, wreaks havoc on your arms, shoulders, back, legs and feet. It may look like an easy job, but it is grueling. Plus, you must always keep mentally alert and focused.

I wasn't drinking nearly enough water because most of the time I wouldn't get a bathroom break but once or twice a day. Unless you wanted to wear an adult diaper and stand around in your own pee pants, you learned to cut back on fluid intake. It was also hard to get in the right nutrition since I had to carry my food around with me. It also had to withstand cold or warm temperatures and be easy to consume while I worked. For the first few years, I didn't eat breakfast and only drank a cup of coffee in the mornings; I barely ate any lunch, and would then be starving and inhale too much fast food late at night. Even though I had a physical job, I gained weight again and felt terrible because I wasn't fueling my body correctly. All of this, plus burying my emotions and feelings, and putting too much pressure on myself to be a good worker and please everyone just wasn't beneficial for me. The bad news is that I didn't recognize the effect all this was having on my body, and as a result my mental state. I felt rundown, tired, in a fog, and any little stressor would tip my anxiety reaction over the edge.

One thing Ray and I both did was join a popular weight loss program in 1995. This was during the "no fat" fad diet phase. Everywhere you turned, you were bombarded with advertisements for no-fat and low-fat foods, magazine articles about losing weight fast and permanently by cutting fat out of your diet, and celebrities spouting off about how it works for them. Since we are both overachievers, we went full force on the low calories, no-fat train. We did lose the weight quickly, but we aren't meant to eliminate good fats from our diet. Without fats, our brain doesn't function correctly, our hormones don't work right, and other organ functions suffer. Since the adrenal glands are part of your hormone system, and I was already exhausting mine with being overworked physically, mentally, and emotionally, I ended up paying the price for going that route. It took a few years, but eventually something had to give.

It was also during this time that my relationship with my family deteriorated. I didn't know how to deal with or express my feelings, I would just cut ties with situations and people that caused me any type of distress or bad feelings; in other words, I avoided or hid from situations that might have made me uncomfortable or would have forced me to face and finally process emotional traumas. In order to protect myself from additional anxiety and conflict, I quit talking to my parents for a few years. It was relatively easy to ignore the situation when I was in Alaska with no permanent address or phone number. Cell phones were becoming more mainstream, but we didn't have one. They were still too expensive and the cost of using minutes was criminal. It was a good excuse for not contacting them for long periods of time, and eventually I just quit calling or reaching out altogether.

Even though it was my choice to cut communications, the situation itself was very painful for me. There was a lot of animosity and hard feelings between my parents and Ray and even myself. I felt it was never going to get resolved, and I hated being in the middle of two very strong-willed parties. I couldn't please them all, and got tired of trying to keep the peace. I loved them, but I wasn't able to step in and stand up for myself and set boundaries or work on the relationships in a healthy way. It made me extremely sad and I worried all the time about disappointing either my parents or Ray. I was walking on a tightrope over broken glass and was terrified of falling. I felt terrible for the hurt that my actions, and inactions, caused many people. I have since forgiven myself for handling the situation in the only way I knew how at the time.

Between 1995 and 1997 we continued the low-calorie, low-fat diet incorporated with a demanding work schedule, and being busy during our off season. I started to have more and more episodes of just not feeling quite right. I would get all these unusual body symptoms that came and went but increased over time. Then it happened; my first major, scare-the-crap-out-of-you, panic attack.

It was February 1997 and we were headed back to Alaska in a few weeks. We got up in the morning, had our low-fat breakfast of a Rice Krispy Treat and coffee. I know, I know - I cringe now just thinking about how I wasn't fueling my body correctly. All that sugar and caffeine was just paving the road to my major anxiety issues. After breakfast, we drove the 20 miles to town and got a latte then headed to the gym to work out. Are you starting to see the problem with this picture? I'm not a senseless person but looking back, I can see I was exhibiting some senseless behaviors.

We got to the gym and started doing our circuit on the machines. Suddenly, I started to feel a bit uncomfortable in my body, but I thought it was just effects of exercising. A guy I graduated high school with came into the room and started talking to us. I hadn't seen him in almost 10 years, and as nice as it was to visit with him, I was feeling so odd that I couldn't even focus on the conversation. I had to excuse myself and go get a drink from the water fountain because I thought I was going to pass out. Instead of feeling better after a drink of water, I felt an overwhelming need to escape. Without saying anything to Ray, I bolted outside. That's all I could think about. Getting out of the building and away from whatever was making me feel this way. I was outside the front doors just pacing and gulping the fresh air. I was trying to talk myself into believing that I was fine and that nothing was wrong.

After about 10 minutes of me doing this, my cousin, who worked at the gym as a trainer, stepped outside and asked if I was okay. He must have seen me though the front windows. I thought *Oh, great! Did everyone in there see me out here being weird?* but I told him I just wasn't feeling well and asked if he could let Ray know that I was outside and needed to leave. I had no idea what was happening to me. My heart was thumping around in my chest so much that I kept rubbing the space between my breasts. I was shaky and unsteady on my feet, almost like how I felt when I was on a boat. I couldn't keep my balance, and I was seeing black around the edges of my vision. There was a multitude of other body sensations going on, but I was too distracted by the need to flee, hide, and cry. Yet, I was working very hard at holding it all together so that no one would notice that I was about to die (so I thought).

It only took Ray a few minutes to come outside, but it felt like eons. I must have had a wild look in my eyes because he immediately asked what was wrong and got a very concerned look on his face. It could also have been the pacing and air gulping that clued him in, I suppose. I told him that something was not right with me and I needed to leave immediately. He kept asking me what was wrong, and I kept telling him that I didn't know exactly but that I needed to get home right away. I told him my heart was racing, and I just didn't feel right.

I think it really scared him too because he wanted to take me to the emergency room. The thought of going to the hospital just made the need to get home that much stronger. I told Ray, "No! I think I just had a bad reaction to something in the gym or maybe the coffee. I'll be fine in a little while." It took some convincing, but he ended up driving straight home. By the time we got there, the body symptoms had diminished, and I was wiped out and weak. I got into the house, drank a glass of water, and laid down to take a nap. I really did think I had a bad reaction to something, sort of like a food intolerance or an environmental toxin. Certainly, I never wanted that to happen again! Sadly, I lived in constant fear that it would.

About ten days later, my fears came to fruition. We were headed into town to do some shopping and run errands. The closer we got to town, the more I started to feel those same body symptoms I had experienced at the gym. By the time we were within a few miles of the hospital, which we had to pass on our way to town, I thought for sure I was having a heart attack and was going to die. My arms felt numb, and I felt very spacey and lightheaded. I told Ray to take me to the hospital and that something was seriously wrong with me.

We were both scared and unsure about what was going on with me. Ray pulled up to the emergency room doors, then walked in and told the person at the reception counter that I was having heart palpitations and needed to see a doctor. He brought out a wheelchair and took me right into the ER. I guess when you say it's your heart, they don't mess around. The nurses took my vitals and a doctor came in a few minutes later and hooked me up to an EKG machine; he asked me a variety of questions about how I was feeling. Truthfully, it's a bit of a blur. My body symptoms had settled down by then and I again felt the fatigue of the aftermath. The doctor said that my EKG looked normal, but that my heart rate was elevated. He never mentioned the terms anxiety or panic attack. He just said that it was probably caused by hyperventilating, to get some rest, and follow up with my regular doctor. I left the hospital feeling like a complete idiot and scared because up until a few weeks ago I had always been in relatively good health.

The emergency room visit must have quelled my fears somewhat because I didn't have another one of those crazy body symptom experiences until a few months later while at work in Alaska. By that summer, I was having full on rapid heart rate episodes, light headedness, shortness of breath (hyperventilating), and feeling weak in my body. I did not know that I was experiencing anxiety and panic attacks. Silly me, right?

I remember being at work, standing on the side of the road in a busy construction zone, thinking I was going to black out. I would call for Ray on the radio and ask him to come take over my flagging station so I could sit down for a few minutes. It really scared me because I didn't know what was going on. We had no health insurance, but I ended up going to a clinic nearby to get checked out. They initially thought I was probably anemic, but that ended up not being the case. The doctor told me to quit drinking coffee because that was contributing to my racing heart rate; he then had me wear a heart monitor for a week. I had also started getting these odd spasms in, what felt like, my heart where I couldn't catch my breath. Then suddenly, my heart would thump hard and I was okay again. The incident would last only a few seconds but terrified me. As much as I tried, I couldn't get one of the incidents to happen when I had the heart monitor on (of course!). I worried that the doctor would think I was just making it all up, or that I was overreacting to what was going on with my body. I didn't want our friends to know that there might be something wrong with me, since I didn't want to answer a bunch of questions or receive unsolicited advice. Plus, I was only 28 years old, which seemed so young to be going through these kinds of issues; so, of course, my mind went to the worst-case scenario thoughts.

I had to go to work with this electronic box, the heart monitor, strapped to me and all these electrode wires attached with those awful sticky pads all over my chest. How do you hide that? Lots of big, bulky clothes, that's how. Having something more visibly wrong with me made me feel like more of a freak than usual. I always knew something wasn't quite "right" with me, and now everyone else would know too. I had to wear the heart monitor for a week, and the day before I went back to the doctor's office, I tried everything I could to bring on one of the heart episodes. I ran around the uphill circular driveway of the place we had our 5th-wheel RV parked. I tried to think of something scary. I asked to work at a high stress flagging station. I even ate sugar and drank a cup of coffee. Nothing. It was so frustrating to get the results of the monitor test and have the doctor say "Everything looks normal, just make sure you keep away from all stimulants, and you should be fine."

I felt relieved, but also not trusting that *that* was the end of it, or that it would be that easy. I did cut out the coffee. It's been 22 years and I still miss the taste and effects of it; at least the effects before I started getting the heart palpitations. As much as I love the smell, taste, and ritual of coffee, the repercussions of what it does to my body is not worth it. Can you hear my long suffering "sigh" here?

I continued to have short periods of anxiety attacks and low-level panic attacks, which I called having "one of my weird heart episodes" as a result of not understanding what was really happening. It was scary, but I was functioning okay and didn't seem to be in any imminent physical danger. We decided that, unless it all progressed to a perilous point, I would wait until we were back in Washington to get further testing done if the issues were still even happening.

As you might guess, the symptoms got worse after we arrived back home in Washington. Why wouldn't they? Between my physical state of stress and exhaustion from doing my job in Alaska and being constantly worried about what was going on with my health, there was now the fear of maybe having to see my parents and deal with that strained situation. I was a mess. We still didn't have medical insurance, but I had to start going to doctors to find out what was going on with my body.

Over that winter, I was poked, prodded, questioned, tested, and saw many doctors and specialists. It was not fun, but I kept hoping that someone would be able to tell me why I was having these episodes of weird body symptoms and generally just not feeling well. I remember one test that a neurologist performed where all these wires were connected to my scalp with a doughy type material, and then I was put in a room where they turned off the lights and show the laser light show from hell just to see if I would have a seizure reaction.

Well, I didn't have a seizure, but it did cause me to have some of my body symptoms and I thought, *Finally! They will be able to see that something is happening to me.* Nope. The test came back that nothing was wrong with my brain functions. I was so frustrated at this point that I just gave up going to doctors and tried to manage the symptoms on my own. Now, what bothers me the most is that not one doctor ever said, "You may be experiencing anxiety or panic attacks." Not one. They also didn't test my adrenal functions or ask about my diet (probably because I was skinny at the time) or even sat down and talked to me. The scariest of the body symptoms was the pounding, racing, and uncomfortable feeling of my heart. It always scared me and it fed the anxiety and panic because I didn't know what it was. My thoughts fixated on the fact that something was wrong with my heart.

These incidents, with the rapid heart rate and discomfort in my chest, were the start of me experiencing health anxiety. It was fixated on my heart, especially. Any little twinge, weird physical feeling, or unusual reaction from my body would have me convinced I had a serious and fatal illness. For years I was obsessed with taking my blood pressure reading. Every time, my blood pressure reading was good (117/75), but my heart rate would be in the 90s and sometimes higher if I was having an anxiety or panic attack. I was afraid to even walk a few blocks since I was convinced I would have a heart attack if I did. It was not a reasonable reaction, but a reaction from the perspective of anxiety never is.

We went back to Alaska that spring, and it was a real struggle for me. My job was incredibly physically demanding, stressful, and sometimes mentally exhausting. I just did not feel good. All the feelings of disappointment in myself came rising to the surface every time I couldn't perform as usual. I continued to believe that my problem was a bodily one, and I just had to deal with it. I believe now that it was easier for me to think it was all physical issues rather than looking at the probability that my problem was mental or emotional. This is because physical disorders and illnesses are more accepted by others – and ourselves. Around this time, my sister-in-law said, "It sounds like you're having panic attacks." My immediate response was "No. That's not it. There's something wrong with my bodily functions." I couldn't even admit to myself that I was dealing with a mental illness. I continued down that road of denial for a remarkably long time.

CHAPTER FOUR

Avoidance

(Ages 28-37)

After another year of trying to do my job and dealing with my "mystery" issues, we decided it was time for a change. One day after work, Ray stated to me, "I think you need to go to college. You're too intelligent to be doing a job that doesn't challenge you anymore and is obviously hurting your physical well-being." Of course, my immediate answer was, "What? No!" because any change was petrifying to me. Even though I knew in my soul that I couldn't keep doing what I was doing and get better, I still fought the change. We talked about it for the rest of our work season in Alaska, and we finally concluded that I would investigate going to school when we got back to Washington. I had no idea what it would cost or what I would want to go to school for. I wasn't good at making decisions about my life because I was always so worried that I would make the wrong one. It was easier, and less anxiety-inducing, for me to allow others to make decisions for me. Not exactly a good life strategy.

There was a substantial sense of relief, once the decision was made, that I wasn't going back to my job in Alaska. It had become increasingly stressful and scary since I was always waiting for one of my "episodes' to happen on the job, which is not a good thing when the actions you take are what keeps others safe. That's a big responsibility, and I was in my own head too much to stay focused enough to do my job properly. Since failing and letting someone down was devastating to me at that time in my life, it just added to the anxiety. Plus, working for relatives can be a tricky thing and our relationship with Ray's aunt and uncle had become strained. I kept bottling up all those unresolved feelings of frustration, hurt, anger, and disappointment that relationship caused, which again added to the anxiety. It didn't help that I still wasn't speaking with my parents and barely talked to my siblings and extended family. I was excellent at avoidance. I didn't realize that the body symptoms I was experiencing were the physical manifestation of all the situations I wasn't dealing with in a healthy way.

At the end of the work season, we loaded up our 5th-wheel RV, enclosed trailer, and our truck and headed home to Washington. We flew a friend of ours to Alaska, and he drove one of our vehicles home for us. He was a logging truck driver, so was the perfect person to help us get back safely. He and Ray would switch off between driving our 1981 Chevy truck pulling our 1978 28-foot long RV, and the Toyota pulling the small enclosed trailer.

It was fun traveling with our friend and sharing the crazy, unique experience of driving the Alaska Highway with him. It felt like a celebration of sorts, since we were driving towards our new future. During the summer our property in Washington was sold; so, when we got home, we ended up selling our Chevy truck and 5th-wheel RV to Ray's brother, Ty, and we lived in our 1985 Minnie-Winnie motorhome for a few months while we looked for a house to purchase. It was during this time that my parents and I started talking again and working on developing our relationship. I didn't find out until probably 10 years later that Ray went to my parent's house, talked to them, and extended the olive branch. It was all because my (paternal) grandmother told him that he would have to be the one to reach out first since my parents just didn't know how to.

God, working through my grandmother and my husband, brought my parents back into my life. I'm not going to lie; it was intense and awkward and scary the first few times we went to their house for a visit. But, true to form for my family, we didn't really talk about the elephant in the room. We skittered about it and hoped it would just go away. So, yes, I was talking to and inviting my family back into my life, but we never resolved why they weren't in it to begin with. It was more comfortable for all of us to move over that speed bump like it never happened, turn the corner, and not look back. I certainly didn't know how to express, or even make sense of, the feelings I had that led me to stop talking to them. They certainly didn't want to hear whatever they thought I might have to say since they probably anticipated it would be hurtful to them.

We moved into our new-to-us house in February 1998. We were excited about the house, but I worried about our ability to keep up financially while I went to school. I felt guilty for not contributing to the family coffers. I'd been working since the age of 14, and it felt like I was doing something wrong by not working. I took everything in my life so seriously and stressed myself out because of it.

Once we got settled, I visited the local community college to talk to a counselor. When I told the counselor that I had no idea what I wanted to get a degree in, she asked some questions about my interests, work background, and what I was looking for moving forward. She told me about a new one-year certification program for Computer Aided Drafting. It was something new the college was offering starting in the fall. It sounded like a good mix of my artistic and analytical sides; plus, I would be able to start working and earning money after a year. It was a field of work that was just starting to expand and would give me the potential to go in many different directions. After taking the entry exam, I decided to start with some courses that spring to get me back up to speed in math, writing, keyboarding, and basic computer skills. It was exciting, as well as petrifying, to go back to school because I love to learn.

My physical symptoms settled down a bit during this time and I thought I was finally over my mystery illness and was getting better. I changed my nutritional habits, was taking high-quality supplements and vitamins, and delving into the holistic and natural side of healing. All of that seemed to help, and I was generally feeling more energetic and hadn't had a weird heart episode for months. I thought that, if I stayed away from caffeine, simple sugars, and introduced healthy fats and more vegetables into my diet, my problems would be fixed. While it did help bring my body into better balance, I still hadn't acknowledged my mental and emotional issues. Those would prove to be the real crux of my problem - I just didn't know it yet.

Ray left for Alaska just after I started school. The plan was for him to work a full construction season and I would come up and work during the summer before starting classes again in the fall. It would enable us to make some money to help pay for my school since we were paying for all of it ourselves. I didn't even think about scholarships until my second year. I was able to then get enough of a scholarship to pay for some of my books. When I was taking classes in the spring, I got a job at a retail clothing store in a nearby outlet mall. It was such a variation from the job I did in Alaska, and it paid a lot less. I was thankful for it though and the fact it worked around my school schedule. It was a fun job, a nice change of pace, and considerably less stressful than the job I had in Alaska.

After finishing my first quarter of college, I headed back to Alaska to work for the summer. We were on a job about 90 miles easterly of Palmer on Highway 1. Palmer was the closest town, so the main contractor built a temporary RV park along the job site. We worked 6 or 7 days a week, 12 to 16 hours a day, which was a typical schedule for us. When we had a day off, we drove to Palmer or Wasilla to do laundry and grocery shopping. Knowing it would likely be my last time working in Alaska, I tried to appreciate the beauty of the area (not hard to do!) and savor the time working with Ray. I only had a few of my "episodes" that summer, but by this point, I was able to deal with them better physically and mentally so the impact was less than what it had been the previous summer. I have many fond memories of that time and am so grateful that I felt good enough to enjoy it.

In early September I was back home getting ready for classes. Ray stayed in Alaska until the end of the season. I was able to fly up and visit him once in the few months we were apart. Even though school kept me extremely busy, along with caring for our (pug) dogs, Pugsey and Nook, and the house, I missed Ray tons.

We hadn't been apart this long since he went to boot camp almost 10 years prior. It was the start of a shift in our relationship. From this point forward, I wouldn't get to spend every day with him. Our work lives would be separate and that was a massive adjustment for us since we had been blessed to see and spend time together every day for most of the previous 8 years. We had some arguments that were born out of frustration and growing pains of moving into this new chapter of our marriage. That was painful.

It was tough finding a balance between what I needed to do and still worrying about pleasing him. I thought that if I wasn't everything that he needed at the exact time he needed it, then he wouldn't love me anymore. I was afraid of this shift in our dynamics, and I carried that fear with me for the next 13 years and more. I put such enormous pressure on myself to please everyone else, and to do everything perfectly, that I didn't understand that I was compounding issues I already had. I worried that I wasn't giving enough of myself to Ray, wasn't doing well enough in school, wasn't working hard enough, or contributing enough, or keeping my house clean enough, or being a good enough friend, daughter, sister…and the list goes on. Even though I love learning and was excited to be in school, I was running myself ragged. Of course, that didn't matter to me, since *I* didn't matter to me. This behavior pushed the limits of my physical and mental health over the next few years when several painful events happened in my life.

Part way into earning the computer drafting certificate, I decided to extend my learning to getting an AA in Civil Engineering/Land Surveying. I was fortunate enough to get a job, part time during school and full time during the summer, at a local land surveying company. They initially hired me the summer before I started my land surveying classes, but I did have my computer drafting certificate. They kept me on after that and gave me the flexibility to set my schedule to work around classes. Many quarters, I would go to work in the morning, then to the college for a few classes, and back to work at the end of the day. Sometimes it was school first, work, and then back to school.

Each quarter, and day during that quarter, was different. This was the time before everyone had a smart phone, and I had to depend on my memory or a calendar that I kept in various places at home, work, and in my vehicle. It was crazy trying to sustain the schedule, and keep it all straight, although being able to have a job in the profession I was studying in was invaluable. It really helped to experience the "why" and "how" of what I was learning and being able to apply it to real work situations.

At this point in time, I was burning my candle at both ends, and in the middle. I was also experiencing more weird body symptoms, that I now know were anxiety and panic attacks, and would often have to call in sick to work or miss a class. I hated, and I mean *really* hated, how this mystery problem was affecting my everyday life. Every time I had to miss work or school, I would beat myself up about letting someone down and worry that people were thinking badly of me. It was hard to explain to others why I wasn't feeling well so often since I didn't know myself. It was aggravating. I didn't realize that all this pressure and being "go, go, go" was making things worse for me and contributing to my issues. My need to be validated by others, by trying to performing perfectly in all areas of my life, was ruining me.

By my second year of college which was Fall 1999 through Spring 2000, I was struggling with the bizarre body symptoms daily, but they were becoming part of my "normal," and I just adapted my life around them. While not a good thing, it did enable me to go about my day-to-day life and handle it. I think part of the reason is that I enjoyed my new job, which at the time was vastly less stressful than the job in Alaska, and it was exhilarating to learn new things. I didn't realize how much I missed challenging my brain. The thing I did miss about Alaska was all the time I got to spend in and around nature. I got some of that in my surveying classes, but it wasn't the same in frequency. I do have to say, I relished being in a climate-controlled environment when I looked outside my classroom or office window, at the cold and wet, or sweltering hot weather. As I got older, I appreciated that more and more.

On May 3, 2000, I went to school in the morning and to work in the early afternoon. By this time, Ray and I had bought cell phones but still weren't really used to having them. I luckily remembered to bring mine to work that day and had it sitting on my desk when Ray called not long after I had settled into work. He sounded strange on the phone and all he expressed was that he needed me to come home right away. That's all he would say.

I instantly knew in my gut that something was seriously wrong. He rarely called me during the day, unless it was something that couldn't wait until I got home; plus, he sounded so unlike himself, almost like it was hard for him to get any words out. Immediately, I told our office manager I had to leave, ran out of the office, and drove home. The whole way there, I had this deep pit of uncertainty and fear in my stomach. I was overheating, trembling, and driving way too fast. My chest felt tight, and my breathing was shallow and fast. My mind was racing around trying to figure out what could possibly be going on. I knew it had to be something dreadful. I was shaking as I got out of my vehicle and made my way into the house through the back door and into the laundry room.

The dogs greeted me, but they were abnormally agitated and ran right back into the living room instead of doing their normal bit of barking and jumping up on my legs. I followed them into the living room and found Ray sitting in a chair. His body was stiff and he was leaning forward a little. He was shaking too. I knelt in front of him and kept asking what was wrong. Finally, he was able to choke out the words, "He's gone. Ty is gone."

At first, I didn't understand, because my brain just didn't want to comprehend that he was telling me that his older brother, Ty, was dead. After a few seconds, it sunk in, and we were clinging together sobbing and keening. The dogs were crowding around us trying to give comfort. Missy, pug no. 3, was just a puppy of 6 months and was frightened by our crying and carrying on. After a bit, we collected ourselves, and I got some details out of Ray. His father had called him and told him the news.

The information was unclear, but we were told that he had been shot in his apartment. It's difficult, because in those moments of grief and disbelief, you want all the gritty, minute details. You want to know exactly how, why, and what. You want all your questions answered right away. Without all that information, it seems unreal and that there could still be hope of mistaken identity. We were in shock. How could this happen? Why did this happen? Ty was supposed to move back to Oregon the next week to start working with his dad since they both did auto body repair and painting. He had been living in McCall, Idaho and wasn't happy or doing very well there. He had been drinking more and hanging around some nefarious types. He was 35 years old, and he was gone. He would never get married, have children, or get to know his niece and nephews. The loss of him was so complete and deep that we couldn't comprehend it.

Ray and I made the decision to drive over to his mom's place near Fruitland, Idaho so we could meet up with his family which was scattered between Washington, Oregon, Idaho, and Alaska. His parents divorced when he was very young, and it was a complicated family dynamic, as most are. Ray's sister had just gotten married the year before and we were thankful she had someone to lean on when Ray called and told her the news. That was the most heartbreaking phone call I ever had to witness. The task of having to call your sister, knowing that what you will say is going to break her world in half, is daunting.

When the miles separate you, and you can't be there to physically comfort them and share your bodily grief, it breaks your heart even more. It all seemed so unreal at the time, like you're watching yourself and everything around you through a hazy filter. I'm sure it was the shock and the mind's way of protecting me from the pain so that I could get on with the business at hand. The worst thing about someone close to you dying is that you must go on living. It's excruciatingly painful. Everything else but your grief seems so stupid and unimportant. How dare the need to eat and sleep disrupt your pain? Those reminders that you're still alive and must do all the things that keep you functioning seem like a betrayal to the person you just lost. Your soul is in pain and you just want to mire in it.

I called a friend that we had helped quite a bit when he was in need due to the fact that he gave over a million dollars to the, in my opinion, cult called the "Ramtha School of Enlightenment". I explained the situation to him and asked if he could come stay at the house and watch the dogs. We had added a puppy, Missy, to our "pack" so we now had three dogs. Having someone house and dog sit seemed like the ideal option for us since we needed to get over to Idaho as soon as possible.

This guy had house and dog sat for us before, so he knew what to do and the dogs knew him. Incredulously, he said that he couldn't because there was a free weekend of teaching at the cult compound, and he really wanted to go to that. I thought maybe he didn't understand why we had to leave, and I told him again that Ty had died. This guy had met Ty a few times, so he knew how important he was to Ray and I. This so-called-friend, who went to a "school" which pontificated about love and enlightenment, chose not to be there for us. He chose the cult over being a good friend and person. I really shouldn't have been surprised, but until that moment, I never fully grasped the hold that cult had on him. That was the last time I ever talked to the guy. He was not, and never was, a friend to us. One more loss for the day.

I had to spend precious time calling dog boarding places nearby to see if we could get the dogs taken care of while we were gone. Luckily, a nearby kennel that bred and trained high end German Shepherds said they had room to board them since all three of the pugs would fit in one of their kennel spaces. I hated leaving the dogs in a strange place with people they didn't know, especially since they were already feeding off our agitated energy and wouldn't calm down.

Once we got the dogs settled, we headed out for the 10-hour drive to Idaho. As we sat quietly watching the scenery roll by, I was trying to imagine what was going to happen in the days to come. Looking too far into the future only causes anxiety since you don't know what's really going to happen. I must have run through 25 different scenarios in my head. All that did was give me tight muscles and a racing heart rate, but it hard not to do that in this type of situation. I was also imagining, over and over, what had happened to Ty. Also, not a good thing to do.

Since we had a late start and were exhausted from the emotional strain of it all, we stopped after 6 hours to get some rest. The last thing the family needed was for us to get in an accident because we pushed ourselves too hard. We barely even slept, but I think we needed to take that time to process our feelings and prepare ourselves for what was to come. This was our first major loss as adults, and we were ill equipped to handle it. We were 31 and 29, and our complete outlook on life shifted because of this experience. Unfortunately, not in a good way.

Before I go on, I feel that I need to talk about Ty so you can understand why we felt this loss so immensely. Ty was four years older than Ray. He was Ray's protector when they were growing up. Even though he did the usual big brother tormenting, he was always there for Ray when it counted. Ty had lived on his own after dropping out of school and learned the auto body repair trade. He was good at it. He and Ray always shared a love of all things muscle car and motors. It was something they could bond over and talk about for hours.

For most of the time that Ray and I were together, Ty lived in the central part of Oregon. Ray lived with Ty his senior year of high school, and they relied on each other as only brothers can. They liked each other and had fun together. They understood each other. Besides me, Ty was Ray's best friend. Ty was a formidable guy in appearance. Not overly tall, but broad of the chest and muscular throughout his body. He had a strong sense of needing to protect those around him and was deeply loyal to those he cared about. Even though he was a big softy, I certainly would want him on my side during a fight in a dark alley.

The best thing about Ty was his loving heart. He felt deeply and was sensitive and intuitive. I think he wanted to hide and protect that part of himself. He was stubborn and a hard worker, as Ray and all his siblings are. In the years between Ray getting back from boot camp and me starting college, we would spend weeks with Ty. We would stay with him while we used his shop to do body work on a vehicle we had, or we went out and helped him cut firewood to sell for extra money. Sometimes, we would just hang out and talk. Their dad lived nearby so we would visit with him and his wife too. Ty became my big brother. He was one of my favorite people. I felt that if I had Ray and Ty around me then nothing bad would happen.

He was funny and had the most infectious laugh I had ever heard. You would never expect it to come out of him, and he would even do it in his sleep. I loved and trusted him; he was a part of Ray and that made him uniquely special to me. He loved animals and always had a dog that was his constant companion. It was heartbreaking for him when they died. One year, after his beloved lab mix Sheba got hit by a car and didn't survive, he was without a faithful companion for almost a year. We knew it was hard on him, so we bought him a Rottweiler from a breeder in Alaska. It worked out perfectly that we were able to bring the puppy to him at the end of our work season. It was a complete match and he called her Lady. She was extremely possessive and protective of Ty. He was her pack. It broke his heart when he had to put her down after she bit the young child of a woman he was dating at the time. Even though he knew it was the right thing to do, I don't think his heart ever recovered from it.

I think that was the beginning of his spiral into depression and anxiety. Over the next year, he started drinking more. We weren't aware until after his death, that he was also taking prescription medication for depression and anxiety and that just doesn't mix well with alcohol. He was self-medicating, trying to hide from his childhood traumas. He was a different person in Idaho. I think he was wrestling with some inner demons and they were winning. I believe that he knew that and that's why he was making the move back to central Oregon, back to what he knew was a better environment for him. I hate that I didn't know then what I know now. I didn't reach out or try to help him because I couldn't recognize in him what I wouldn't recognize in myself. I didn't yet know the amount of inner torture that anxiety can inflict upon you, but he knew and was trying to deal with it the best he knew how.

By the time we got to Ray's mom's place, we were emotionally drained and physically tired. My whole body felt tight, and I was trying hard not to break down so that I could be strong for Ray. After the rest of the family showed up, we drove to McCall to meet with the police detective in charge of the investigation. I think he was surprised that he would be meeting with eight family members, and he scrambled a bit to find a room for us to meet in that would be private. I don't remember where the room was located, but I do remember that it had a few folding tables and chairs in it, like those used at events or church bake sales. He told us that the statements they received from the other people in Ty's apartment at the time of his death indicated that Ty had shot himself in the right back side of his head.

Wait! What?

There were other people in the apartment? None of what he was telling us sounded like truth. We told the detective that Ty would never have killed himself, and was actually making plans to move back to Oregon the next week and that no matter what, he would never take his own life. That just wasn't who he was. The detective looked at us like, "Yeah.... that's what they all say."

It was frustrating, and we didn't know the right questions to ask or our rights at this point. We were all still walking around in a fog and none of it felt real. In what alternate reality are we sitting in an ugly musty room talking to a police detective about the circumstances surrounding the death of our loved one? Not one I ever thought I would be in.

Sadly, we made many mistakes that day because we didn't have the knowledge needed for this type of situation. We should have insisted that the state police take over the investigation. We should have insisted that a real coroner handle the autopsy and handling of the body. They used the local funeral director who just put "suicide" as the cause of death on the death certificate before a real investigation was even completed.

We were burying him within a week of his death. It's like they couldn't release the body and get him buried fast enough. Our understanding now is that the City of McCall Police Department made many mistakes. Knowing that they were not equipped to handle this sort of death situation, they should have immediately called the state police to take over, but they chose not to. Years later, we did get the state police to do their own investigation, and they ended up arresting one of the people in the house who they believed killed Ty. She was a woman he had dated for a short period of time while she was separated from her husband. She was a drug addict and was mad at Ty for not giving her his prescription medication. Such a stupid thing.

Unfortunately, the woman was let go because McCall said they couldn't afford the trial. All that McCall did was change the death certificate's cause of death to "accidental death by own hand". The woman went free and ended up killing another man in California and going to prison for that murder. After being caught up in the whole drama of this for years, and trying, to no avail, to get the state governor, reporters, and anyone else to listen to us. We finally gave up.

We got tired of not being able to end our grieving and move on with our lives. Every time we had to deal with the mess, we would feel angry, hurt, and sad all over again. After the whole fiasco with McCall refusing to accept the outcome of the state police's investigation, we let it go. We had done all we could, and it wasn't going to bring Ty back to us. Frankly, the stress of it all was doing considerable damage to Ray's mom and dad, both physically and emotionally.

One of the hardest parts of the few weeks following Ty's death was the funeral itself. During the service, we were sitting in the front row of the pews at the funeral home. The casket was sitting just feet away from us. I had Ray on one side of me and my sister-in-law, Judy, on the other. Judy was shaking so hard at one point that I thought she was just going to break into a million little pieces. The struggle to hold in all the emotions we were feeling was just too much. I couldn't sit still. The need to release all the nervous energy I had was overwhelming. My knee was bobbing up and down and my heart was racing up into my throat. I could only stare straight ahead because my senses were being overloaded. Ray's mom was sort of rocking back and forth with tears rolling down her face. I don't think she could have stopped them if she tried. I was so worried about all of them and trying to comfort and be there as a support, but that's hard to do when you're constantly on the verge of a major panic attack. I wanted to escape from that room so badly that I almost screamed.

Once the service was over and the men were preparing to carry the casket outside, I practically ran out of the side door where the casket would be carried out. I just stood against the exterior wall, trying to calm myself down. I remember it being cold outside. It felt good on my flushed face. The fresh, crisp air burned in my lungs. The sobs were coming out in bursts as I tried to hold them back, almost like releasing the steam on a kettle. What I didn't know is that, right after I practically ran out of the room, Ray threw himself onto Ty's casket and was crying and carrying on. I was so mad at myself for not being there for him because I had to escape outside due to the overwhelming grief and panic that I was feeling.

I have no idea how we drove in that funeral procession 12 miles down a windy steep roadway to the cemetery. Once there, we huddled together as we watched Ty being lowered into the earth. It felt so final and so wrong. Dealing with death is exhausting, and dealing with the business of it is soul crushing. I hated "shopping" for a casket and talking about the costs of this and that. I am thankful for a friend of Ray's mom who let us stay in her quiet, tranquil cabin the night before the funeral. She was a massage therapist and gave us all massages that evening. Her taking the time and energy to do that for us was amazing and what we all needed to get through the next day.

To add salt to the wound, we had to clean out Ty's apartment. There is something so surreal and wrong about going through someone's intimate and personal belonging. We were seeing all those little things that people usually keep to themselves and that no one else is privy to. Things like bank statements, personal letters, the little things that we use every day – much like what we keep in our nightstand.

We had the added torturous bonus of needing to go into the space where he died, knowing it wasn't a peaceful death. We didn't want to look too closely at anything in the living room in case we saw something the cleaners had missed. I remember grabbing the coats Ty had hanging near his front door and one of them was a newer insulated Carhartt coat Ray and I had given him at Christmas. I saw that and the memory of Ty's smile when he opened the gift washed over me. I just couldn't do it. The coats smelled like him and after I took them out to his van, which we were using to transport his stuff back to our place, I just laid across the seat and cried and kept saying, "I can't go back in there. I'm sorry. I just can't!".

Ray's mom, sister, and I stayed out in the vehicles while Ray, his other brother, and cousin cleaned out the rest of the apartment. Again, it all seemed so final and unreal. I felt as if I was in this weird limbo of thinking I would never laugh again and knowing that I would because sometimes laughter is what heals us the most. I found out that, during intense emotional upheaval, I tend to use humor to deflect from the pain. Sometimes that is received well by others, and sometimes it is not.

By the time we got back home, all I wanted to do was crawl into bed with Ray and the pugs, sleep for weeks, and not see the light of day. The world felt even less safe than before, and I wanted no part of it. Life doesn't work that way. I had to get back to the business of living, which meant going back to school and work, taking care of the dogs, the house and myself, whether I wanted to or not.

Spring was starting and the flowers were blooming and the sun was beginning to shine brightly. I hated it. I wanted the dark clouds and gloom. I wanted the world around me to match how I felt inside. It seemed wrong to be around the cheerfulness of nature, but Ray and I went on with life and tried to grieve but not dwell on our loss.

The Saturday after we got home from Idaho, I heard a knock at our front door. It was my grandparents. Usually they called before coming over, so it was a pleasant surprise. I was touched that they were worried about us and wanted to stop by and see how we were doing. Grandpa saw a television set of Ty's that we were going to put in the garage sale we were having that weekend. He asked if he could buy it since theirs was so old. He wanted me to meet them for lunch on Sunday and then deliver and set up the TV for them afterwards. It was out of character for my grandfather to initiate that kind of thing. Most of the time, I would just stop by their home every week or so to visit and see how they were doing. If I hadn't been so wound up in my own head and grief, I probably would have seen the signs that something wasn't quite right with Grandpa.

I had a lovely lunch and visit with them that Sunday. I'm so thankful for that because a few days later, on May 30, 2000, we were hit with another enormous loss. I was at school all that morning and rushed to work just before lunch time. When I walked in the door at work, the owner's wife said that my sister had called for me twice in the last 10 minutes and that she would call back again. I instantly got a bad feeling and before I could even sit down at my desk, she said my sister was on the phone again. It was one of those times when you know you must take the call, but you also know you really don't want to.

My hand was shaking as I reached for the phone and picked up the handset. My sister said that Grandpa was at the hospital and had suffered a stroke. She said I needed to get there right away. To the bewilderment of my coworkers, I ran out the door yelling that my grandpa was sick and I had to go. Luckily, the hospital was only a 10-15-minute drive from work, but I probably made it in 7 minutes. I was hunched over the steering wheel of my Jeep and couldn't seem to catch my breath. I just kept praying "Please God. Please God. Please God." I didn't even know what to pray, but God knew what my heart was saying.

My sister's husband met me in the parking lot of the hospital and was trying to calm me down and give me information to prepare me for how Grandpa was. Looking back, it was a bit humorous because he was not known for handling stressful medical situations very well. He passed out while my sister was in labor with their first child. He was notorious for fainting if he even thought he was going to see blood, or any bodily fluid. I appreciate that he did try that day.

My sister was in the waiting room ready to grab me as I walked in. My mom was in the ER room with Grandma and Grandpa. He had gone into a coma in the ambulance. When I went in to say goodbye to him, I was dazed and didn't know what to say. My cousins, sister, mom, and grandma, plus a nurse and doctor were also in the room. They had taken out his false teeth, and I teased him and asked, "Where's your teeth?" because when I lived with them, I would sometimes see him without them and we would get goofy about it. Everyone else thought I was being serious and proceeded to explain to me that they had to be removed so he wouldn't choke on them. I let it go and didn't explain because I knew that Grandpa heard me and understood what I was trying to say.

    I kept thinking that they would get him in a room, he would wake up, and I would be able to talk to him again. My dad was working on the other side of the state at the time, a 7-hour drive away, and he was trying to get home as soon as possible. I thought for sure that Grandpa would hang on until Dad got there. My sister, me, and our two cousins were sitting in a private room near the ER. My sister and I were trying to contact our brother who was living in Portland. His car was broken down at the time, and we were working out how to get him to us. We all thought we had time, but of course Grandpa had to do it his way. He passed away about an hour after I got to the hospital. I remember my cousin, who had stepped out to use the restroom, came back in the room crying and saying "He's gone. He just went. Girls, he's gone!" We huddled together crying and clinging to the feeling of family. A rush of childhood memories spent with the four of us at our grandparents' house came flooding back to me. Good memories, but the feeling of loss was deeper than soul deep. I felt deflated and numb.

    Two unexpected major losses in three weeks left me feeling raw. The next few hours were a bit of a blur. We went to my grandparents' house and waited for Dad to arrive. There were family members to call and plans to make. My sister and I drove to Portland and picked up my brother. It was a somber drive there and back. I distinctly remembering them being so quiet and closed off and me not being able to stop talking. Not a normal behavior for me in those types of instances. I was hysterical inside and was trying to keep it all in, but my emotions were leaking out when I let my guard down. By the time we got back, Dad had arrived. The house was crowded and I couldn't stand the sound of my loved ones crying and the stupefied looks on their faces.

    I went outside and was sitting on the front steps. I was trying to catch my breath and bring some order to the chaos inside my head. My dad came outside a few minutes later and sat next to me. He asked me the most incredible thing. He said, "Are you okay? I'm worried about you." All I could think was *Why are you asking me if I'm okay? You're the one whose father just died, and you weren't there to say goodbye.* I was so used to making sure everyone around me was okay, that it never occurred to me to make sure I was okay. I told Dad that I was fine, just trying to process all of it. He gave me a little side hug and went back inside. I don't think he will ever know how much that meant to me. My dad isn't one to talk about his feeling or be overly demonstrative with affection, so that gesture meant everything to me.

Ray and I were still grieving Ty's death, and now, we were starting the grieving process all over again. I was trying to support him and he was trying to support me, but we were just living in a fog of tears. I would go between the extremes of feeling too much and doubling over with the losses, and not feeling anything and putting on a brave face. There was no in between for at least the next month. Time doesn't heal the wounds; it just distances you from them so you can get on with your life. It's always still there, if I poke at it. I can tell you that I've been crying on and off while writing this part of the book. It's been over 20 years, and when I think about it, all those feeling of sadness and loss come rushing back.

Grandpa's funeral was surreal, but I do remember that my husband and brother were pallbearers and they were standing off to the side during the gravesite portion of the service. They both looked so sad and alone, and I felt wobbly without Ray by my side. As soon as the minister was done talking, I walked over to Ray and got folded into a big hug and then reached out to hold my brother's hand. I needed to be connected to these two great men I loved that I knew were hurting as much as I was. Sometimes feeling the heartbreak of those around you is worse than the heartbreak you're feeling. I know it was that way for me. I also realize now that sometimes feeling someone else's energy and being empathetic to what they're feeling is too much for me, and I can't handle it and sometimes it helps in the moment to distract me from my own pain. It's always puzzling to me why it's one way or the other and I'm never sure which way it's going to be in any given situation. I almost always end up having heightened anxiety or a panic attack after getting down in the emotional trenches with someone else.

The months and years following is when the anxiety and panic started escalating. I would get up in the morning and "not feel good". I still didn't know that my issues were caused by anxiety. I would just tell my husband that I was having one of my "episodes". I know. It sounds like something a woman in the 1700s would say, such as "Oh, dear me. I'm having one of my spells." As ridiculous as that sounds, that's how I felt. I couldn't articulate what was going on with my thoughts and body because it was different every time.

I would feel light-headed, shaky, and sick to my stomach; I also had a myriad of other varying body symptoms. I tried not to miss too much work or school, but it was hard. Just pure perseverance and the fear of failure kept me going on most days. Not feeling quite right became the standard for me, but it's such a slow process that I didn't really notice what was happening. I was pushing the grief down and not dealing with it, because that is what was acceptable to the people around me. The attitude of "be strong, don't inconvenience others, and deal with it privately" is a message I was taught at a young age, and it was reinforced for me throughout my life. So, that's what I did. I added one more thing to my garbage can of emotions and situations, that I never acknowledged or dealt with and clamped that lid back on tightly.

During the time between Ty and Grandpa's deaths, and my graduation from college in June 2001, there were other extremely stressful life events. Our neighbor started harassing us, including taking covert pictures of me while I was mowing the lawn, or calling the police when we had a garage sale. Then 9/11 happened which shook up the entire world and changed how we all lived. We were in the process of purchasing a piece of commercial/residential mix property, with Ray's cousin as half partner. There were two commercial buildings on the property, and Ray and I were going to open an off-road motorcycle repair and sales business; his cousin was going to open an automotive repair business in the other building. It was an exciting prospect, but very stressful since we would essentially be giving up all our savings for the down payment, remodeling, and opening of the business.

I was trying to finish up school and wasn't sure what direction my career was going to take. My employer, that had kept me working all through school, wanted me to stay on and work full time for him. That was an easy decision for me, since I was already comfortable there and could just seamlessly transition to full time. All of these normal life stressors should have been doable for me to handle, but when you throw in the fact that I was still hurting from our losses the previous year, the uncertainty of the world at large, and dealing with my strange health issues, you would be right to guess that anxiety started to control my life even more.

After graduating (Wahoo!), I was able to focus more of my time on work, both at my job five days a week and at our new business on Saturdays. I was in my early 30s, and my world kept getting smaller and smaller. I was comfortable going to work, home, my parent's, my sister's, and maybe doing things with a few close friends on occasion. What I didn't notice, is that I was starting to avoid certain places and social gatherings.

Looking back, I can see that the avoidance of places or situations had always happened, but I was expanding that list and as a result, shrinking my world. I started to not like going to movie theatres, large shopping stores (such as Wal-Mart and Costco), gatherings with more than just a few people, shopping malls, and any place that was new or unknown to me. I came up with all kinds of reasons and excuses that would seem acceptable to other people. I would say, "I prefer to shop small local businesses," or "It's much cozier and relaxing to rent a movie and watch it at home." I'd even say, "Sorry, I can't make the <insert event> because I think I'm coming down with the flu."

I can tell you that a person with an anxiety/panic disorder gets good at hiding the truth and lying. We don't do it maliciously, but to protect ourselves from questions like "What's wrong with you?" and to appease other people. We're usually very big on pleasing other people, which is part of what gets us to the point of anxiety and panic in the first place. I had no clue that my avoidance of places was agoraphobia. I never even realized it was happening. It was just so automatic to stay away from anything that I felt would trigger an "episode" of bodily symptoms.

Life moved along the next few years with Ray and I both working long hours six days a week. My job was going well, and I enjoyed being a draftsperson and not having the load of responsibility that I had at my job in Alaska. The mix of analytical and artistic thinking that occurs in Land Surveying, and particularly the drafting aspect of it, was a good fit for me. I liked the people I worked with which included my employer's wife who came in several times a week to do the billing and other paperwork. I especially found a true mentor in our office manager, Diana. She is an amazing person who had such a wealth of knowledge that I tried to absorb like a sponge. She probably got tired of me asking so many questions, but when you have a person willing to share what they know, you take advantage of it. Even though she moved to another state in 2007, I still call her at least once a year to catch up.

At the time, my employer was also a good mentor. He would go over all the mark ups on the maps I drafted and explain to me why something had to be a certain way. I know that I would never be where I am now in my profession without the help and guidance that they gave me during the years I was going to school and the first few years after I graduated. I felt appreciated and safe at my job.

All that changed one late morning in 2003. There were a few people out sick, or had to leave early, and Diana had to go record maps at the courthouse and do some research at the title company. It was just me and my employer in the office. No big deal. It had happened many times before. It was a small company and if a few people are out, you're down to a skeleton crew.

My desk was an old drafting table that faced a window, so my chair was a high stool with a back. It's a regular office chair, it just sits up higher. There were two other drafting tables in the room and a built-in desk.

Usually there were at least two other employees working in the drafting room, but that day it was just me. Because my desk faced the outside wall, my back was to the room's entry door. I'm one of those people that isn't very good at situational awareness since I tend to have either tunnel focus on what I'm doing or in the throes of anxiety or panic and the world around me becomes a buzz of blurry activity.

That day, I was in tunnel focus mode when my employer came into the room. Next thing I know, he's awkwardly standing next to me, asking what I was working on. It was a strange question since he had just given the project to me earlier that morning. I instinctually knew that something wasn't quite right. The energy he was giving felt "off", and his body language instantly felt wrong. He was standing too close and was in my personal space. He was saying, "I know that we're both married, but that doesn't really matter." Then, he stands behind me, puts his hands on my shoulders and kept squeezing them. I was penned in between him and my desk. I was afraid of what he might do next.

I have dealt with all kinds of situations where men made a pass at me or made colorful remarks when I worked road construction in Alaska. Sometimes it would originate from men working on the construction crew or driving the big trucks, but mostly from the public who would yell things out the window as they drove by. I usually just laughed it off and never felt threatened or uncomfortable by it. This was completely different. This was a serious come on by an older man who was my employer. I hadn't seen this coming, didn't know what to do, and I went into shut down panic mode. I firmly told him "No!" and said that I wasn't that kind of person and that he needed to stop. He did back away but kept rubbing my shoulder and talking about how no one would have to know and that we wouldn't be doing anything wrong. All I could think was *Hello?! It is wrong! It's not something I want to do!*

I thought that, if I just walked away into another room, he would leave me alone. I grabbed my lunch out of the fridge and walked into the conference/break room to heat my lunch up in the microwave. He followed me in there and kept standing close, touching my shoulder. It was making me horribly uncomfortable. I tried changing the subject and was asking about a coworker who was on vacation and if she would be back in the office the next day. He said, "Why? Do you think she can rescue you?" I remember saying, "No. I don't need anyone to rescue me. I can take care of myself." I was trying to put on a tough "Don't mess with me!" persona, but inside I was running around like a startled rabbit in the road. All I could think was *What do I do if he tries to rape me?*

He followed as I walked back to my desk and loitered in the doorway for a minute as I kept my back to him and tried to eat my lunch. I really thought I was going to throw it up. He finally left and went back to his office. I numbly went back to work, but my mind felt like it was frozen, and I couldn't concentrate. About twenty minutes later, he must have realized I might tell someone, like his wife, about what had just happened. He came back to the doorway of the office and said "Thank you for saying no." I said something inane like, "Of course, no problem" because I was still dumbfounded and couldn't believe it had even happened. He thanked me again and said that he doesn't know why he propositioned me and promised that it would never happen again. I said, "You're welcome" and turned back around as he went back to his office.

Diana came back about an hour later and then field crews filtered in as the day went on. I didn't say a word to anyone. I have no idea what my behavior was like the rest of that day, or the next few days, but inside I was terrified. I didn't want to tell Ray because I didn't know what he would do, and we really couldn't afford for me to quit or lose my job. It took me three days to finally tell him. He handled it a lot better than I thought and asked me how I wanted to deal with the situation. He would step in if I wanted him to. I told him that I wanted to just let it go and only do something if it ever happened again.

I ended up working there for a total of fourteen years, and it never did happen again, even though there was often inappropriate conversations and comments made in general, but not made directly to or about me. I think on some weird level, he respected me for saying "no" because I don't think that happened very often. I found out a year later that he'd been having an ongoing affair with the coworker that had been on vacation during that incident. No wonder he was laughing at the thought of her "saving" me from the situation. Little did she know that he was also seeing a few other women at the same time. When she found out by accident one day at work, she rushed out of the building and never came back. All of this came to light and my employer ended up getting a divorce. After that, he and the business were never the same. It's like his heart just wasn't in it anymore and he was too focused on his personal life drama. I am glad to say that he did seek help for his problems a few years before I left the company, and he apologize for being inappropriate towards me. It was inexcusable behavior on his part, but I am glad he got help.

After my co-worker's abrupt leaving, I had to take over many of her projects and was trying to learn on the go. Since my employer was distracted with his personal issues, I turned to other people in the company to learn from. I'm thankful to a couple of other licensed surveyors that worked there, one for a long time and one for only a year or so. They both stepped in and mentored me at a time when I desperately needed access to their experience.

We never really get to where we are on our own. Along the way, I've had so many people give me a helping hand just when I needed it. I see now that this is God loving me through other people.

The result of being sexually harassed was me asking myself what I had done to make him think I would be open to the idea of an affair. I felt more fearful at work; I looked at the men around me differently. I gained weight to protect myself, and the anxiety ratcheted up another level. I was regularly having high anxiety bodily symptoms at work such as tight stomach, light headedness, and a rapid heart rate. I felt drained physically and mentally. To this day, I don't like sitting with my back to a doorway. Sadly, the whole incident with my employer was just one more thing I added to my emotional garbage can. Once again, I didn't deal with the situation, or my feelings about it, when it happened.

The next few years were a haze of work and regular life happenings. I went to doctors for more tests to find out what was wrong with me. Still no answers. I was told to manage my stress better but wasn't given any ideas on how to do that. Short of quitting my job and living as a hermit in the woods, I saw no relief from the stress I was under. I was still working long days at my job and then helping at our business, the motorbike shop, on Saturdays.

It was nice being part of Ray's world at the shop and spending that time with him. It reminded me of when we worked together in Alaska. The dogs were also a source of comfort and happiness. I've read studies that show having a pet lowers blood pressure and helps relieve stress. I believe it! It was always comforting for me to have all three dogs snuggling on the couch with me or heaped on me when I was in the reclining chair. I thought that life was finally settling down, and we could breathe without feeling like the other shoe was going to drop. But it didn't last for long.

For fun and exercise, a friend of ours built a motocross track on his property that was just a street over from our house.

He and Ray rented heavy equipment and built the track themselves. The property would be open for riders on certain days, free of charge. Some of the consistent riders, generally friends of ours, would donate time or money occasionally to help cover the cost of grooming and upkeep of the track. I would go over there sometimes to watch Ray and others ride, and it was a nice place for socializing that didn't usually trigger anxiety symptoms.

Ray raced dirt bikes most of his childhood, took a break during his teen years – mostly because all his time, attention and money was spent on me – and then took it up again in his mid-twenties. He would race at the tracks in Alaska if we had a day off, and at a local track when we were home during the winter. He also raced ATVs, both motocross and flat track. By spring of 2005, Ray was mostly just riding for fun and exercise. He had recently bought a new bike and was looking forward to taking it through its paces at the track. A few of his riding buddies were there too, just having fun on a nice sunny spring day. Ray was taking it easy since he was still breaking in the bike.

While Ray was doing his thing, I decided to go over and visit with my parents and have my mom wax my eyebrows. I had bought one of those home waxing kits, and it was easier for me to have mom do it than try to sit in a salon chair and feel trapped if I had a panic attack. Plus, it gave me a chance to visit with her and Dad if he was around. Mom had just finished my eyebrows and I was chatting with my parents in their kitchen when my cell phone rang. It was a friend of ours. I knew he was at the track with Ray, and it was odd that he would call me. I picked up the phone and said, "Hello." He said "I don't want you to worry, but Ray had a little accident on his bike, and the ambulance is here now. You can just meet them at the hospital." The minute someone tells me not to worry, you know that's not what's going to happen. I told him that I was coming to the track and would be there shortly. My parents could see the panic on my face, and when I told them what happened, Mom suggested that Dad go with so that I didn't have to drive.

I'm so glad he did. I was not in any frame of mind to be behind the wheel. The "What if!?" thinking was in overdrive.

The track was only a few miles from their house, so we got there in about 10 minutes. We pulled up, and I saw Ray laying on the ground with the paramedics and his friends gathered around him. I wasn't even thinking at this point; I was just reacting. This, for me, was probably a good thing, as I was dealing with things in the moment and not thinking too far ahead. I ran over to Ray with Dad right behind me. They were trying to pull off his riding boot, and he was screaming.

The paramedics told me he might have broken his leg and they needed to see if it was a compound (through the skin) break. I remember yelling at them to just cut the boot off. A $300 pair of boots means nothing when your husband is crying out in pain, and you don't really have a clear idea of what the damage to his leg is. I was holding one of Ray's hands, and my dad had the other. I don't even know if I was crying, but I think so. They finally got the boot off and thankfully there was no bone through his skin. It was apparent though that his leg was likely broken, and it was quickly swelling.

The paramedics had given Ray morphine before I arrived, and it wasn't working. Once we loaded him in the ambulance, he was still crying out in pain, so they gave him another dose. I rode in the front of the ambulance and my dad followed in my truck. Later, Dad told me my truck was close to empty on the fuel gauge, which is so unlike me. He was worried he would run out of fuel before we got to the hospital. I rarely let my vehicle get below one-quarter of a tank low, but of course the one-time I let it slide this happens, which of course justified my *Always be prepared because something bad is bound to happen* philosophy on life.

When we hit a particularly curvy and bumpy part of the freeway, Ray started moaning again in pain. The paramedic said he couldn't give him any more morphine or it may stop his heart. Ray says that that ride to the hospital felt like it took hours when in fact it took about 30 minutes. The ambulance came from our local fire department, and I can't express how thankful I am for their kindness and professionalism. First Responders truly are exceptional people.

Once we were in an ER room, and Ray wasn't being jostled about anymore, he was able to take some deep breathes and talk to me a little. He told me he was in terrible pain, and I could see it in the fact that his face was white, he was sweating, trembling from shock, and his muscles were all tense. They took him for X-Rays and shortly after, the doctor came into the room. He was the orthopedic surgeon on duty that day and thank God that he was since he proved to be an exceptional surgeon. He showed us the X-Ray image and pointed out the multiple breaks in Ray's left leg. He had essentially broken his tibia and fibula above the ankle and below the knee. There was nothing holding his lower left leg together except muscle, tendons, ligaments, soft tissue, and skin. No wonder it hurt so much when they were trying to pull his boot off. It still makes me queasy just thinking about it.

He was admitted to the hospital, and they scheduled surgery for later the next day. They couldn't fit him into surgery before that. They hooked him up to an IV with the narcotic Dilaudidd (which to my understanding is a synthetic morphine) that could be administered by Ray with the click of a button when the pain got too bad, but not more than every few hours. Unfortunately, Ray is a person with a high pain threshold. He shouldn't have been feeling much of anything, but he was still in constant pain but never expressed how much. He was hitting that pain killer dispensing button as much as he could. That should have clued me in that something was wrong, but it didn't. I thought that the nurses and doctors would know best and be able to recognize when someone was still in extreme pain.

It was a rough 24 hours until Ray went into surgery. I was trying to do everything I could to make him comfortable. I washed him since he still had dirt on his face, in his hair, and along his lower back and arms. I was so concerned about his welfare and making sure he was taken care of, that I kept ignoring my own signs of emotional and physical limits. Ray went into surgery late afternoon the day after the accident. My parents came and sat with me in the waiting room. The surgery should have only taken an hour or so, but after almost 2 hours had dragged by, I was pacing around and having to step outside every 15 minutes to get some fresh air because I kept experiencing anxiety and panic attack symptoms. My mind conjured up all kinds of horrific scenarios where they had to cut off the leg, or that Ray had died during the surgery. Finally, after 3 hours, the surgeon came and let me know how Ray was doing.

He said that the surgery took longer because when he tried to insert a steel rod into the middle of his bone, which meant that the bone marrow was pushed out, they didn't realize his heel was cracked, and it ended up blowing out his heel. They had to abandon the steel rod idea, removed it, and then put the bones together with three steel plates and thirteen screws. The doctor said that Ray was starting to come out of the anesthesia and would be back in his room in about fifteen minutes. My parents left, but a good friend of ours, who had stopped by after work, stayed, and went up to Ray's room with me. She wanted to check in and see how he was going. Her mother worked in the hospital administrative offices, so she was familiar with the hospital. I felt such relief that the surgery was over and that we could move forward in Ray's healing and recovery. I was exhausted from dealing with the anxiety, plus it was late in the evening and I hadn't even eaten anything because my stomach was so upset and tight.

Ray was wheeled into the room a few minutes after our friend and I arrived. He was groggy, but also very restless. He kept saying that he was in a lot of pain. I could tell the anesthesia from the surgery had almost worn off, and that the Dilaudid wasn't helping him. He was thrashing around, which was not good for his leg, and crying out and moaning in pain. He was trying to bang his head on the handrails of the hospital bed, trying to knock himself out. He kept begging me to make the pain stop. Seeing someone you love in unbearable pain is one of the absolute worst things to experience, especially when you can't take it away for them. My heart was breaking, and I was scared for him. I was also angry that he was in so much pain. I was frantic to find him some relief.

I kept trying to soothe him by touching his head, his hands, and rubbing his right leg and foot. After about a half hour of this, I went in search of the nurse to see if she could contact the doctor and find out why Ray was in so much pain. The nurse came back into the room with me, took one look at Ray's condition, and I could see by the surprised look on her face that he should not be suffering so much. She couldn't understand why the pain relief medication wasn't working. Our friend, who had stayed in the room with Ray, mentioned to us that he asked her to punch him in the face as hard as she could so that he could pass out. Most of the nurses I've been around are very calm in the face of situations that us mere mortals freak out over. This nurse, bless her, was frantically checking his IV, his chart, his vitals, his leg, and trying to find out what was going on. She was as affected by Ray's visible pain as our friend and I were.

My fear for Ray was increasing, and I was frustrated with not being able to help him. The nurse started asking me questions about Ray's history with pain killers, which was none. She asked about his family medical history, how he handled pain, etc. I suddenly remembered Ray's mom telling us years ago that morphine was like aspirin to her and that when she had a surgery, they had to use Demerol for pain relief. I told the nurse about it, and she said that likely Ray had the same tolerance to morphine that his mother did. Apparently, there is a small percentage of the population where morphine has no effect on them. To think that Ray had gone over 30 hours with no pain relief is astounding to me. He is one tough guy. The nurse left to call the doctor and see about getting Demerol prescribed for Ray. It took over two more hours for her to reach the doctor, for him to call the hospital pharmacy, and for them to get a syringe of Demerol to the nurse.

Thank God that our friend stayed with me and even had the foresight to follow me into the bathroom where she let me have a good long cry on her shoulder. I was shaking and hyperventilating, and thought I was either going to throw up or pass out. I wasn't going to let Ray see me break down, as I didn't know the effect it would have on him. His physical, emotional, and mental state was precarious enough. Finally, the nurse came rushing into the room and administered the Demerol to Ray. It was amazing. Within five minutes he quieted down and quit thrashing about. Within fifteen minutes he was sleeping and finally no longer in immense pain. It was strange to watch his face go from tight, clenched, and taunt, to slack, calm, and smooth. I had never been so relieved in all my life.

I stayed with him for another half hour just to make sure he was going to stay pain free. The nurse, who was pregnant, and who had told me this was her last shift at that hospital since she had gotten a job at a hospital closer to where she lived, was standing with me and our friend in Ray's hospital room as I was about to leave. We all had tears in our eyes and looked like wrung out dish cloths. I felt bad for her, since she was obviously concerned for Ray and was as frustrated as I was about the steps she had to go through and the time it took for her to get him pain relief. She told me she would check in on him often and for me to go get some rest. I wasn't about to argue with her.

I had to go home each night he was in the hospital because I had to take care of the dogs, and stop by the business to pick up and drop off the bank deposit. As our friend and I were leaving the floor Ray was on, I stopped at the nurse's station and told the two nurses that were there to call me immediately if there were any issues with Ray. One of them looked at me incredulously and said, "You're leaving?" I instantly felt like a bad wife and a horrible person. I could immediately feel my stress level going up, along with the anxiety, about twenty notches. Tears started running down my face and I just stood there mutely not knowing how to respond to her question and their looks. Thankfully, our friend stepped in and said, "She doesn't have to explain to you why she's leaving, since it's technically your job to take care of her husband while he's in this hospital. Besides, she's just been through a horrible experience and needs to get some good rest." She then guided me to the elevators and walked me to my vehicle. She gave me a tight hug and said to call her if I needed anything.

That whole ordeal would likely have resulted in me needing a hospital room if she hadn't been there to support me. I thank God for people who care, and are there just when you need them. I cried almost the whole forty-minute drive home, and I truthfully don't think I should have even been driving. I was in a state of suspended consciousness. I was so glad to see the dogs that night and have them all in the bed with me for comfort. At first, my mind was spinning, and I couldn't get to sleep. I kept reliving the last few days. I was feeling all the fear, stress, and worry over and over again. You know when you're so tired that you can't even sleep because your body is in some weird state of primal exhaustion; well that's how I was for the whole week that Ray was in the hospital. That was the first time I remember having the odd feeling of my body being in control to where it was hard for me to function. I didn't realize that the effects of the constant heightened sense of anxiety was pumping cortisol and adrenaline into my system so much that I never had a chance to recover from it. It felt like my body was humming all over. I had this horrible sense of dread, and I don't think my stomach unclenched for a month. I was experiencing continual bouts of disassociation, but described it as feeling "spacey" since I wasn't yet aware of that term.

The next morning, I headed to our business to take care of the bank deposit then back to the hospital. Ray was resting more comfortably but was still in a lot of pain. The surgeon came in to look at his leg and told Ray he was concerned about the swelling. He stuck a needle in the leg to measure the pressure and said it was too high and was probably part of the cause of the intense pain Ray was still feeling.

They would have to perform another surgery later that day to relieve the swelling in order to prevent compartment syndrome. If the pressure in the leg became too high, then permanent damage to nerves, muscle, and tissue would happen. The surgeon explained that they would have to slit open the leg on both sides and leave the slits open until the swelling went down, which could take several weeks or longer. Because Ray had so much trauma to the tissue at the time of the accident, waiting for surgery, and during the surgery, it was expected that the swelling would last for at least a month. This other surgery and complications are not what we were hoping for. I could tell that Ray was upset and concerned, especially since the hellishness of the night before was still fresh in his mind. I tried to be calm and supportive and reassure him that it would all be okay, but what I really wanted to do was sit down and cry for days.

I hated that he had to go through more pain and suffering. I was praying, but probably not as much as I should have been. I was a Christian but didn't have a close relationship with God. I was going through the motions but not really believing or having faith. I can tell you now that the whole ordeal would have been easier to get through if I had. I felt very alone that day and for many of the days to come. No one was at the hospital with me. All my family was working, as were my friends. We didn't attend a church, so there was no church community to lean on. I had called Ray's family the day before, but they were all living more than a state away and were busy with their own lives. When I talked to Ray's mom, she barely even seemed concerned.

After I told her what was going on with Ray, she went on to give me an update on some medical test she had received results about the day before. My expectation was that she would drop everything and come to her son's bedside because she wanted to comfort and help care for him. Instead she told me to keep her posted. I don't know why I had that expectation, since I knew she wasn't that kind of mother. She loved and cared for Ray, but she was not someone to show affection or love easily.

So, I was on my own when they came to get Ray late that afternoon for his second surgery in 24 hours. The nurses told me I could wait in his room, and that they should have him back in a few hours or so if all went well. I kept reminding all the hospital staff that encountered Ray that morphine/Dilaudid didn't work and that he had to have Demerol. I was terrified that we would have to relive the nightmare of the day before.

I tried to read a book while waiting, but just couldn't concentrate on the story. I decided to burn up some time and nervous energy by going to the cafeteria for dinner. I wandered aimlessly around the looking at the food choices and finally settled on a chicken Caesar salad. I got it to go, so I could go back to Ray's room and wait. I wanted to make sure and be there when he got back. As I stepped into the elevator, I looked up and saw the parents of my friend that had been with me the night before. They were there for a nutrition class since he was recovering from open heart surgery. I had met them several times but didn't know them well. They asked how Ray was doing, and when they heard he was back in surgery and that I was waiting alone, they said they would come and visit with me while I waited. I tried to tell them they didn't have to, but they insisted. Their kindness overwhelmed me, and I felt so grateful in that moment for their kindness. They stayed with me for almost an hour, which helped distract me from my worrying.

Thankfully, Ray was back in the room about 30 minutes after they left. I was so relieved to see him resting comfortably that tears came to my eyes. Even though he was out cold, I hugged on him for a good five minutes. I stayed for a few more hours, just to make sure he was okay, before heading for home. As hard as it was to leave him every night, I think getting out of the hospital and being able to regroup at home helped keep me going. The love I received from the dogs each night was a balm to my sore and chaffing soul. They could sense that something was wrong and stayed close by my side whenever I was home.

One of our pugs, Nook, was especially keen to my moods. We had a close connection, and she was always the one to actively reach out and give snuggles. I always joked that she thought she was human. I would wake up an find her underneath the covers with her head on Ray's pillow just staring at me. It was kind of unnerving but in a weirdly sweet way. At least she made me laugh when I didn't feel like laughing.

Ray was in the hospital for about a week, and I was petrified of bringing him home. His leg was in a temporary cast from the last surgery and he was still in a lot of pain. It was hard for him to get around because putting the leg down made the pain worsened and any little bump to it would cause him to clench his jaw. He was weak and cranky and felt generally awful from all the effects of the pain medication and strong antibiotics they had him on. Getting him into the back seat of the truck was especially tricky. I had to stop at a pharmacy on the way home to get his prescriptions filled, and I'm sure he was tired of me asking "How are you doing? Are you okay?" At one point he said, "Kris. I'm not okay, but I'll make it."

It took over an hour for the prescriptions to be ready, and I can't even fathom the kind of fortitude it took for him to sit in the back seat of that truck quietly and patiently while we waited. I was glad that my dad was waiting at our house to help me get Ray up the steps and into his recliner. I must take a moment and explain about the recliner, which I think was a gift from God. I never spent a large amount of money without talking it over with Ray first, but I wanted to get him something nice for his birthday which had been just a month or so before he broke his leg. I decided to get him a fancy recliner. It was big, comfy, well made, and had heat and massage. I went all out and bought it on payments so he wouldn't know. I picked it up myself and surprised him with it. I cannot tell you how thankful I was for that chair during Ray's recovery. He was able to sit in it comfortably, with his leg elevated and apply heat and massage to his sore and aching back. He slept in it the first few weeks he was home from the hospital. I look back now and know that God had a hand in me buying that chair for him.

Due to the fasciotomy surgery, which had his leg split open on both sides, Ray had to have a new cast put on twice a week. It would exhaust him every time we had to take the trip to the orthopedic center for them to remove the old cast, clean up the wound, and then apply a new cast. You must remember, he had exposed muscle, tissues, and nerves. Any change in pressure on it, or just air blowing past would cause him to clench his hands and jaw muscles. Because Ray is a very driven person with a strong work ethic, he had one of our friends take *my* recliner down to our business so that he could go to work for at least half the day. He was only a week out of the hospital when he concocted that plan! He was still so weak from the surgeries and trauma that he couldn't even use crutches. He had to use a walker, which he hated. I bought him some leopard print fuzzy handle covers to try and "pimp his ride". He wasn't amused, but used them anyway since they did make the grips more comfortable.

It was difficult for me to let him out of my sight. I thought that if I wasn't there then something bad would happen. I was tired all the time, even when I woke up in the morning. I found it almost impossible to separate myself mentally and emotionally from the trauma of the experience. The responsibility that I felt to make sure Ray was alright and that I had to keep everything else running smoothly was slowly wearing me down. My capacity to handle the situation emotionally and mentally was deteriorating by the day. I'm one of those people that will hold myself together during crisis, but then fall apart days or weeks later and wonder "Why?"

We argued about him going to the business since I was concerned that he would overdo it or pick up an infection. It was an off-road motorcycle repair shop. I shuddered to think of the dirt and grime he would be around. My schedule for the next few weeks was grueling. I woke up early to get myself ready for the day, then I had to get Ray ready. I had no idea the amount of time it takes to help someone do something that they would normally be able to do on their own. Plus, it's frustrating for both parties. I took Ray to the business, then did the 30 minute drive to work. I would work three or four hours, go pick up Ray and head back home. Once I got him settled and as comfortable as he could be, I would take care of dinner and any chores. There were also the dogs that had to be taken care of, although at this point, they were pretty low maintenance since I could just let them out to run around in the fenced yard for an hour while I was cooking dinner.

    I don't even know the word for the type of exhaustion I felt. I was worried about Ray since he kept getting more and more depressed about his situation. For an extremely independent person, it was tough for him to be so reliant on other people for such a long period of time. He was also in excruciating pain for a few weeks as his body rebuilt the bone marrow that had been pushed out when the surgeon tried to insert the metal rod, which ended up not working anyway. My heart ached as I watched him writhe around on the floor groaning and crying out because there is no way to alleviate bone pain. You're just forced to deal with it. This was especially hard for me because I'm such an empathetic and highly sensitive person. I didn't know how to distance myself from his pain. All I could do was be in it with him as much as I could.

    There was one evening that I heard a vehicle pull up and by the time I got to the sliding glass doors, I saw my parents standing there getting ready to knock. I motioned for them to come on in, and as soon as they stepped into the room and my mom said "How are you doing?" I burst out into uncontrollable crying. She just stood there hugging me and letting me get it all out. Ray said, disbelievingly, "Why is she crying? What's wrong?" Really?! I still can't believe he even had to ask. I heard Mom reply with "She'll be fine, she just needs to let it all out." Truthfully, I was not expecting that outburst. I had no idea that I was going to have that reaction right then. It makes sense now, but back then I really thought I could be strong and tough and power my way through the whole situation. Oh, silly girl.

About a month after the accident, Ray's mom, Jessica, came to stay with us for a week. I thought I would finally be able to get some relief from the daily caregiving. What I forgot was that she is not a caregiving type of person. I also noticed that she wasn't her usual "energizer bunny" self and that she had a gray pallor to her skin tone. In the past, when she visited, I would come home to find that she had cleaned all my windows, had used pumice stone on all my toilets, and had cooked a delicious dinner. Keep in mind, I never asked or expected her to do these things, that's just how she was. This time, she didn't do any of those things except make dinner. Plus, Ray said that she was taking naps in the day. She also complained a lot about her back hurting.

We knew she had been seeing a doctor trying to figure out why her back was aching so much but hadn't gotten any real relief. I noticed all these changes in her but was so distracted with what was going on with Ray that I didn't question her about it as I normally would have. Ray expressed to me later that he was relieved when his mom left because he never felt he could relax when she was around. That made me sad. He did like it when my grandma would come over and sit with him when I had to go to work or run errands. She was a wonderful, caring person who had a comforting presence about her. She would brush his hair away from his forehead and give it a little kiss before she would leave. It was so sweet. Ray has always liked those little morsels of affection from people he loves.

A week after Jessica left to go back home to Idaho, we got a phone call in the middle of the night from Ray's oldest brother. He said that Jessica was in the hospital and was diagnosed with leukemia. One of the tests came back with such alarming results that the doctor called her and told her to get to the hospital immediately to be admitted for treatment. She was in stage 4, close to death, and didn't even know it. Ray needed to get to Boise right away, and as much as I wanted to be there for him and her, we didn't have anyone to take care of the business, or the dogs, on short notice. I also had my job and had taken off so much time with Ray's accident that I needed to stay. Medical insurance was very important to us at this time, and we couldn't afford to lose it. Since Ray still couldn't drive, he reached out to one of his longtime friends who said that he would gladly drive Ray to Boise. Thank God for friends!

We were distressed about Jessica's condition, but it explained so much about how she looked and behaved when she had been at our place the week before. At this point, I was worried about Ray travelling, since he was still in a cast with his fasciotomy and using crutches. I didn't want his leg to keep swelling, since that was something he continued struggling with. Even though, by the time Ray left, we knew that she was in stable condition and responding to the initial treatments, I felt awful that I couldn't be there to see her. Ray was gone for about five days, then had to get back to have a new cast put on. Again, I had real concern about infection, especially with him going over a week with the same cast and bandages and being in a hospital which is full of germs. I was praying every night for Ray and Jess. I do have to say that it was a relief to get a few nights of good sleep, since I wasn't being woken up every time Ray moved and moaned in his sleep from pain. I was on such high alert that every time I felt the bed shift, or he made a noise, I would wake up. All of that added to my exhaustion. The pugs and I hogged the bed and were asleep early every night that Ray was gone. I felt guilty for feeling good about self-care when those I loved were going through such horrible experiences. I was – and still can be – such a worrier, and my worry muscle was getting a workout.

It didn't help matters that my job was overly stressful during this time and it would continue to get worse as I worked more hours and had more clients I was trying to please. The word "NO" was not in my vocabulary. I was taking on increasingly more responsibilities at work since my employer was still dealing with personal issues, and the work kept piling up. I was good at juggling multiple projects with varying timelines and degrees of complexities, but my need to please and be perfect was adding to my stress load. With making Ray and his recovery my priority, I felt I was letting down people at work. If I stayed at work too long or didn't call to check in on Ray, then I felt I was letting him down. I had no life outside of work and caregiving.

I was so drained by the time the weekend rolled around that I didn't want to go anywhere or do anything except veg out at home where I felt safe and comfortable. But of course, that isn't real life. I had property and a house to maintain and clean. There was grocery shopping to do and errands to run. There is always laundry, dogs to bathe, family to see, or any other number of obligations. I felt as if my world would implode if I didn't keep up the pace while making everyone else happy. It was also during this time that Ray and I bought property just across the alley from our commercial property where the business was. The house on it was in shambles. We were going to completely gut and remodel the house and then move into it. The selling of our current home would put us in a good place financially. At least, that was the idea.

One of the reasons Ray was so upset about being hindered by his injury was that we couldn't stay on track with getting the remodel done. We had a specific timeline due to a high interest, short term loan. We were losing money by the day. On top of me not working as many hours, Ray not being able to contribute as much at the business, and the medical bills, we were feeling the pinch. Of course, that all just added to the stress and feeling of being overburdened. I wish I would have focused more on the scripture Matthew 11:28 which says, "Come to Me, all you who labor and are heavy-laden and overburdened, and I will cause you to rest (I will ease and relieve and refresh your souls.) AMPC version. I could have really used some of that rest and soul refreshing right about that time. It would have made my life a little more joyful during all of this if I had shared my burden with God. But as you'll see,

I lived and I learned – the hard way, which appears to be my preferred method of learning.

After Ray got back from visiting his mom in the hospital, I noticed he was showing signs of discouragement and feelings of depression. He was having a harder time staying positive, and could you blame him? Between dealing with his physical limitations, concern about his mom's health and not knowing what direction it was going to take, worry about getting the house remodel done, and knowing that he had another surgery coming up, he really struggled to see the light at the end of the tunnel. Feelings of impending doom and fearful thoughts were particularly overwhelming for me during this time. I felt like something bad was just around the corner and that I better think of what it might be so that I could be prepared. Since I had so much negative talk going on inside my own head, I fought to keep him uplifted. A depressed person relying on an anxious and depressed person. We were quite the sad pair.

The good news is that the upcoming surgery was to close the fasciotomy incisions, which was one step further in Ray's healing process. When the surgeon explained to us that he would be closing the right side of Ray's calf and then doing a skin graph on the left side we thought, *Ok. No big deal. It can't be as bad as the first two surgeries.* Wrong. If you've ever had a skin graph, you understand how excruciatingly painful it is at the donor site. We should have gotten a clue when the surgeon said he was going to take the top few layers of skin off a couple of patches of Ray's upper thigh by using an instrument like a cheese slicer. You know what's exposed when you remove the first few layers of skin? Nerves. Exposed nerves.

It was an outpatient surgery, and Ray was looking forward to only having his cast changed every week instead of every few days. It felt like progress, and it was a huge morale booster for him. Thankfully, my dad was able to be with us the whole day. He drove us to the hospital, kept Ray and I company while they got him prepped for surgery, then during the surgery he and I got some lunch. The waiting was the worst. I was trying to hide the effects of the nervous energy I was feeling, but my body was always in motion. I was either my foot tapping, wringing my hand together, or shifting around in my seat. Sitting in the hospital waiting room with nothing to distract my brain wasn't helping with the anxiety. Finally, we got word that the surgery went well, and Ray was back in his recovery room. This time around, his post-surgery cast was sturdy and the bandages on the donor graph area appeared to be able to survive the trip home and last through the night.

I was given instructions to remove the bandages later the next day and to replace them with lubricated (non-sticking) bandages. The nurse gave me a few to take home and said I would need to pick up enough to last a few weeks as the bandages would have to be changed every day. I was told that the bandages put on post-op were lubricated and would remove easily. Well, that didn't happen. Just when I thought Ray had gone through the worst of it, we encountered the reality that dry bandages had been put on the wound. Ray was lying on his right side, with his head at the foot of the bed when I attempted to remove the bandages. When I went to remove the first bandage, he cried out, started twitching, and passed out for about 10 seconds. By the time I got half of the first bandage off, he was crying, I was crying, and I think even the dogs were crying. I was panicking and kept holding my breath which only caused me to think I was going to faint.

Even laying a warm, wet washcloth over the area didn't help remove the bandages. We finally decided that getting him into the bathtub and soaking in warm water would be the way to go. After filling up the tub, getting a trash bag to wrap his cast in, reassuring him that it was all going to be okay, and then manhandling him into the tub, I just sank to the floor next to it with his casted leg resting on my shoulder. I felt as if I was a balloon and someone had deflated me. After 15 minutes of soaking, we were finally able to peel off the bandages (while he was in the tub) with less pain infliction than before. It was still horribly painful, but at least he didn't pass out again. Once I got him up and out of the tub (Thank God for big open garden tubs!) and back on the bed ready for rebandaging, he kept asking me, "Are you sure the bandages you're using are lubricated?" It was almost like a mantra at this point. It was awful, because when the wounds were exposed, even the slightest brush of air around it would make Ray tense up and bring him to tears. We were both so wiped out after that fiasco, that he took a pain pill, and we both took a nap.

The pressure to get the house across the alley from our commercial property remodeled, so we could sell our current home and move, was weighing on Ray so much that I found him one Saturday digging fence post holes in the rain while hopping on one foot and trying to balance on a crutch. I pulled up next to him in the alley, rolled down my window and said "Well, this is an interesting sight. What in the name of all that is holy do you think you are doing!" I wanted to yell at him but controlled myself because I understood that he needed to feel useful and productive. I told him to get in the truck. He said, "No. I have to get this done. No one else is going to do it." I know him well enough to know there was no use arguing, so I parked the truck and got out to help him. The very last thing we needed was for him to fall and hurt himself or overdo it and cause the leg to swell up again. There is no way I could handle living through any part of the last few months over again. I think I would have ended up having a complete mental breakdown if that happened. I'm not being dramatic when I say that.

As Ray started to heal and gain back his strength, remodel of the house continued. We ended up selling the house we were living in before the carpet was installed in the remodeled house. We moved all that we could into a storage unit nearby and the rest of our stuff had to be crammed into the kitchen so the flooring could be installed a few days later. It was not ideal, but it worked. Thank God for friends and family that helped us move because at this point Ray was in a walking cast and boot, but still had to be careful.

As you can imagine, the stress of everything that was going on was making me more and more ill. I was having daily episodes of heart palpitations and an elevated heart rate. I was fatigued all the time. I would get dizzy and spaced-out. My neck and back hurt every day. I was gaining weight, and when I tried to exercise, I would get light-headed and panicky so I just wouldn't do it. I was back to going and seeing different doctors and specialists.

Ray and I were struggling as a couple, but of course we wouldn't talk about it. I learned growing up to not talk about issues or problems, but instead to sweep them under the rug and never let yourself get riled up. I never saw my parents argue or fight, or have a constructive conversation about anything that made them upset. As a result, I didn't know how to clear the air in a healthy manner. I was like a kettle on slow burn that would eventually blurp out a snarky comment. If I did express anger or frustration, I immediately felt stupid and awful about it. On the other hand, Ray grew up around fighting and arguing, so he hated it. If he even detected a change in my tone of voice, he would shut down or leave. As a result, we did not deal well, or even at all, with issues that would come up. For the most part, I did what I had always done, which was to keep my feelings and thoughts to myself and just go along with whatever made others happy. My emotional garbage can was getting jam-packed, but I kept that lid on tight. As you'll find out later in my story, there are consequences to these types of behaviors.

Not only were we trying to recover physically, mentally, and emotionally from Ray's accident, we were also trying to recover financially. Downsizing to a different house helped us pay off some debt and put a little money in the bank, but having our own business was a drain on our personal finances. The business would do well one month, then no so well the next month. It's hard to budget when your income is unpredictable. I ended up paying all the household expenses with my paycheck. I felt a lot of stress and pressure to provide. We were so busy at my job that even working 10 or more-hour days, five or six days a week, still wasn't getting me caught up. I was feeling pressure at work to produce and keep the customers happy. My mentor and good friend at work, Diana, had moved to Montana, and I was acutely feeling the loss of her presence.

This was especially true as I was working towards getting my LSIT (Land Surveyor-In-Training) certification through the state. In Washington, and most states, there is a two-step process for getting your Professional Land Surveyor's License. The first is to have a minimum of four years of experience and/or education in land surveying. Then you must apply to take an eight-hour exam. If you pass the exam you become certified as an LSIT. The LSIT exam is given by a nation-wide survey exam company, so it's valid in any state that accepts it. Fortunately, there was another employee at work that also wanted to get certified, so we studied together at lunch time. My employer and other people I talked to in the profession told me that most people fail the exam the first time, so to just think of it as a practice test. Surprisingly, instead of that giving me a defeatist attitude about the test, it took some pressure off me because no one was expecting me to pass the first time. Meeting other people's expectations, and my own unreasonable expectations, was a problem for me. I know that it was a factor in the causes of me feeling anxious all the time.

The test was in Seattle at a building in the Seattle Center, which is where the Space Needle is. My co-worker and I went up the night before and stayed in a hotel just across the street from it. I barely got any sleep that night because I was anxious about forgetting the many math formulas that were running on a reel in my head. Plus, the sounds of downtown Seattle are extremely different from the small town I live in. Every little sound in the alley outside my hotel room would jostle me out of my dozing. The morning of the test, my stomach was so tight and full of butterflies that I thought I was going to throw up. I get horrible anxiety the days leading up to, and right before, I start a test. Once the test starts and I can concentrate on completing it, then the anxiety subsides as my mind is focused on something else. The first thing I always do is read through the test questions. Then I address the ones I for sure know the answer to. Then I move onto the iffy ones and save the *What the heck?!* questions for last. This has always been a successful method of test taking for me. The one problem with this method is that I tend to obsess over the *What the heck?* questions while I address the ones I am confident about answering.

Unfortunately, on this test there were quite a few of the *What the heck?* questions that were about things I never even thought to study for. Things that I didn't believe had anything to do with land surveying. When time for the lunch break came, we were instructed not to talk about the test to anyone and to be back in an hour. My co-worker and I walked silently to his truck, got in, grabbed our water bottles and protein bars, took a bite and a sip, then looked at each other. I said "What the hell was that all about?!" He started laughing and said "Thank God! I thought it was just me." We didn't say anything more about the test, but it made me feel better knowing I wasn't alone in the struggle. By the time we finished, it was after 4:00 pm, and we were ready to get home and crash. We ended having a hard time getting back to the freeway because of traffic and the fact that we were mentally tired. It took us 40 minutes just to get out of downtown Seattle, and by the time I got home that night I was thankful that the test was over. Not only was the stress of the test contributing to the increase of anxiety symptoms I was experiencing such as fatigue, clenched stomach, and shallow breathing. Plus, being in such close proximity to so many people for an extended period really wears me down. I also felt, many times during the test, that I needed to escape from the room. Knowing that I couldn't without failing the test made the panicky feeling worse. The good news is that I found out six weeks later (I know! It was horrible having to wait so long.) that my co-worker and I both passed the test. We were extremely relieved.

While all of this was going on, us moving, work being busy, taking my certification exam, and Ray's healing, we were still dealing with Jessica being in the hospital for over two months getting treatment for leukemia. She was in a hospital in Boise, Idaho, so it was a 10 plus hour drive one way. We were able to go for a long weekend visit a few times those first few months. She was responding well to the chemotherapy and was finally forced to quit smoking.

Ray and I had a hard time leaving the business and my job because we had taken off so much time to deal with his injuries. Ray's sister lives in Arizona, had one toddler and was pregnant with her second child, and Ray's brother lived in Idaho but couldn't afford to take much time off because he works construction, and you have to build while the weather is good. Really, what we all wanted to do was drop everything and be there for Jessica, but unfortunately that isn't how life is. That's why it was so great that Jessica's sisters were able to be there most of the time.

The uncertainty of Jessica's health outcome was always weighing on us. I think especially at this time it was extra hard on Ray's sister because she had to give birth to her second son without her mother being there with her. The stress of dealing with a new baby, a toddler, a husband that was gone for work two or three weeks at a time for work, and a mother with a serious life-threatening disease that lived states away was a lot to deal with at one time. Whenever I would start to feel overly stressed about all that was happening, I would say, *Well, so and so, has it worse than me and they're handling it well so I need to suck it up and be stronger.* Comparing myself to how others handled stressful situations is something I did, and still do, often. What I need to remember is that maybe I don't see the crying breakdown they had in the car on the way home from work, or the unhealthy ways they don't deal with emotional issues; such as arguing with family members, yelling at their children, staying absurdly busy with unimportant things, drinking, smoking, binge eating, escapism with entertainment, gambling, or sleeping all weekend because they can't face life. Hey, I've used a few of these so I know that I'm not the only one who does. It's just easy for us to feel alone in our hurts and sufferings. I've often felt that way in my life, alone, since no one could possibly understand my issues because I didn't even understand them.

After we had settled into our remodeled home, I started going to doctors again to find out the cause of my mysterious bodily symptoms. One doctor put me on Beta Blockers. It was great for about a week or so until I was so lethargic, I could hardly move or think but at least I felt relaxed. It took getting close to death for my brain to finally stop overthinking. I had Ray buy a blood pressure machine and when I measured my blood pressure it was so low that I promptly called the doctor's office. The nurse I talked to, after hearing my blood pressure reading, told me to immediately stop taking the medication and to get to an emergency room if my blood pressure didn't normalize within 24 hours. That was scary. It certainly didn't help my trust issue with doctors. I would make appointments because I knew I needed help, but would cancel them because I was too scared to go. Someone always had to take me and go with me. I was also trying homeopathic and natural remedies to try and fix whatever problems I may have.

I researched and read about all kinds of possible causes of my physical issues. It was my digestion, liver, kidneys, parasites in the blood, a lack of minerals, a lack of B vitamins, hormonal issues, and the list goes on. I was in such denial about my mental health issues, that I kept trying to find a physical cause to my problems. It makes sense. If your body feels bad, it must be a bodily issue. The problem with that thinking is that everything is connected, mind, body, and soul. The mind controls the body, and believe me, it is a very strong force in your physical health.

Yes, I was having physical health issues, but as I would find out, the main cause was the mental and emotional health issues. And around and around we go. Just as I thought I found "the thing" that was going to fix me, it would either not work or quit making a noticeable difference in my health after a short time. I really did feel broken but was too scared to share these thoughts with anyone. It got to the point where I would only go to a medical doctor after my husband had a strong conversation with me about it. I was drained from always being tired, having no energy, and not feeling well.

This is about the time that my "issues" (aka: anxiety and panic) were really making an impact on my life and how I lived it. We made plans to go to a boat show in Seattle with another couple. I really didn't want to go because I knew it would be busy and crowded which was a situation that made me feel extremely uncomfortable. I knew it was going to trigger my light-headed and rapid heart rate symptoms, but I went anyway because I sure wasn't going to tell Ray or our friends that I couldn't go because the thought of it terrified me. So, I put on my "Hey, everything is super!" mask and went.

Instead of being able to have fun, enjoy the time with friends, and see new things, I was constantly looking for a way out and worrying that I would have some sort of weird attack in front of all these strangers and *Oh my gosh, how embarrassing would that be!* I was miserable. By the time we got home that evening, I was completely worn out. My muscles were tense and I wanted to just go in the bathroom and cry. I was mostly frustrated because I did not know what was wrong with me. I was making decisions on where to go and what to do based on the probability of it impacting my bodily symptoms. Large stores with fluorescent lights were "bad". If I had to wait in a line for checkout, it was "bad". If I had never been there before or if it was a place that I had experienced an onslaught of symptoms it was "bad". I also avoided social situations, crowds of over 20 people maximum, drawing any kind of attention to myself, and any place that was too hot. I had no idea that this was agoraphobia. I was already starting to make my world smaller and, what I thought was, safer.

Another thing happened as Ray was healing from his accident, and while Jessica was sick. We bought a trailer park in Idaho. It was a mobile home park that Ty had lived in. After his death, Jessica bought it and fixed up the mobile home he had owned. She also built a building on the property and fixed up the park. I think it made her feel closer to Ty, living in what had once been his home and completely remodeling it to pay tribute to him. It was her way of finishing or doing something he would never be able to do, but that had been a goal of his.

Prior to getting sick, Jessica was living in the lowlands of Idaho so that she could keep her business going during the winter. The mountainous area of McCall and New Meadows aren't hospitable to wintertime construction. After she got sick and was in the hospital, the family realized that any assets that she had would be taken to pay off medical bills. We needed to keep the mobile home park to eventually sell and use the profits to help with her living expenses. Ray and I were the only ones, at the time, that could financially pull off purchasing the mobile home park. It was a stretch for us and we had to use a high interest loan from a personal lending company to do it. Jessica and Ray's oldest brother vouched for a person they knew in New Meadows that would live in Jessica's mobile home and be an on-site manager for a reduction in rent. It was a small mobile home park, and the rent income from one mobile home and a few spaces barely covered the monthly payment, taxes, and insurance.

At first, it was just occasionally that we would have to put some of our personal income towards basic expenses to keep the park going. Again, I had one more thing to do and worry about. Every month I would spend time keeping track of rent payments, rental agreements, expenses and making sure I had some extra money set aside just in case. After we had owned the mobile home park for about a year, we received a very generous offer for it. This was supposed to be a short-term thing anyway, and I felt the offer was more than fair. The input from Ray's family was not to sell. They thought that in a few more years we could get even more for it, and that we would lose much of the money in taxes, and since Jessica didn't need the money right now, it was best to hold onto the mobile home park. I think there was also this thought that it was inheritance for Ray and his siblings for when Jessica passed away. I argued vehemently against not selling, but Ray decided to do what his family wanted instead. Not gonna lie, that was a blow. Suddenly it wasn't what was best for us that was driving our lives. I get it - Ray wanted the approval and love of his family. Once again, I acquiesced to someone else's wants and didn't fight for myself or us. I didn't know how to explain to Ray, in a healthy and clear way, why I wanted to sell the mobile home park. I didn't like being in additional debt. It put more financial pressure on me and on us. I didn't like being a state away and having to rely on people I didn't even know to take care of our investment. It was a lot of added stress, which I felt we didn't need at the time. I couldn't honestly say that I had a bad feeling in my gut about keeping it because frankly I had a bad feeling in my gut all the time.

We ended up keeping that mobile home park through the recession, dumped a ridiculous amount of our own money into it that we never got back, and finally ended up selling in 2014 for a fraction over what we still owed on it. Since the loan was high interest, a minuscule amount of each payment went to the principle, if that. We practically had to give it away just to get out from under the drain of it. We ended up with just enough money from the sale to buy outright a used vehicle for me to drive. Lots of lessons learned with that experience, but I had bitter feeling about it for many years.

Overall, the three years we lived at the remodeled house in town were awful for me. I did like the house, it was comfortable and laid out well, but I don't ever remember feeling good while living there. The stress I was feeling was amping up, and my ability to handle it was dwindling. The house was only a half block from a busy two-lane highway and our bedroom faced a side road. Being right in town, it was a busy and noisy area. We had no front lawn, and a small back yard area. The wooden privacy fence helped, but it wasn't a very relaxing place to live. There was no shade trees or air-conditioning, so it got very hot inside the house in the summer. We would have fans blowing, but it was bad.

We had one of the hottest summers I could remember while we lived there. We had one week where it was upper 90° to 100° during the day and only cooling down to low 80° or high 70° at night. That might not sound hot to those of you living in places where you have over 100° weather for months at a time, but to those of us in the Pacific Northwest it is HOT. Plus, we have high humidity here, so it really zaps your energy. For some reason, the anticipation of, and then actually being in, hot weather makes me feel very anxious. During that blistering hot week, I couldn't cool down. I was miserable, cranky, and fell down in our back yard as I tried to get the motorhome plugged in so the dogs and I could stay cool. The motorhome had air-conditioning, thank God! I ended up staying in the motorhome with the dogs for two days because I was terrified to go outside in the heat. I seriously thought I would die if I went outside for more than a few minutes. It didn't help that I was taking in enough water, but was retaining it and not sweating. I couldn't cool myself or regulate my temperature. My fear of being in hot weather became worse after that incident. I still deal with it today, though not as severely.

We were in the house maybe six months when Jessica and Ray's sister came to visit for a week. Jessica was there to visit the Seattle Cancer Care Alliance and see if she could get a bone marrow transplant and treatment there. She had a pic-line in her chest, which is a tube that is used to administer fluids or medication so that she wouldn't need a new IV line each time she was in the hospital or getting chemotherapy. She had some color in her face, was in good spirits, and had more energy that she had the previous two years. Prior to her diagnosis, her skin color was more gray than rosy. That should have been an indicator that something was wrong, but we didn't know that at the time.

Jessica had a real eye for interior decorating, and I would tell her she missed her calling. She had this gift of being able to make a space feel comfortable and inviting. She said my house, and especially my kitchen, needed some decorating, so we went to a home interiors store and she helped me pick out pictures to hang on the wall, accent pieces, and things I had no idea what she was going to do with them. At this point, I was able to go into small stores, where I could quickly get to an exit if I started to feel anxious. I'm glad for that because it's a memory of time with Jessica that I hold near and dear to my heart.

    I came home from work the next day and Jessica, with help from Ray's sister, had the kitchen fully decorated and pictures hung in the living room. My kitchen looked like an English countryside cottage. I still don't know how she saw the vision of that and then made it happen. Ray has that similar ability with things that need fixed up. I guess that's where he gets it from. A few days later, I came home to find another surprise. Jessica had completely rearranged my kitchen drawers and cupboards. She said the way I had it just didn't work right. At first, I was offended and felt like she was judging my ability to manage my own home. Now, it's something I laugh about when I think of it. I knew that it came from a place of her wanting to help and make my life easier. Only Jessica would do something like that. It's part of what made her so unique.

    I continued to have odd health issues. One day I woke up, and my right eye felt sore and extremely dry. I went into the bathroom, and when I turned on the light pain exploded through my eye and head like nothing I had ever felt before. I quickly turned off the light and when I looked in the mirror, the white of my eye was so red, I looked like something out of a horror movie. It felt like there were a million grains of sand between my eyelid and my eyeball. Of course, the first thing I did was completely freak out. I instantly thought that something was horrifically wrong that I must have been dying. I felt my heart beating faster and faster, the cold sweat of panic on my skin, and I couldn't catch my breath. I called in sick to work, then called the eye doctor that I had seen a few weeks prior, explained my symptoms, and they said to flush it with a saline solution or drops and see how it goes. No help there. I called my mom to see if she would stop by and look at it. Moms know everything, right? I don't care how old you are, when you're sick you want your mom. She stopped by, took one look at it, and then toted me to the chiropractor. She thought that maybe I had a pinched nerve in my neck. The chiropractor saw it and said to get to the emergency room.

At this point, I'm doing the whole rapid shallow breathing thing and trying not to display any outward sign that I'm completely freaking out inside. We went to the local hospital, and the ER doctor looked at the eye, went and talked to someone else, came back and had me stand on one foot with my eyes closed. I started to tip over. I didn't realize it then, but when anxiety and panic hit me hard, my equilibrium gets a bit squirrely. The doctor went out of the room again, came back and said he thought I needed to get an MRI because I might have a brain tumor. I'm glad my mom was with me because all I could think about after that was *Holy Smokes! I have a brain tumor and I'm going to have to get brain surgery and then will probably die!* Not very conducive thinking to keeping calm and having some perspective on the situation. Mom told the doctor, "Thanks, but no thanks!", then ushered me out of the hospital. I was crying and shaking and hyperventilating. Mom called Ray, explained the situation, and suggested that he take me to the emergency room at the hospital in Olympia which was a 40-minute drive away from where we were.

Mom dropped me off at the business and Ray hauled me up to another ER. On the drive to Olympia, I answered Ray's questions or conversation with as few words as possible. My worst thoughts were coming true, and didn't I just know that something like this would happen! After sitting around, again, in an ER waiting room, I finally got in to see a doctor. He took one look at my eye, did a more thorough examination, and then said "I think you have iritis, which is inflammation of the colored part of your eye. I'm going to call and talk to our on-call ophthalmologist to confirm. I'll be right back." As soon as he left the room, all the tension whooshed out of me, and I sagged like a sack of seeds.

When the doctor returned with confirmation of the iritis, he set up an appointment for me to see the ophthalmologist the next day and gave me some drops to use in the meantime. I was so relieved that I just kept nodding my head like a bobble-head doll. I spent a whole day in two hospitals, which cost me $1,000.00 for the second visit because insurance will only cover one visit per day per issue. It also took about 30 visits to the ophthalmologist over the next three months while my eye healed. I couldn't drive for over a month and had to wear sunglasses all the time because of the light sensitivity. Having to rely on others to help me, and the fear that people would think I was weird, on drugs - or worse - added to the intense anxiety I was feeling. The whole experience just confirmed to my anxious and suspicious mind that the medical profession could not be trusted to take care of me. I was let down by my eye doctor, and an ER doctor, before finally finding a doctor that cared and wasn't an idiot. The ophthalmologist told me it was rare to see iritis in someone so young (I was 35 at the time). To date, I've had iritis several times in both eyes; at least I can now recognize the early warning signs and can get help right away so that the recovery time is shorter and the damage to my eye is reduced.

While I was going through all that, Ray was having trouble with the plates and screws in his leg. There was an especially long screw that went in just under the front of his knee and angled upwards. It would occasionally hit his sciatic nerve and cause him great pain and his leg to collapse under him. A few days later things would shift and the pain with lessen or go away. He had to wait two years after his accident before he could get the plates and screws removed.

Once again, we trekked up to the hospital early in the morning and waited around in a pre-operation room for a few hours while they got him ready for the surgery. My grandmother went with us this time. She and I kept Ray entertained and distracted while we waited around a few hours for the surgery. Even though it was a minor surgery, it brought up all the feelings and fear I had when the accident happened and during the months following it. I was so thankful Grandma was there keeping us company, praying with us, and generally lending support and comfort. It was an outpatient surgery so we were home by early evening. The recovery was considerably shorter and less dramatic than his other surgeries, which we were vastly relieved about. I'm happy to say that from then on, Ray worked hard for years at rehabilitating his leg and now he mountain bikes, trail runs, and rarely has a pain in the leg. It's still quite a sight with the Frankenstein scars and skin graph; it has a bit of an odd angle to it, but he was able to keep the leg and have it fully functional. The doctor said it's probably even stronger than it was before the accident. I'm thankful to God for watching over Ray that day and for giving us an amazing surgeon and medical care people at both the hospital and doctor's office.

It wasn't too long after Ray's final surgery that we noticed our oldest pug, our male Pugsey, was eating less and seemed to be in some discomfort. He was 16 years old, mostly blind, but still such a joy to us. I made an appointment for Ray to take him to see the vet. I told Ray that morning to call as soon as he was done with the appointment so I could get an update on what was going on with Pugsey. The time of the appointment came and went and I hadn't heard from Ray, so I called him. I could tell in his voice when he answered the phone with a "Yeah?" that it wasn't good news. Ray tearfully told me that on the way to see the vet, Pugsey started crying out in pain and wouldn't stop. By the time Ray got to the vet's office, he was so distraught, that he took Pugsey in, told them to put him to sleep, and he left. I couldn't say much because when I cry, it's hard for me to speak – like literally no words will come out. I took a few minutes after I hung up the phone to dry my tears and try and pull myself together. A short time later, my employer came into my cubicle and said, "What's wrong with you? You look like your dog just died." I said, "He did just die,." and then burst into tears. I had to go out to my truck for about 10 minutes so I could cry and grieve in private. His death was a hard hit. He had been a part of so much of our lives and was the cause of many wonderful memories. I was angry at Ray for not staying with him during the euthanizing procedure. Pugsey should have been with someone who loved him as he slipped into eternal rest. I held onto that anger for a long time, but finally let it go when I realized that Ray handled the situation the best that he could, and I'm not the one that went through it so shouldn't judge him for his actions. It still hurts me to know I wasn't there for Pugsey, and that was probably most of where my anger came from - guilt. We still had Nook and Missy, and they helped lessen the feelings of grief by giving us comfort and continued companionship.

A year later, I knew it was time to have Nook put to sleep. She was 14 years old and having trouble with her back legs and going to the bathroom. I didn't want the same thing to happen to her as what happened with Pugsey. We waited too long for him and he suffered because of it. I would not do that to another one of our pugs. During my lunch break one day, I called and made an appointment with the vet for the coming Saturday which was just a few days away. That would give us the chance to say goodbye and spend some final time with her. I came home that afternoon and didn't find the dogs in the house. Sometimes Ray would put them out in the back yard when he came home for lunch or later in the afternoon if the weather was nice. I figured that's where they were.

I put my bag down, popped my dirty lunch dishes into the dishwasher, and walked to the back door to see my girls. I was looking forward to snuggling with them that evening. My sister and her husband were visiting from out of town, for their 20-year class reunion. They were mostly busy with all the activities, visiting with friends and other family. It was probably part of the reason Ray put the pugs in the backyard; we were afraid that visitors would accidentally let the dogs out the front door which was near an alley and two busy roads. When I looked through the glass of the back door, I saw Missy huddled under the patio swing. I thought that that was odd behavior for her. I stepped out onto the concrete patio and there was Nook lying on the concrete. At first glance I thought she was sleeping, as pugs often do. It took mere seconds for me to realize her body wasn't quite right. It's something I think we instinctually know, that lizard part of our brain that recognizes when someone is dead. I ran to Nook to see if I was wrong, but I wasn't. My girl was gone. I ran my fingers lovingly down her back again and again as I cried, telling her how much I loved her and thanked her for all the comfort, love, and beauty she gave us. I then kissed the soft spot on her head just between her ears. I was shaking. I grabbed Missy, sat on the swing, and let the grief pour out of me.

Once I settled down a bit, I went inside and got Nook's favorite blanket and covered her up with it. I tried to call Ray at the business, but there was not answer. For some reason, I called the vet's office and told them what happened and cancelled the Saturday appointment. They were extremely kind and empathetic. In fact, a few days later we received a condolences card in the mail from them. They did the same thing when Pugsey died. It's nice to know that someone else understands and cares. Having no children, the dogs were family to us.

When I couldn't reach Ray by phone after calling repeatedly for 15 minutes, I went out to the alley and walked to the back of the business. There is a chain-link fence surrounding the property, and I was hanging onto it crying and attempting to get the attention of one of our friends that was there. I asked him to get Ray right away. Ray was busy with customers, but our friend must have told him there was something wrong with me because he came rushing over to the fence to see what I needed. I told him about Nook. He opened the gate, gave me a hug, and said he would send our friend over to get Nook's body. Our friend came and scooped her up in her blanket, put her in a box, took her home and buried her for us. We didn't have anywhere on our small lot to bury her, and he had a place where his dogs that had passed had been laid to rest.

For the next hour or so, I was inconsolable. I laid on my bed with Missy and wailed. My sister came home, found me on my bed, hugged me, and let me talk about it. The pain of that day is something I still feel very strongly. The loss of Pugsey and Nook weighed heavily on me, and my thoughts of impending doom were frequent for months after both their deaths. We still had Missy and that did help; she was sad and lonely being an only "child," but we weren't quite ready to add to the family again.

In 2006, we decided we wanted to move to a more pastoral setting. We started looking for land to buy since we wanted to build a house. We eventually found just over 6 acres next to forest land and a stream. The property had a well on it but nothing else. It was tucked in off the road and was just a half-mile from the first house we ever owned. Ray would still only have a 15-minute commute, and my commute time was just 10 minutes longer. Even though the property was ridiculously expensive, or so I thought at the time, it was the middle of the housing boom and bare land was hard to find. We figured we would be our own contractor, hire the people to do the framing, electrical, plumbing, etc. and be able to save some building cost. I don't know if it saved us a ton of money, considering that being the project manager of building a house in addition to our regular jobs made our lives even more hectic. Thankfully, Ray wasn't too far away during the day and could be at the property to coordinate and check on things as needed. We sold our house in town, moved out to the property, and lived in our motorhome while the house was being built.

Since we've been married, Ray and I have lived in recreational vehicles, a shed, an apartment, a single wide trailer, a triple wide mobile home, a remodeled house, a remodeled double wide mobile home, and finally we were building a new house. We felt we were on the life trajectory that we were supposed to be on; the one that we were told, from a young age, by our parents, society, media, and other people, that we were expected to be on. The whole path of working hard, building up your credit, having a nice house and nice vehicles, having good jobs and keep doing better is what we strived for. This was supposed to make us happy. Right? So, that's what we did and building this nice new house with a big shop was one more step on that path.

    We had to get a high interest, short term building loan since the one with the bank fell through at the last minute because we hadn't hired a contractor to manage the project. The pressure to make sure the ridiculously high interest rate payment was made on time, and that the house was built and refinanced in six months, was stressful. We put tens of thousands of our own saving into the development of the property, such as the septic system, well upgrades, site preparation, gravel for the long driveway, and other things that were needed before the actual building of the house started. We were good at saving money, but it still depleted our accounts. Worrying about money, packing up, moving our things into storage, and getting everything done to get the house started, in addition to my busy job was hard on me. I tend to try and over control situations when I feel out of control. This is not a good way to be, especially since there is so much out of our control and it's just foolish to think we're in charge of everything anyway.

CHAPTER FIVE

Zenith

(Ages 38-43)

There was so much work to be done to get the house built that it was daunting just thinking about it. We were excited though and ready to tackle building a new house. We picked out a two-story plan from a local architecture firm which, conveniently enough, was the exact same floorplan our framer had used when building his house. Ray was able to take time away from the business, as needed, to get the building sites cleared off and gravel spread. For me, work was still demanding and busy; plus, I had decided to sit for the exam to become a Professional Licensed Surveyor (PLS) in the State of Washington. It was a 6-hour national test and then a 2-hour state specific test. It was taken in one grueling long day.

Admittedly, it was hard to find time to study the way I needed to or to find a quiet place to spread out my study materials. There was no way I could study at work. Between the workload and the constant interruptions, that just wasn't an option. Home was a construction zone with people coming and going, and the motorhome was just too cluttered. By this time, my parents had bought the property next door, and they were in a complete gut and remodel with their house. No chance of going there to study. I did the best I could and studied where and when I could. I packed my study materials in the car just in case I happened to be somewhere I had a few minutes to kill. Once the house was framed in with a roof, plumbing, electrical, drywall and light fixtures installed, I would go in there for an hour or so in the evenings and study.

I was juggling a lot of "can't let anyone down" balls, and it was wearing me out. Failure at anything for me was not acceptable. From a young age, it was expected that I would not do anything to make the family look bad. That same way of thinking hitched a ride with me into adulthood. I was pushing myself so much mentally and emotionally, that I was physically worn out. I was eating better with a main diet of vegetables, protein, and healthy fats. I had lost some weight and was more active. I thought I was "better" and not "sick" anymore. I seemed to be handling all the pressure and stress without any derogatory effects on my health. Yeah…. that lasted for about four months. As the deadline for me taking the PLS exam and for getting the house completed loomed nearer, the more I started to see some of my health issues pop back up. I also got the surprise announcement that Ray's 14-year-old niece would be coming to live with us in August right before school started. We had nowhere to put her, so there was added pressure to get the house finished. Ray and I don't have children and now we were taking in a teenager. What were we thinking?! We certainly weren't equipped to go from a couple with no children to having a struggling teenage girl in our care.

I'll just wait here a second while all you parents finish laughing.

Your late 30s is not the age to start learning how to parent someone. Since there was no additional room in our motorhome, and for privacy's sake, we borrowed a friend's tiny old hunting travel trailer to use as our niece's bedroom. That worked for about 6-weeks and then the friend needed his trailer back. Our niece had to sleep in a tent in our completed shop/outbuilding for over three weeks because we didn't get our occupancy permit for the house until mid-November 2007. The rainy and stormy season was upon us and it was so frustrating having to move all our stuff from the shop to the house in torrential downpours. We had moved everything out of the storage units into our shop a few months prior once the final permit was issued on it. Storage unit fees are no joke. Those can really add up over time, and we were pinching pennies as it was. I thought, *Finally! The house is done, we're moved in, and now I can relax a little.* How delusional was I? Uh, "hello!" - I just welcomed a teenage girl into my household, and I hadn't heard the results of my PLS exam yet. I had too many balls in the air – no relaxing for me.

I found out just a few weeks after we moved in that I had passed the national portion of the exam but had failed the state specific portion by two answers. I was devastated. I had never, ever, failed a test. Ever. I was mortified. I acted mildly disappointed and like it was no big deal, but inside I was screaming horrible things to myself.

Loser!

You could have done better if you'd just made the time to really study!

Everyone is going to think you're stupid now.

What will my family, friends, and co-workers think when they find out? They'll be whispering and talking badly about you behind your back.

I'm such a disappointment to Ray and my parents.

You probably shouldn't even be licensed. What do you know anyway?

The negative and destructive self-talk was never ending. I was expected to be better, or at least, as good as everyone else. I was determined to get licensed though, so I signed up to retake the state specific exam in the spring of 2008. I was so terrified of failing again, that I spent money on additional study material in the two areas pertaining to the questions I'd missed. I didn't give myself the positive self-talk that I should have. I should have reminded myself that I only missed by two answers, and that the two subjects I missed the answers on were extremely complex portions of surveying in Washington State. It didn't matter to me. The unrealistic expectations I had for myself overruled any rational thought on the subject. Once again, I was extremely anxious leading up to the test and was ready to bolt out of the room right before it started. I was able to calm my nerves as soon as my brain was preoccupied and focused on the task at hand. I'm sure the pressure I gave myself of not failing was a good motivator though, whether I like it or not. I am happy to say that I did pass the exam and was granted my PLS status in June 2008.

The burden I put on myself to achieve carried over into all aspects of what I did, including making a positive difference in our niece's life. I had no clue what I was doing, but I tried. I really did. It was painful trying to bring a minor into our household when they are so different from us. Ray and I have always been extremely responsible people that understood that our actions affect other people. It was hard for me not to compare myself at her age, versus how she was. It wasn't fair, but that's what I had to rely on for experience. At her age, I was completely independent in knowing when I needed to go to sleep, getting myself up in time to get ready and be picked up by the school bus, get my homework done, clean up after myself, and worked by myself on Saturdays at my parents' laundromat business.

We struggled with our niece staying up late, not getting up on time, missing the school bus so that Ray would have to come back home and take her to school, or she would impose on my parents and ask them to do it. She was also not getting her homework turned in, and other types of typical teenage behavior. Ray had no understanding and would get extremely frustrated to the point that they would get into arguments or just quit talking to each other. I felt caught in the middle and tried to be the mediator and fixer of the situation. That wasn't working for me because it caused the anxiety symptoms that I was feeling to get worse and worse. I didn't want to be at home because it was a hotbed of bad feelings, disappointment, anger, frustration, the silent treatment, hurt feelings, and tension. I felt all of that. All of it. For once I didn't mind the long hours at work.

I love my niece. I think she has a good heart and so much love to give. Sometimes I would come home and find that she had cleaned the bathrooms, vacuumed, cleaned the kitchen, and straightened up. I would feel so bad for being frustrated because I knew she was trying. It was a monster of an adjustment for her, and she was only 14 years old. Life with her mother was always unstable at best, and her father was great with her until he had a steady woman in his life. She was never the focus of the love and attention she needed and deserved. I wanted to fill in all those gaps for her, to be a mentor, and someone she could count on to be there when she needed reassurance or the hard truth. I wanted to do all of that, but unfortunately, I was not equipped to do it. I didn't realize I had a lot of work to do on myself before I could truly be there in that way for someone else.

She stayed with us for six months, then moved back in with her father and stepmother #3. I know that it was unrealistic to think we could have made a noticeable impact on her in such a short time, but I still felt like I had failed her. I understand that it was just the worst timing for us and maybe even her. She needed unlimited, unconditional love, and we weren't the people that could provide that at the time. I think it really hit home to me that maybe it was a good thing we didn't have any children. I don't think I would have handled it well at all.

Shortly after our niece moved out, we got a new pug puppy and named her Isabel. From the first moment I held her, I knew she was special. The day I picked her up to bring her home, I stopped by my employer's house so he could meet her. He was a "dog person" and lived just a few minutes away, plus he was instrumental in us meeting the breeder. She was so tiny – fit in the palm of your hand, tiny – and when my boss held her up to his chest he said "She's so little! You're bringing her to work with you, right?" I stuttered, "Uh…sure…Is that an option?" So, off to work she went with me for the first month she was with us. I'm extremely grateful to my boss for letting me do that. Being able to spend that time with her forged a bond between us that was magical. She was also very helpful in calming down irate customers. It's hard to yell at someone when the other person is holding an adorable puppy. My co-workers would borrow her when they were feeling stressed, and she quickly became the office therapy dog. The workplace was just a little bit brighter when she was there and my stress level at work was considerably less when she was on my lap. Once she started to sleep less during the day and needed more attention, I left her home with Missy when I went to work. Luckily, Ray came home for lunch every day, so the dogs weren't home alone more than 4 hours at a time.

While our niece was living with us, Jessica's health kept declining. She no longer had leukemia, but the toll the cure took on her body was devastating. She had symptoms of graft versus host disease, and the cells of her organs and skin were hardening, so they had her on steroid medication. She struggled with moving around, had low energy, and plenty of pain throughout her body. Jessica moved in with her mother in Coeur 'd Alene. The drive for us was about six or seven hours, so we ended up going over for a weekend every month or so.

She was on oxygen at this point, was rarely driving, and eventually not at all. Ray and I would stop on our drive over and buy his mom and grandmother gifts because it gave them such joy to receive them, which always put a smile on our faces as well. By the third time we visited, Ray's grandmother would sign (she was deaf), "Where are the gifts?" once we greeted them and sat down to chat. She would always sign it with a mischievous smile and a twinkle in her eye. Ray would intentionally say, "What gifts?" just to drag it out and tease her a little. It became the thing I think they both looked forward to every visit.

As glad as I was to see Jessica and Ray's grandmother, those trips were draining. I went into full on caregiver mode when I was there and wanted to direct all my emotional and physical energy towards being present with them. I felt that I wasn't allowed to have complaints about my wellbeing because it couldn't possibly compare to what Jessica was going through. I continued to push myself and not practice any self-care because I didn't feel I deserved it. I felt I was a whiney slacker if

I couldn't be at least as tough as she was. I was also caregiving to Ray when we were there. It was his mother, and I needed to support him in all the ways that I could no matter what. As it so often happens, one of my strengths was also one of my weaknesses. Because I have such empathy for other people, and truly care about their wellbeing, I tend to put others' needs above my own. I'm much better about it now and have a robust self-care regimen, but at the time I wasn't even aware I was doing it. That's just how I had always been. I think that even if someone, at that time, had explained to me the whole "You can't fill someone else's glass if your pitcher is empty" thing, I probably would have dismissed it. That meant me looking, I mean really looking, at myself and that was not about to happen anytime soon. I did not want to open the lid on my emotional garbage can and see the soupy mess inside.

One time when we were visiting Jessica for the weekend, I was so weary that I had to psych myself up to do anything. I remember sitting on the couch listening to Ray talk to his mom and thinking, *I should ask if anyone wants any lunch, and then make lunch*, but the thought of expending that much energy made me want to slide into a boneless puddle on the floor. Of course, I didn't slide to the floor but got up and made lunch. I wanted to be there for Jessica, Ray, and everyone else, but I had nothing left in me to give. I was emotionally empty. That night, when we finally went to bed, all I wanted to do was curl up and sink into oblivion.

Even though it can't be seen from the outside, I was fighting myself internally all the time. Fighting to not panic, fighting to not let anyone see my struggles, fighting to do tasks that someone without anxiety doesn't realize are terrifying to me. All that internal fighting is exhausting! I had never felt that much despair and deep weariness before. That weekend was just a hint of what was to come.

I didn't grasp it at the time, but the agoraphobia was worsening. My avoidance of places and situations was so gradual that I didn't even notice it was happening. Looking back now, I can see that I hid my avoidance by working 50-60-hour weeks so that I never had to do anything except work and go home. By the time my downward spiral into anxiety and panic hell had reached its peak in the fall of 2010, I was barely able to function. My social life was dead. I only spent time with my husband, close family, and people at work. I had no hobbies. I hadn't picked up a sketch pad or set up my paints and easel for years. Pretty much the only thing I did in my spare time was read, watch tv, or do household chores. I didn't take good care of myself. I wasn't consistently eating the way I knew I should, and I was at my heaviest weight ever. I wasn't getting any exercise because I would have a panic attack whenever I exerted myself. The elevated heart rate during exercise mimicked what it felt like to have a panic attack, so it scared me. I barely had enough energy to get through a day. I was a mess, and not even a hot mess.

I started to dread driving and the minute I got in the car, I started to panic. I would tense up and hunch over so much that I was practically curved around the steering wheel. I would try to take a deep breath and couldn't. My mind was darting around and all I could think of was keeping myself from passing out so that I could reach my safe place, which was either work or home. I became so fearful of driving that I started altering my driving routes to avoid stop lights, heavy traffic, and unfamiliar roads.

A trip from my place of work to my chiropractor should have taken 40 minutes via the freeway. I had to give myself 60-90 minutes because I would travel back road routes that bypassed all the things that would trap me in my car. Every time I was stopped at a lighted intersection, I would get so panicky that I could feel myself on the verge of blacking out. The freeway or multi-lane traffic was the same. I felt trapped between exits or places to pull over. All the awful things I thought would happen never did, but it certainly felt like it would. I think I avoided driving on the freeway for almost a year. I never told anyone what was happening or that my behaviors had become so extreme. I was embarrassed and felt so ridiculous for being that way. I cried every time I had to drive, and I thought that if I shared my struggles with anyone else, they would judge and ridicule me.

Some pivotal things happened in the months between October 2010 and May 2011 which sunk me even deeper into the downward spiral of anxiety. One of them was the death of my mother-in-law, Jessica. She had been fighting the good fight for many years, and it was not an easy battle. It was physically and emotionally taxing on her, and even though she gave all she had, and then some, it all came to an end in November 2010. My husband and I received an emergency phone call telling us that she was in the hospital and that we needed to hurry and get to her side. Every time we received one of those phone calls, of which there were many over the previous seven years, it gave my stomach a turn and ratcheted up the anxious feelings about 1,000 percent. It didn't matter though, because I wanted to be there for her, my husband, and my extended family. It was a nerve wracking 7-hour drive to the city she lived in, and by the time we got to the hospital, I was already worn down by my worrying and "what if?" thinking.

I remember telling myself, as we walked into the hospital, that I had to suck up my own tiredness, anxious feelings, and just be there for everyone else. Unfortunately, we didn't receive good news from the doctors. She had tumors all throughout her lungs and abdomen resulting from one of the treatments used to cure her leukemia. She was done fighting, and it was heartbreaking. That evening they had to put her on life support so that we could all say our goodbyes. Let me tell you, when a family must make the decision to take someone off life support, it breaks something inside of you. It's that fragile part that knows we aren't God and shouldn't have to make these types of decisions. I think we all wanted to hold onto that hope that she would pull though once again and be that miracle she always was in the past.

Once we knew this was the beginning of the end, I sat in one of those uncomfortable plastic chairs in the hospital waiting room and broke down into uncontrollable crying. I was mortified because I had done it in front of all my husband's family. He had just gone to say goodbye to his mother and the thought of him having to do so was my last straw. I felt that I didn't have the right to be so emotional about it since I was just the daughter-in-law. My job was to be there for everyone else. Plus, none of them were breaking down, and I felt ridiculous for not being able to hold it together. Being vulnerable and feeling like a freak in front of all of them just made the anxiety worse. I had this running dialogue in my mind saying *Oh my gosh! You're so weird. Look how uncomfortable you're making everyone else. Suck it up you fat ugly cow.* So, I did just that; I sucked it up and buried those emotions.

By the time it was my turn to go and say goodbye to Jessica, I could barely even verbalize all that I wanted to convey to her. I had so many memories I wanted to share with her and things I wanted to make sure she knew, but it was all jumbled up inside of me. I knew that if I let it out, it would break the dam, and all my emotions would come flooding out. I knew that couldn't happen because the thought of me being the weak one in this situation did not go along with my brain's instructions to "suck it up". I do remember thanking her for always treating me well and for giving me such an amazing husband. I also told her that she would be in God's arms soon and all her pain and suffering would be over. Even though she couldn't talk, I could see in her eyes and by her facial expressions that she was ready to go.

Once she was taken off life support, she went into a coma. Ray and I left for home while his sister and a close family friend stayed with her until the end a few days later. For any of you that have had similar experiences, you know how horribly sad and painful it is to physically lose someone. I have always felt guilty for not staying and for leaving my sister-in-law to essentially deal with it on her own. The sad thing is that if I had not been in this downward spiral of anxiety and panic hell, I would have been able to stay and provide comfort and support. I really was not physically or emotionally able to do so. But wait, it gets worse.

Fast forward a few weeks to right before Thanksgiving. I was preparing for a house full of guests, cooking Thanksgiving dinner and helping my sister-in-law put together the funeral and Celebration of Life for Jessica. I was having panic attacks daily and the anxious feelings were going on 24/7. I could not get my mind to stop spinning over the memories of her death and the constant worrying about getting everything together so that the funeral and Celebration of Life went off without a hitch. I had also spent days cleaning my house from top to bottom because I was so worried about people judging me, and I wanted to look like I had it all together. Which of course, I certainly did not!

I cooked Thanksgiving dinner by myself and was so worn out from trying to function while at a high level of anxiety, that I took an hour to lay down in between prep work and waiting for the turkey to get done. Instead of resting, however, I had such a bad panic attack that all I could do was lay there with silent tears running down onto the pillow. In the middle of my panic/crying jag, I heard my bother-in-law and niece come in. I pretended to be asleep when she came to check on me, so that I wouldn't have to talk to anyone. I didn't want them to see me having a panic attack. I was ashamed and didn't want anyone to know how much I was struggling. I got up about 15 minutes later, washed my face, gave myself a pep talk, and went downstairs to greet everyone with a smile on my face. I thought that I had to be strong for everyone else. I didn't think I had the right to be such an emotional and physical mess. I look back at the pictures of us at Jessica's Celebration of Life, and I can tell you that I felt as horrible as I looked, and I looked awful. I got by that week, but my downward spiral was just starting to pick up speed.

In the months that followed the death of my mother-in-law, my mental, emotional, and physical health drastically declined.

My world kept getting smaller and smaller. The agoraphobia was advancing at an alarming rate. I used to be okay going into stores I felt "safe" in. The ones that I knew where everything was and that had quick checkout lines. The big ones posed the risk of getting deep into the store and having a panic attack and not being able to get out of the store before the bodily symptoms got too bad. God forbid anyone would see me freaking out. Believe me, if you deal with panic attacks you know that feeling of the need to escape and hide. It's so overwhelming when you're having a panic attack.

There was a grocery store next to where I worked and a drug store a few blocks down, and those were my "safe" stores. The places I could go to without having a panic attack. But that all started to change. I was having panic attacks daily and was having anxiety attacks all day long. Panic attacks would wake me up several times during the night. I tried to hide all of this from my husband and people at work, but they could see something was wrong with me. My husband was getting frustrated because of my odd behaviors; plus, he was still dealing with grieving the loss of his mother. I kept thinking that it was all caused by a physical deficiency and that once I figured out what that deficiency was, then I could get better. I would be fixed. Yup…I was totally wrong about that. Oh boy, was I wrong! No matter what medication, diet change, nutritional supplement, or miracle vitamin I tried, the anxiety and panic episodes kept getting stronger and more frequent.

The time between November 2010 and June 2011 were the most miserable eight months of my life. Every day I thought I was going to die…. I didn't want to……yet I wanted to. Your body wants to survive. It is programmed to survive. The brain has other ideas sometimes. My brain had hijacked my body. Specifically, it was my subconscious that had hijacked my whole being. I, *me*, the essence of who I am was not in control. Some trauma-riddled part of me was running the clown show. I didn't trust my body anymore. I didn't trust that I had any way to come out of this whole fiasco alive. I was my own worst enemy at its most fundamental level. I was literally killing myself with my thoughts, but because it was all manifesting in a physical way, I kept thinking it was a physical issue or cause. I had researched my symptoms online numerous times and all kinds of horrible diseases would pop up in the results. Often, panic attacks would be in the results lists too. It was easier for me to believe that I had a horrible disease because at least people would be accepting of a physical issue. I didn't want to face or admit that I was mentally ill.

Eventually, my only safe place was home and then my bedroom at home. At one point, the agoraphobia was so bad that I struggled to leave my bedroom and go downstairs. It didn't help that going up or down the stairs wiped me out. I barely had enough energy or breath by the time I reached the landing. I would get light-headed, which just caused more anxiety. I was starting to miss days at work because the thought of leaving the house would be so overwhelming that I would wake up in the middle of the night having an intense panic attack just thinking about getting through the next day. At this point, I started to accept the fact that I was having panic attacks. I just didn't want anyone else to know how bad they were. I let my employer know, but only because I had to tell him why I couldn't make it to work every day. He was kind enough to let me work from home when I could, but my portion of our income took a hard hit. That was just one more thing that I was stressing and feeling guilty about.

On top of the daily panic and anxiety, I also started to experience depression. I had never felt it on this level before. People tend to think that depression means you feel sad. For me, that wasn't it at all. Depression made me feel nothing. Absolutely nothing. Depression is not an overwhelming feeling of sadness; it is an overwhelming lack of joy. I know it sounds like the same thing, but it's not. You can feel sad and yet still experience joy in something.

This was a total lack of caring about anything, even myself. I no longer had interest in things I used to enjoy. I didn't want to be around people, especially if they were laughing or reacting with feeling to anything. I didn't get joy from playing with my dogs, a sunny day, flowers blooming, a good book, a funny show, or time with a friend. It was less painful to cut out the world, and people, than it was to try to be in it and pretend that I was alright. This lack of feeling and joy scared me more than all the panic and anxiety. It petrified me on a soul deep level. I didn't know if I would ever come out of it. When you're so far distanced from what it is that connects you to all other living things in this world, then you no longer see a point in being part of it. Because of my faith in God, I never planned out or seriously considered taking my own life, but I can tell you that the thought of being released from the inner torment did appeal to me a few times. The heavy burden of carrying around all the anxiety, panic, and depression while desperately trying to hide it eventually broke me and my greatest fear was realized; I got found out.

Three years prior to her passing, Ray and I bought Jessica a new vehicle. It was one that was easier for her to get in and out of and was generally more comfortable for her. We had been making the payments, but after Jessica died, we had no need for it and didn't want the extra financial burden, so in March 2011 we put it up for sale. The interested buyer lived in the Seattle area and needed us to drive the vehicle to her lending institution where we would be signing papers and handing the vehicle over to her. In order to do that, I had to drive the vehicle over 90 minutes on Interstate 5 through congested traffic with my husband following in his vehicle so that we had a way to get back home. This would be no big deal, just an inconvenience, for most people. For someone in the throes of constant anxiety and panic, it's a very big deal. Especially for someone who has been hiding the fact that driving on the freeway induced severe panic attacks. Since I didn't want to disappoint my husband, I gave myself yet another "Suck it up and just do it!" speech and got in the vehicle.

I can't leave out that, when my husband told me what we needed to do, I was internally freaking out so bad that I argued and asked why she couldn't bring the paperwork to us, and threw up any other roadblock I could to get out of doing this. He got extremely frustrated and by the end of the conversation, we were raising our voices, and I was holding back tears of frustration. I gave in because I didn't want to admit to him how bad the anxiety was for me and didn't really know what was wrong anyway, so I couldn't explain it; plus, I did not want to fail him or myself.

It was a hard thing, this battle that went on inside my head, because of how disgusted I was in my inability to just get better. I really did want to make this drive and not have any anxiety issues, but the nervous stomach, muscle tension, and fearful thoughts started days before I even got out of the driveway. The trip started out okay. I was able to barely hold it together for about 30 minutes, then my arms and hands started to tingle and go numb as the massive panic attack I ended up having was building up. After 15 minutes of reverently hoping that it would subside, I was forced to call my husband and let him know that what was going on.

There I am, on the side of the freeway with five lanes of traffic roaring by, crying, shaking, and completely locked up. I couldn't go any further. Ray was upset. He couldn't understand. He asked if I could at least make it to the next exit a mile up the road. I was able to do that, but it was the most terrifying mile of my life. We pulled into a gas station parking lot, and I got into his truck. He kept asking me what was going on and why couldn't I keep driving. I struggled to even explain it. I must have seemed liked a crazy person to him; a weird version of the girl he had married 22 years before. I was devastated that I had let him down. It was the lowest point in my life so far.

He was scrambling trying to figure out how to proceed and get the vehicle to where we needed to go. After some very tense silent minutes, he finally called the person buying the vehicle and explained what was happening. I was ashamed. Now, my weakness had been exposed to not just Ray, but a stranger. What I didn't realize was that even then, God was watching out for me. The woman buying the vehicle said that she herself had experienced panic attacks in the past and completely understood. She offered to come and meet us if we could get to a place that was ten miles closer to her. She would then drive the vehicle the rest of the way to the lending office. With relief in sight and a few minutes to let the panic attack subside a little, I was able to drive ten more miles, and then go into the lending office and sign the paperwork. Not to say it was easy, I was still anxious and my body was feeling the effects of the adrenaline that was pumped into it during the panic attack, but I did it. The drive home was not fun either. It completely scared Ray and when he tried to talk about it, I got defensive and shut down. After this whole incident, the downward spiral picked up even more speed, and I realized in June of 2011 that the anxiety and panic had won. I was ready to die rather than go one more day in complete lifeless misery.

That might sound dramatic to some people, but that's truly how I felt. It crushed my spirit that I was not living my life to the fullest, and that I was allowing the anxiety and panic to control my decisions. I felt guilty for the impact that my issues had on my husband and family. Ray was spending less and less time at home. He was out mountain biking the majority of the one day a week that we had off together. For his own sanity, he needed to get away from me. I was not an easy person to be around. I thought I was failing God and could just get better if I was stronger in my faith. I believed that I wasn't doing enough to fix myself and that I had failed everyone. I didn't like feeling weak. I had always been the strong one, there for everyone else and able to lend a helping hand when needed. I absolutely HATED who I had become. My self-loathing hit an all-time high. I didn't even know this pathetic person. I saw no way out of my circumstances. I had lost all hope and had hit rock bottom, but that was just where I needed to be in order to finally invite God to the party (pity party, that is).

On a Saturday in mid-June 2011, I was wandering the house trying to disperse some of the anxious energy I was feeling. I finally settled onto the couch in the living room and turned on the television. At this point, the only thing I could watch on TV that didn't cause the anxiety to jack up was the shopping networks. I never bought anything, I just watched them because they had a calming effect on me. I couldn't even watch the weather channel because it would have stories of terrible storms and calamities, and I would imagine for days all the horrific things people had gone through. So, the innocuous shopping channels were my go-to entertainment. I now have a hard time watching them because they remind me of this terrible time in my life.

I was staring at the television, petting Isabel and suddenly a rush of acute panic came over me. I starting crying because I just didn't have it in me to handle one more big panic attack. I was done. I shut off the television and sat there crying, blowing long and hard out of my mouth, attempting to lessen the tightness in my stomach and chest. I started praying out loud and crying out to God for help. I slid to the floor, got onto my knees, and cried out for God to take this burden from me. I cried out to Him "I surrender! I can't do this anymore. Please just take me now. I would rather be dead than live one more minute in this hell on earth." I kept telling Him that it was all too much for me to bear, and I was giving it all to Him, surrendering my worthless broken life to Him. I was okay if He saw fit to take me right then and there, and I would be forever grateful if He did.

I waited a few minutes, and when I realized He wasn't going to take me, the panic eventually started to subside. For the first time in a long, long, time I felt the presence of God. I became very quiet and still and reveled in the feeling of His peace and love. I then told Him that since I had messed up so badly on my own, that from that day forward I would do whatever He directed me to do, and take the opportunities He sent my way. I wouldn't question it. I continued to pray and thank God for loving me enough to save me from my sin and asked that He use me in whatever way He sees fit. By the time I pulled myself up off the floor, blew my nose and wiped away my tears, I felt better than I had in months. I was still a complete and utter mess, but I finally had some hope, and that is no small thing to someone in such dire straits as I was. No small thing indeed.

I sat back down on the couch, turned on the television, and what blipped onto the screen was an infomercial for a program called "Attacking Anxiety and Depression". I know it wasn't a coincidence, especially since the channel that the informercial was on was not the same channel – not even close in the channel lineup – from the home shopping network channel it was on when I had shut it off just a short time ago. I knew, down in my spirit, that this was from God. He was sending me help, and it was up to me whether I followed through on my part and kept my promise of doing whatever He directed me to do.

I gladly took that first tiny step on my way to healing by picking up the phone and ordering the program. What's funny about this whole situation is that about a year or so earlier, Ray had come home with this same program which consists of audio sessions and a workbook to go along. He said he bought it for his mom since she was struggling with anxiety due to her illness, but she said she didn't want it. He thought maybe I would want it. I emphatically said, "Why would I want that? I don't have that problem!" I wouldn't even look at it, and after a week of it sitting around the house, he sent it back for a full refund. That right there was a missed opportunity, and even then, God was trying to send help my way. I just wasn't ready yet. I was so scared of addressing my issues, and that cost me severely. I often think about how much pain and suffering I could have avoided if I had just acknowledged I had a problem and had been open to receiving help when it came along.

As I waited for the program to arrive in the mail, I was afraid to be optimistic about it helping me. I was so far down into the pit of despair that I didn't trust that the ladder out reached to the top. What I did know, is that I was no longer alone is the pit. For the first time in over twenty years, I felt God with me. He always had been; I just didn't allow myself to feel His presence or to connect to Him. After my surrender, I was renewed in my desire to have a close relationship with Him. When I had to get in the car and drive to work, I started talking to God. Any conversation with God is a prayer, and as I talked to Him as the friend, protector, and savior that He is, the more comforted I felt. The anxiety and panic attacks were still happening daily, but I finally felt that there was hope for a better outcome in my life. Having existed for so long without hope, I can assure you that when it finally comes to you, it is life changing.

Finally (even though it had only been a week), the "Attacking Anxiety and Depression" program arrived. I was excited and nervous. I wanted so badly for it to help me. I told God I trusted that He sent me to this program and that there must be something of value in what I was going to hear or read. I decided that I would listen to the audio session all week in the car, then do the workbook portion on Saturday. That Monday morning, I excitedly popped in the first CD, said a prayer, then headed into work. The audio sessions are about an hour long, so I generally would hear half of it on my way into work and half on my way home. After a few minutes of the program's creator talking about how the program works, she started talking about the statistics of how many people deal with the symptoms of anxiety. I thought to myself *Wow! That's a lot of people. Is that number right?*" Then she said something that made me cry so hard I had to pull off the road because I couldn't see though my tears. She said, essentially, "If you are listening to this and you suffer from anxiety and panic attacks, I want you to know that you are not alone. I've been through some version of what you are going through. I understand."

I hadn't realized until I heard her say those words that I had felt so immensely alone in my suffering. No one around me could relate, and I was too ashamed to talk about it to anyone; even if I did, I just knew they wouldn't understand. She then proceeded into an interview with a doctor that talked about common fears that someone suffering from anxiety and panic attacks have. The fear of having a heart attack, passing out, or dying from the panic attack. He went through the whole physical aspects of what transpires in the body when a panic attack happens. At first, it was hard for me to hear what he had to say because it made me think about how my body felt during a panic attack.

    I especially had a fixation about my heart, the rapid heart rate, and feelings of tightness in my chest area. I would obsessively take my blood pressure reading. I was always in fear of having a heart attack or passing out in public. My heart was my physical focus in a negative way. I was unaware that this is common, but when I first heard this audio session, I had no idea other people felt the same way. The second half of the audio session was a group discussion which involved the program's creator and about four or five other people. I listened to these people talk about their experiences with anxiety, panic attacks, and the depression that comes with it. I, once again, had to pull off the road due to the tears flowing out of my eyes. They were describing exactly (exactly!) what I had been going through and what I had dealt with most of my life. I could not believe it! It was such a relief and a comfort to know, I mean really know, that I was not alone in what I was going through. It was a tremendous moment of hope for me. It was like I had been wandering alone across a vast desert for decades, and had finally found my tribe.

    About halfway through the whole program, I made an appointment with a naturopathic doctor. This was a huge step forward for me, but I knew that the intense, constant, anxiety was taking a toll on my physical health. Even though I was starting to put some tools in my new "managing anxiety" toolbox, I was still physically weak, not sleeping well, having heart palpitations/irregular heartbeats, had no energy, and in general, felt dreadful. Going to doctor appointments were still severely anxiety inducing, so I asked my mom to go with me to the first appointment so she could fill in any blanks in my medical history, but really, I wanted her there for moral support. Plus, I still needed someone to drive me since we had to take the freeway and go to downtown Olympia which I was not familiar with.

Meeting with the naturopath doctor was such a different experience than any I'd had with a regular doctor. She spent an hour talking to me, asking in depth questions about my physical and mental health. She dug into my medical past, even into childhood. I had never had a doctor show such care, concern, and compassion. She ordered extensive bloodwork for me and then said she wanted to give me a B-Vitamin shot before I left, and depending on what the bloodwork showed, may end up prescribing these shots for a short duration of time.

It's probably a good thing she sprung the shot on me at the last minute so that I didn't start worrying about it beforehand. She gave me the shot, we talked for a few more minutes, I paid my bill, and got my paperwork, all of which took about 10 or 15 minutes. As we walked from the building to the car, I suddenly stopped in my tracks, turned to my mom, and exclaimed, "I think the B-Vitamin shot just hit my system. For the first time in years, I feel amazing!" I could not believe how much better my mood was, how much energy I had, and I wasn't on the verge of a panic attack. I was even, surprisingly, somewhat relaxed. After feeling those positive effects of the shot, I thought, *Now this is something I could get addicted to*. It was that good. I'm not even exaggerating. Amazing!

I went back to see her a few weeks later to go over the results of the blood tests. I appreciated that before she even went over the results, she explained that even though the results indicated severely adverse effects on my body, the good news is that it was all things that could be improved upon with supplements, diet changes, and exercise. All my vitamin and mineral levels were depleted (especially D and the Bs) and came in well below the low end of the advisable range. She explained that one of the effects of constantly being in the "fight or flight" mode is the burning up of all the vitamins and minerals in my body. Even though I was taking supplements, I was using them up faster and in a higher quantity that what I was ingesting. My "bad" cholesterol was fine, but my "good" cholesterol was way too low. She explained that what brings the good cholesterol up is exercise, which I hadn't been able to do because of the anxiety (fear of how exercise made me feel), and low energy. She immediately started me on a high dose of daily Vitamin D, and a daily dose of trace minerals, magnesium, calcium, and a combined B12 and B Complex shot. I can't even explain to you how excited I was about the B-shots. Ray was at the appointment with me, and had to learn how to do it. Thankfully, he wasn't squeamish about it and was able to administer it every three days over the course of a few months. My butt muscles were bruised by the time I was able to stop the shots, but it was well worth it.

The naturopath doctor prescribed supplements for adrenal support, digestive aids, and hormone balance. I was starting to feel better physically and mentally, and it was such sweet relief to finally have hours at a time that I wasn't totally consumed in the throes of an anxiety or panic attack. Just being able to take deep breaths because my abdomen wasn't so constricted, not being completely hunched over the wheel when I had to drive, or being able to finally watch something other than the home shopping networks was a true blessing. I continued to see that naturopath doctor on and off for the next year, and I will always be thankful to her for saving my life, which I truly felt that she did. Between her help and the help that I was receiving from the program, I was starting to get - dare I say – excited about my future.

There were fifteen sessions in the program, and by time I finished it in mid-September 2011, I couldn't believe how many small steps forward I had taken in my healing expedition. Most people say "healing journey", but I feel like the term "expedition" is more appropriate, as we are exploring new ways of doing things as we heal. The program forced me out of a few of my comfort zones, made me look at some aspects of my upbringing, and my thinking and behaviors that got me into the pit of despair. It was grueling and mostly very uncomfortable. I was being forced to make changes, in myself and in the relationship that I had with myself and the people around me. I was still experiencing high anxiety and panic attacks, but they were becoming less severe and not as frequent. I also now had some tools in my toolbox that could help me manage through the anxiety and panic attacks.

For some reason, grocery stores were particularly difficult for me to go into. I had acute anxiety and numerous panic attacks while in grocery stores that I was previous able to go into with no issues. As I spiraled downward, it became so bad that I can't count the number of times I left a full grocery cart in line as I fled from the building. Waiting in the checkout line was a panic trigger; in fact, waiting in any line was a trigger. After several failed attempts to walk out of the store with my groceries, I resorted to going shopping with my mom and sister on Saturdays so that, if I had to flee, at least I could give them my debit card and they could finish the checkout process. I know this appears as if they were enabling the anxiety and panic behaviors, but forcing me to do it just made it worse.

While going through the "Attacking Anxiety and Depression" program, I was able to start making it closer and closer to checking out on my own and eventually making it through the checkout process sometimes. I cannot express how thankful I am to my mom and sister for helping me with something that is so easy for most people, but was terrifying for me. I appreciate the patience and care they showed me. I felt embarrassed enough by not being able to perform a task that I had done thousands of times before with no issues; if they had ridiculed me or made light of my struggle with this task, I would have been crushed.

After finishing the program, I would listen to certain lessons again and again on my drive to and from work. They helped me maintain the progress I had made, but I wasn't making any additional progress. God knew this, and once again sent me some help.

Ray came home one day and was telling me how he had repaired a four-wheeler (quad motorcycle) for one of the neighbors. As most people do with Ray, she ended up telling him her life story, which included a bout of panic attacks that started a few years prior. She had learned to manage them with the help of a psychiatrist. I made the usual "oh" and "interesting" responses to the story, but hearing about other people's anxiety still got me anxious. Unbeknownst to me, Ray had shared with her that I was dealing with anxiety issues. He didn't tell me this part because I was still so secretive about my struggles and didn't want anyone to see me in a bad light or to think less of me because of it. We were at home one weekend afternoon sitting in the living room when a car that I didn't recognize pulled up. Ray noticed it was the neighbor and got up to answer the door. I stayed hidden in the living room but could hear the whole conversation. She said that she was dropping off the name and contact information of the psychiatrist she used, since she hadn't been able to drop it off at the shop the day before. I got a horrible squishy feeling in my stomach when I realized they were talking about me. I could tell Ray was worried that I was not going to take too kindly to him blabbing about my problems. He was right. I was mad, defensive, and didn't even want to entertain the notion of seeing a psychiatrist.

I had been raised hearing my parents, my father especially, make derogatory comments about "shrinks". I distinctly remember him saying that he saw no need for it, that it did no good, and that all you needed was God. There was always a negative stigma attached to anyone that had gone to see a psychiatrist. The thought of me going to see a mental health professional started all those external opinions and feelings about it yapping in my head. I was raised knowing not to air your dirty laundry, talk about problems, and certainly not to do anything that might cause others to think badly about me and therefore my family. I was a reflection of, an example of, a product of, who they are; if it was known that I wasn't perfect, then neither were they. That's an impossible standard to try and live up to, but it's what I had automatically been doing my whole life.

What finally prompted me to call the psychiatrist that the neighbor recommended was my husband. He reminded me that the anxiety and panic I experience, and therefore some of the limitations and issues that spread from it, affect him too. He is a casualty of my trauma. I may be the one physically, mentally, and emotionally experiencing the effects of anxiety, but he deals with the aftermath and the limitations that puts on his life. So, for the love of the good man that had done his best to support me, I said a prayer and made the call. I left a message and anxiously (because, how else am I going to be?!) waited for a return call.

The psychiatrist called me back later that day, asked a few questions about what I wanted to see her for, then told me she wasn't taking any new patients. I asked her if she could recommend anyone else, and she suggested looking into a Psychiatric Nurse Practitioner. I went to my health insurance's website and looked under "find a doctor", filtered it to mental health, and started looking through the list. As I scrolled up and down the page, one name kept jumping out at me. She was a Psychiatric Nurse Practitioner with an office in a nearby city. I called and was able to set up an appointment for the following week. Making that appointment was an enormous, but necessary, step forward for me.

I still had difficulty driving without having a panic attack, especially if I was headed to a place or experience that was making me overly nervous. Since I wasn't sure what kind of shape I'd be in after my therapy appointment (I had no idea what to expect!), I asked my mom if she would drive me to the appointment. Ray had to work, and my mom was the logical option since she was self-employed and able to adjust her schedule. As thankful as I am for her support that day, and the next few appointments that she took me to, it was difficult for me not to imagine that there was some judgement from her about me going to therapy. I think though, at this point, she was just glad that I was getting some help.

As I was sitting in the waiting room before that first appointment, my knees were bobbing up and down, my hands were sweating, my throat was dry, I felt light-headed, had the urgent need to pee every few minutes, and I was ready to bolt out the door any second. I was praying for God to bless and guide the conversation and to give me the strength to do my part of the process. You see, talking about the anxiety, panic, depression, and what my day to day life had been like the last year, caused me to panic. I was so used to hiding how I was feeling, mentally and physically to avoid judgement from others, that I wasn't sure if I would be able to do what I anticipated was necessary to make this work. Adding the fact that I had no idea what to expect regarding therapy, and you can maybe understand why it was so ridiculously anxiety-causing to try and seek help for the anxiety. Hey…I never said it made sense.

After a short wait, a woman opened the door leading back to the offices and called my name. She had a very pleasant voice, beautiful dark hair, and a calming presence about her. This was Jeanette, my therapist. She led me to her office which had a small loveseat couch for me to sit on with a low coffee table in front of it. She sat in a chair opposite me and settled in behind her laptop. I looked around and noticed wall art with writings of scripture and uplifting messages. There was a box of tissues on the coffee table, which I would avail myself off quite frequently in our sessions. I immediately felt comfortable despite all the feeling of anxiety.

The first session started with Jeanette asking the question "Why are you here?" Such a simple question, right? I was trying to figure out how to explain what I had been going through, the last year especially, and I kind of locked up. We sat there for a minute, staring at each other while she allowed me to collect my thoughts and calm my mind. That was the first time anyone had done that for me, giving me time and not rushing me into the spotlight. I finally blurted out, "I have severe panic attacks, am afraid to drive, have a nervous tight stomach all the time, and don't want to live like this anymore." Then, I burst into tears. Jeanette, blessedly, let me cry for a few seconds, then asked me some questions to get details out of me about the severity and effects of the anxiety and panic attacks. I told her I didn't want to take medication; going into this, I was afraid that she would try to force medication on me instead of giving me tools to cope with the situation.

The hour flew by, and when her assistant knocked on the door to give the 10-minute reminder, Jeanette said that she thought we would be able to make progress without the medication, and that she wanted to see me twice a week for the next month or so. I walked out of that room feeling relieved that the first appointment was over, and with a knowing in my heart that once again God came through on His promise by sending me to the right person.

After a few weeks of therapy, I was able to drive myself to the appointments. It may seem like a silly thing to be excited about, but it was a monumental step forward for me. Being able to drive myself to an appointment, especially one that wore me out emotionally, gave me such a feeling of accomplishment that it motivated me to not give up. For me, having felt so much despair at the loss of the independent and strong person I always thought I was, this put a tiny spark back into my soul.

I did get to a point about six months into the therapy where I wasn't making much progress with the tools Jeanette had given me. I was still not able to go grocery shopping without having a panic attack, and driving was still anxiety inducing. I prayed about it, and had peace with the decision to ask Jeanette to put me on a medication for a short time in order to get me over this "hump". She prescribed Buspirone at a low dose. It made me throw up the first few weeks, and my stomach hurt horribly. I took DGL – Deglycyrrhizinated Licorice – to help protect my stomach. I felt spacey the first few days, to the point that my co-worker picked me up and drove me to and from work the first week I was on it. I took the full prescription strength for about

7 weeks, which enabled me to have enough successful outings that I felt I was over the "hump". It took me 12 weeks to ween off the medication because you must do it so slowly.

When you take something that alters the chemistry in your brain, it's disastrous and possibly life threatening to go off it too quickly. Since Jeanette had me lower the dosages at such a slow rate, I had no adverse effects from stopping the meds. Even though I've always tried to address my mental and physical health issues from a standpoint of natural approaches and medicine, I know that the medication is there to help when needed and that there is no shame in that. No one lives your life except you, and only you can decide what is best for yourself at any given time. **Someone reading this book needs to hear this: you are not weak for needing help.** Even though it may feel like you're giving in, or are not strong enough to handle your own issues, you're stronger for asking someone for help. It takes much more strength to receive help than it is to give it. Giving makes all of us feel needed and important, but it's just an imperative that we ask and receive help knowing that it will positively impact the giver's life and not just our own.

At the start of my time climbing out of the anxiety and panic pit I was in; I was leaning heavily on God to get me through each day and to comfort me when I was pushing the boundaries of what felt comfortable. I particularly remember an incident in which God reached out and literally touched me as He comforted me. I had a chiropractic appointment that was 31 miles away via the freeway. Usually, I would take a longer route where I could avoid driving on the freeway. On this day, I was held up at work and didn't have time to go my alternate route. I had to take the freeway in order to get to my appointment on time. Once I knew that was the case, I started devising ways I could get out of it. I could reschedule my appointment, but that didn't work because my body really needed the adjustment. After scheming with myself about how I could get out of driving on the freeway, I employed some of the lessons I had learned from the 'Attacking Anxiety and Depression" program and told myself *I can do this!*" False bravado anyone? I was shaking by the time I got to the freeway on ramp and was feeling the start of a panic attack by the time I merged into traffic.

    I was talking to God, as if He was a friend that I had called on the phone. I was telling Him how scared I was, that I needed to know I was going to be alright, and that I knew He was with me in that vehicle. Suddenly, I felt a grip on my right shoulder, as if a passenger in the seat next to me had reached over and given it a squeeze. I continued to feel the weight of that hand on my shoulder for another minute or so. I knew, without a doubt, that it was God assuring me that He hears me when I cry out to Him and that He is there to comfort me when I need it. My panic attack subsided and I started to cry out of awe and happiness, as I thanked God for never letting me go and for always being with me. I can tell you with certainty that it was not my imagination. As strong as my mind is, I know what it's capable of and this was not something I conjured up myself. If you've ever really felt God, Jesus, the Holy Spirit move in or around you, it is something you have a sense about in the deepest, most private part of your spirit. I never forget those moments I have with God because when I need to, I ruminate on them to sustain me in my darkest times.

    When I was in the middle of doing the "Attacking Anxiety and Depression" program, my mom gave me a book written by Joyce Meyer called *Be Anxious for Nothing*. Mom said that a woman from her church came up to her, gave her the book, and said that it had really helped her and asked if Mom would give it to me. I didn't know this woman. During a conversation the previous week Mom shared my struggles with her, after which this woman told Mom that she had gone through a difficult time in her life and started having panic attacks. She told Mom that this book had helped her break free from the panic attacks. I'm always a bit leery of accepting certain types of help from my family and those close to me. I see it as if they're implying that they don't like, or can't accept, who or how I am, so they must find something that will fix me. Sometimes, it ends up making me feel worse when it doesn't pan out. I feel, once again, like I have failed those around me. In keeping with my promise to God to look at or do whatever He sends my way, I read the book. Nothing. No bolts of awareness lightness in my soul. No "ah-ha" moments of understanding. I put the book on my bookshelf and forgot about it. My experience with this book was about to become a lesson from God that has imprinted itself into my psyche.

Fast forward six months or so. I had finished the program and had started therapy. I was still listening to the audio sessions from the program and could have probably recited them word for word at that point. I was in the office at home one day, doing the usual paperwork and filing necessary to keep the lights on, when I happened to look over at the bookcase. My eyes instantly lasered in on the book *Be Anxious for Nothing*. I had an instantaneous message go through me that said, "Read the book again." I didn't really want to. It hadn't done me any good the first time, so why read it again? I ignored the message and went about my life. A few days later, as I was scrolling through the guide on the television, I saw a show called "Joyce Meyer: Enjoying Everyday Life". I thought *Hhhmmm.... how come this has never jumped out at me before?* I watched the last 10 minutes of the show and felt such a strong connection to the teachings from Joyce that I wanted to read the book again. So, I did. This time, the Bible verses and Joyce's message really resonated with me. This whole experience taught me that God has a timing for everything, and that if I ignore what He is telling me to do, then He will keep pestering me until I do it. Every single time.

One thing that God has sent me an immense amount of help for is the guilt I feel about missing functions that are important to my family and close friends or not being able to be there for them when and how they need it due to my struggles with anxiety and panic attacks. In May of 2011 my sister's ex-husband died in a car accident. They had been married for over 20 years, and he is the father to my three nephews. They had only been divorced a few years, and my nephews were still young men. They had a complicated relationship with their father, but at such a young age still had hope that it could all turn around someday. Unfortunately, they never got that chance.

    For her boys, my sister helped plan all the funeral proceedings and dealt with all the business that comes along with death. The morning of the funeral, I woke up with every intention of going. I showered, got dressed, grabbed my keys, headed down the stairs, and then stopped. I couldn't get myself to take that last step off the landing and head out the door. I felt the beginnings of a panic attack move through my body. I was shaking, couldn't catch my breath, felt weak in my limbs, and lethargic all about. I thought that if I could just get into the car, I would be able to go and be okay. Instead, it got worse. I despised myself every minute of the time leading up to, during, and for days after, the phone call I made telling my sister I wasn't going to be at the funeral. As much as I envisioned myself being a solid rock my sister and nephews could lean on that day, I wasn't equipped to do it at that point in my life. Even though I realize that me going in a heightened state of anxiety and panic wouldn't have done her, or me, any good, I still feel shameful about not being there. It's something I carry with me, and even though I have forgiven myself approximately 50 percent of the way, I still get angry at myself about my "weakness". Being angry and ashamed at yourself is not a good feeling. I know I cannot change my past behaviors; I just try to do better each time a situation that challenges me comes up. If I fall short of my goal, I try to forgive myself right away so that I don't keep carrying around that heavy sack of guilt and shame.

    Dealing with the struggle of never knowing when you're going to have a panic attack leaves you hyper vigilant for places and experiences that might trigger one. Then, something will happen that would make you think, *That would definitely cause a panic attack for someone with anxiety or panic disorder, let alone someone that doesn't!* yet no panic attack. I have a great story about that comparison.

It was about a year after the peak of my downward spiral, and I was doing better, but still had frequent anxiety and panic attacks. I was driving home from an after-work appointment with the chiropractor. My route home from his office was different than my normal route home from work since his office was in a different city than where I worked. At the time, we lived way out (I mean WAY OUT) in the country, and the road home was narrow, curvy, and only had one or two short distances where you could pass. I got behind a car that was doing 30 mph below the speed limit and then would speed up and then slow way down, and then kept doing that cycle. I think the person was drunk. After a while, there was a line of cars behind me, and I was losing my patience, which is not something that most of us with anxiety disorder have an abundance of anyway.

As we approached one of the passing areas, I saw my opportunity and sped up to get past this horribly annoying driver. I didn't immediately slow down once I passed the car because I knew others would try to pass too and wanted to make sure they had room to get back into our travel lane. What I did not know is that an officer from the county sheriff's office had been doing speed patrols on that road for the last few weeks and was happily handing out tickets. Well, next thing I know, I see lights behind me and a cop car on my tail. YIKES! Surprisingly enough, I was upset instead of afraid. I found a spot to pull over and as the officer was talking to me, the drunk driver (I swear that person was drunk or horribly impaired and should not have been driving!) with about 10 cars behind it poked on by at about 15 miles an hour. I pointed that out to the officer, but he ignored me and proceeded to give me a ticket for not slowing down fast enough after passing the vehicle. I was so mad, but I was not fearful, and I didn't have a panic attack during the whole episode. Even I can't understand why. It makes no sense. I'll have a panic attack just going to Home Depot, but not when getting pulled over and given a ticket? It's no wonder it's so hard to understand anxiety and panic disorders. But of course, that was not the end of the story.

I paid the ticket, which was only the second ticket I had ever received in my 25 years of driving, and thought that was the end of it. It was not. About a year later, I was driving to work at 5:30 in the morning. I came down a hill into town and was going a bit over the speed limit, and didn't see the city cop sitting in a parking lot. You know that feeling when you pass a cop and just know you're getting pulled over. I had the normal "pit in the stomach" feeling, but nothing too bad when I pulled over to the shoulder of the road and the cop pulled in behind me. I got my license and proof of insurance ready and was thinking *Great! Now I'm going to be late for work. ARG!* The officer took my information and went back to his car to presumably write me a ticket. He comes back and says, "I need you to get out of the vehicle." My first thought was *What?!* He had to ask me twice because I was so stunned.

I got out and he put handcuffs on me and said my license was suspended for not paying a previous speeding ticket. At this point, my brain was scrambling to come up with a logical reason why this officer would think I was a criminal. He must have me mixed up with someone else. I even asked him that. Looking back, it was quite funny. As he was escorting me to his vehicle, a couple of elderly women walked by staring and shaking their heads. It was mortifying. The ridiculousness of this whole thing is that I am the squarest, do it by the rules, don't get into trouble person that most of my friends and family know. He put me in the back seat of his car, which by the way is not very comfortable when your hands are cuffed behind you. Plus, it's really cramped back there and the seats are a hard plastic. All I could think at that point was, *That's probably because people bleed, puke, poo and pee back here. EWWWW!*

The officer asked if there was someone that he could call to come get me and my car. If not, he would have to impound the car and take me to jail. JAIL!!! Oh my gosh. I was thinking *I can't do jail. I'll have a massive panic attack, then freak out, they'll taser me and I'll have a heart attack and die!* or something along those lines. My husband didn't pick up the phone and the only other number I could remember in that moment was my employer's cell phone number. It was a surreal moment. There I am, handcuffed in the back of a cop car listening to the officer ask my boss if he knew a Kristina Horton and that he had her in custody. I could hear my boss say, "Are you sure?" I was horrified!

Thankfully, my boss was able to come get me and my car. He had to be driven there by two of my coworkers on their way out to a job, so they got to witness my humiliation first hand. I think the only reason I didn't have a panic attack is because I was in shock. It didn't seem like it was really happening. I fully expected to start hyperventilating and babbling in the back of that cop car and get carried off to the insane asylum. Which, by the way, is a very real fear that many of us that experience anxiety disorders worry about. Anyway, my boss talked to the cop for a minute while I'm placed in the passenger seat of my car and when he gets in to drive us to the office, he just looked at me and said, "Well, this is an interesting morning" and chuckled.

When we got to the office, I called Ray and told him what happened and that he'd have to come get me and the car after work. I seemed to be okay and just got on with my day. A couple of hours later, my boss popped into my office to give me a folder and made joking comments about the incident. Normally, I would joke right back, but instead, the delayed reaction of what happened hit me, and I started to sob. He got a panicked looked on his face, and that made me feel bad, so I cried even harder. I can tell the story now and laugh about it, but it still amazes me that I didn't have a panic attack during both incidents. By the way, I found out that the county never updated in their system that I had paid the first ticket and so I had been driving around for almost a year with a suspended driver's license. As unpleasant as that situation was, I thank God for having it happen. Otherwise, I would never have known my license was suspended, and it could have resulted in an even bigger problem later.

By the fall of 2012 I was handling the anxiety episodes better, and they were becoming fewer and further between. I was finally settling back into work and feeling good in my comfy little "safe" zone. As I soon found out, being stuck in my "safe" zone was not where God wanted me. I wasn't even looking to change my work or move out of my current job position, but God decided I was needed elsewhere. It was such a foreign concept to me that I would be needed somewhere, because I felt so broken and useless. As Joyce Meyer likes to say, "God uses cracked pots to let His light shine through" or something along those lines.

I had received a text message from a former coworker saying that the state agency she worked for was getting ready to post a job announcement for the manager of the survey research office, and she thought I would be a good fit for the position. I was so terrified of switching jobs and having to work through all that change. I'll clue you into something; most people with anxiety disorders do not handle change well. We tend to go into super control mode elsewhere in our lives. Believe me, it's about as much fun for us as it is for those around us. Anyway.... I really prayed about it, because I just felt in my spirit that I was supposed to apply for this job. So, I did.

I thought, *There's no way they'll ask me to interview. I'm sure there are other people better suited for that job.* I think it was me just hoping I was wrong about what God wanted from me and I could stay in the job that felt safe and comfortable. Of course, if God wants something to happen, it's going to happen! I was selected for an interview and was offered the job a few hours afterwards. When the division manager called to offer me the job, I wasn't even prepared for the word "Yes!" to pop out of my mouth when he asked if I would accept the position. I had such a stunned look on my face that I turned to Ray and said, "Well, I guess I have a new job."

I started work at the state agency in February of 2013, and even thought it was bittersweet leaving a place, and the people, who had been so good to me, it was a beneficial change. It catapulted me into some serious growth. I also met one of my closest and dearest friends there, and forged professional and personal relationships that will forever be a part of me. Portions of that job were very challenging and caused me great emotional discomfort. Many days I felt like someone poured a big glass of self-doubt down my throat.

One of the questions that was asked during the interview for this job was if I was comfortable doing public speaking. My answer was "yes", but I don't know why. The thought of it should have sent me into a panic, but instead I felt reassured that if God had me get the job, then He would equip me for the work. Three weeks after my first day on the job I found myself at the yearly conference of our statewide professional association. I didn't have to do a presentation that year, but I did have to be at a booth in the exhibitor's hall and interact with people all day long for the four-day duration of the conference.

I also had to be in crowded rooms with people moving about and constantly encountering me. In other words, I had to be "ON" all day. I went to my room in the evenings and just crashed. The emotional and mental exhaustion was astounding. It was like full sensory overload and every 10 minutes I wanted to run outside. It was also anxiety- inducing to be away from home in a hotel without Ray. Just staying in hotel rooms usually caused me high levels of anxiety because I was not in a "safe place". I was doing okay, probably because I was so exhausted after having to process so much energy from other people all day. I am an introvert and can push myself out into an environment of people, people, and more people, but it takes a toll on me if I do it for too long without a chance to recharge with time alone.

The following year, I did a four-hour presentation in front of a room full of my fellow professionals. I made sure to get plenty of rest the night before and got up early enough to have my time with God, to eat a decent breakfast, and go over my presentation one more time. When I stepped into the elevator, with my heart pounding, I plastered on a smile and repeated over and over in my head, *Help me, Jesus!* I entered the presentation room, got my computer set up, grabbed a bottle of water and a cup of herbal tea, all the while chatting with a few people that had wandered in or were standing out in the conference area great hall getting morning refreshments.

One of my staff members, who knew how nervous I was, came in and checked on me to make sure I had everything I needed. That helped ground me a little, especially when he made some jokes and made me laugh. As I stood at the front of the room, and the seats started to fill up, I felt my abdomen tighten so much that I was having a hard time taking in a full breath. Even though I had taken 0.5 mg of lorazepam (Ativan) that morning, it certainly didn't feel like it. I was on the verge of a panic attack, and I knew it. Just when I was ready to run out of the room, I got the signal from the room attendant that it was time to get started. I thought *Well...if I pass out or topple over, at least it'll give everyone something exciting to talk about.* So, I said one quick prayer, forced myself to take a long, slow breath, tried to steady my shaking legs, and got on with it.

I found that most of the anxiety and panic happens in the lead up to the public speaking. Once I get going and am engaged in the information and communicating with the audience, the anxiety gets pushed to the back of my brain. When I'm actively involved with a task, then it distracts my mind and interrupts the thoughts that are causing the anxiety and panic. Thankfully, I got through the presentation with only one moment where I felt my heart skip a beat, and my vision got a little gray around the edges. It was when someone was asking me a question, and it's a marvel that I was able to even hear enough of the question to answer it correctly. After the presentation, I had to go to the exhibit hall booth for an hour before I could head up to my room and take a much-needed nap.

Even though that first presentation was terrifying, I was so proud of myself afterwards. I did it!!! I conquered one of my Goliath's. David's got nothing on me.[5]

During my six years at that job, I did countless presentations and bits of public speaking. Some occasions were more challenging for me, and some barely gave me any anxiety. I did start to notice that when I had to speak to a group of my peers, it was more anxiety-inducing to me than when I presented to stakeholders. Working through some of my insecurities in therapy helped me with that. I came to realize that I did have something to offer, and it didn't matter if everyone liked me or not. How they felt about me was none of my business. I still struggle with those issues, but I continue to make forward progress with letting go of those limiting beliefs and insecurities. I also discovered that the more I did public speaking, the more comfortable I got with it, and that sometimes it was easier to talk to a large group rather than a small group of people.

Another way that this job pushed me into uncomfortable growth was in the supervising of people. Suddenly, I had a staff of five with very different personalitie, to contend with every day. Not only was I trying to figure out my job, adjust to working for a government agency, but I also had to learn what job tasks my staff did and how they did them. I spent the first year mostly learning from my staff, observing what was working well and what wasn't, and educating myself on how to be the best leader I could be. Every time I had to make a decision that I thought someone else might not like or agree with, I would second guess myself and make sure I had looked at the situation from every possible angle.

I felt overwhelmed by the work I was doing in therapy, on my own, and what the job was teaching me about myself. I was being forced to make hard changes about my own thoughts and behaviors if I wanted to continue healing and stretching myself in all the ways that God was asking me to. Believe me,

---

5   See the book *Goliath Must Fall* by Louis Giglio.

it was not fun. Doing the hard work on yourself never is. It's painful, and scary. It tears you down in order to build you back up, and yet is some of the most rewarding work you'll ever do. I came to realize that I had to sort out some of my issues before I could be the kind of leader I wanted to be.

I don't like to hurt people, and I don't like seeing people hurting. Having to discipline staff and sometimes go down bumpy roads with them was painful for me. I knew that I had to do it in order to support the rest of the staff, but I also knew it was likely to cause pain for the individual. I'm a stubborn person and have a very strong sense of what I think is the right thing to do. Once I start on that path, I doubt dynamite would throw me off it. Sometimes the outcomes were not what I wanted, but I also knew that I couldn't sacrifice the cohesiveness of the team by letting unhealthy behaviors from one person affect everyone else. Ultimately, I came to realize that they made their choices, just like I had. I blamed myself for a long time; somewhere deep in my subconscious I felt vulnerable and hurt by their actions. It was the age-old thought pattern of *It must be my fault that this is happening. I didn't do enough, I didn't help enough, I missed something, right?*

I realized that one of the continuing trauma patterns that I learned early on in life was to not say or do anything that might trigger someone else's trauma. If I even thought my actions might cause them to hurt, then I wouldn't do it. It could be something as simple as not wearing a piece of clothing that I really liked but that my husband said he didn't like; or if there was a behavior they were doing or something they said that hurt me, I wouldn't say anything and would just make excuses about why they might have done or said what they did. I could see their trauma and excuse it even if it hurt me, but I never protected myself from it. I made their health, well-being, and comfort more important than my own. Sometimes it wasn't even something they said or did, it would be something I didn't think I could say or do because even though it was truth, or something that needed to be discussed, I wouldn't do it because it might be uncomfortable for them. I've come a long way in changing this pattern, but it's such a core false belief of mine that I still fight it, especially when dealing with those closest to me.

With this job, I had to learn to break that pattern. I found this easier to do with people that I cared about but weren't necessarily close to. It opened the scab of my deepest wound, the fear of hurt and rejection and of being unlovable. I was going to have to sit in a room and tell someone that they were behaving in a way that was not good for others, whether it was personal behaviors such as talking in a demeaning way, or they weren't meeting their work standards. I just knew that I would be to blame. They would say the problem was me, that I was being too extreme in my evaluations of the situations, and that I was just out to get them. At least that's what I thought they would think. I wanted my team to like me, to respect me, to appreciate the opportunity to grow as a person. Those are unrealistic expectations. I did get that from most of my team eventually once I dealt with the personnel issues head on, but that required me to open that scab and be vulnerable to someone else which was terrifying to me. The anxiety, which had been manageable for a few years, came back to haunt me. Dealing with other people's trauma reactions were stirring up my trauma reactions. I was a mess inside. I worked hard at keeping a cool and collected exterior at work, but my emotions were bouncing around in me like the inside of a pinball machine.

God did send me a new saving grace. He sent me to someone that helped me trust my body again. I had recently lost about 30 pounds, but wanted to get strong. I was petrified just thinking about joining a gym, especially since I had no clue what to do or how to begin working out. I was also carrying around the lingering fear of gyms since the massive panic attack I had at a gym 15 years earlier. One of my staff happened to mention that he started going to a gym where he knew the owners. I asked him some questions about it and decided to stop by one afternoon on my way home. I told myself I was just going to look, get a tour, and see if I liked the feel of it.

I walked in, stood in the entry area looking like I was lost on another planet, when a gregarious guy, who looked to be my age, greeted me, and started chatting with me. He introduced himself as Rodney and asked me my name. I told him I was just looking, but as he started to give me the tour, I felt an overwhelming urge to tell him what was really holding me back from joining the gym. So, I did. I still wasn't comfortable telling people about the anxiety and panic attacks because I thought it made me look pathetic and weak. My hands were shaking a little and I felt tears well up in my eyes when I told him of my struggles and that I really wanted to trust my body again and get it healthy. He was so kind and shared that he too had dealt with some anxiety and panic episodes. He acted so excited about wanting to help me, and I have to say, it started to get me optimistic and comfortable with the idea of working out again. I left the gym with a feeling of relief and some excitement.

I ended up hiring Rodney for personal training sessions. Initially I had two or three sessions a week with him. It was slow going at first. I was so out of shape! I would start to panic if the warmup on the treadmill went over a certain speed or time. I am forever thankful that Rodney was patient with me, distracting me with conversations and jokes, so that I wouldn't think so much about how my body was feeling or reacting to something we were doing. Most of the time, I felt comfortable enough to tell him when I needed a minute to get the anxiety under control or if I was starting to panic. He never judged me or made me feel bad or worthless when those things happened. He had a strong faith in God and as a fellow Christian, we had some great discussions about our beliefs. In many ways, those training sessions were making my body strong but were also feeding me spiritually with praise and worship.

After six months, I quit the personal training and had a go at doing the workouts myself. Months later, I noticed that I hadn't seen Rodney at the gym for weeks. I asked one of the other trainers if he had changed his schedule. They said that he had quit and didn't know where he was working. Since I knew that I still needed a trainer to keep me on track, I reached out to Rodney, and he said he was at a different gym now. Fortunately, it was a gym that was right on my way home, so I made an appointment and stopped by to see Rodney and feel out the gym. Even though it was a chain gym, it was independently owned and the people there were friendly and of all shapes, ages, and genders working out. The gym was busy, but not too busy. I signed up and continued my training with Rodney on and off for the next few years.

I eventually stopped with the personal training since I needed a new vehicle and it was a financial choice that I had to make between the two. I figured I was comfortable enough at this point to work out on my own consistently. Through Rodney, God gave me the gift of feeling good about my body again, and not always thinking that it was conspiring against me. Even though I'm not as diligent about my workouts as I was a few years ago, I am no longer afraid of working my body or experiencing all the strange sensations that happen when I do. I no longer belong to a gym. I made one of the spare bedrooms in our house a workout room. It's a tiny room with a low ceiling, but my treadmill, yoga equipment, and weights fit in there and that's enough for me. I continue to struggle with being consistent and liking to work out, but that is a self-sabotage story for another time.

CHAPTER SIX

Reconstruction
(Ages 44 – 50)

Shortly after starting my new job we decided that to take some of the financial pressure off us, we would downsize. We sold our three-year-old car, and I drove our older single cab, no frills, small truck. We put the trailer park in Idaho up for sale. We bought an 11-year old 36-foot 5-wheel RV with three slide outs, put it on our commercial/residential property, and moved into it so that we wouldn't have a mortgage payment. When we packed up the house, we sold, gave away, or threw away lots of stuff we had been dragging around for years and didn't really use or need. These changes, my new job, moving out of our house, moving into the RV, were scary but also very liberating. We had lived in RVs before during our time in Alaska and when we were building the house, so this was not a difficult adjustment for us. The bonus was that my commute was at least 15 minutes shorter each way, and Ray's commute was a 50-foot walk.

Taking all that financial pressure off us, especially me, helped with my level of anxiety. I was able to go into the new job with a sense of knowing that if it turned out to be a bad work environment for me, then I had the freedom to walk away and know we would be okay, money wise. I didn't feel trapped in the job. I believe that made a significant difference in my ability to succeed by being able to focus on it and not feel unnecessary pressures elsewhere in my life. I'm not saying it wasn't still a struggle for me, but that taking away quite a few of the things that tipped my stress and worry scales in the wrong direction helped me better handle the job stressors.

By the time 2014 rolled around, I had hit a period of what I like to call "reprieve from the anxiety". I wasn't waking up every single day with a horrible nervous stomach. I had attacked the root causes of my anxiety from every angle I could find. I took my therapy homework seriously. I had Bible verses and affirmations memorized that I would say to myself throughout the day. I exercised to release anxious energy; I ate clean foods and balance my diet. I took supplements to support my body functions. I regularly got chiropractic adjustments and massages. I wrote in my journal at least every other day. All that work payed off, and I was able to get the reprieve from anxiety that I was longing for.

I went months without even a hint of a panic attack. I consistently had more positive thoughts. I was gaining confidence in my ability to manage the anxiety symptoms. I was working out three days or more a week, and just felt good in my body. The anxiety was still there, it just wasn't something I was aware of every hour of every day like it had been for most of my life. We went on a three-week trip to the United Kingdom and Ireland in the fall of 2015. We went to Hawaii the summer of 2016 with my family to celebrate my parents' 50th wedding anniversary. I couldn't believe I was the same person that just a few years prior wasn't able to drive or leave her house without having a completely devastating panic attack. I started to think I was fixed. I was cured of this horrible ailment! That happens, right?

The trouble with that kind of thinking is that I got complacent. I became lazy about my mental and emotional health. I thought I was fixed, so I focused instead on my physical health. I forgot that in everything there is a balance to be kept. I came to realize that I don't have the luxury of setting aside my mental and emotional health for any amount of time. It is an ongoing and constant process.

I bought into the messages that came at me from my childhood, books, programs, other people, and social media that said things like:

You're only acceptable if you don't have this problem.
If you just did_____, then this will all go away.
You're only lovable if you _____, look this way, accomplish this certain thing, and conquer your fears.

So, when the anxiety symptoms started creeping back in, I ignored them because "I was fixed!" Right? I wasn't going to have anxiety and panic attacks anymore. I had this all under control. Of course, thinking I had it under control should have been an indicator to me that some of my old thinking had crept back in. Control. Control. Control. It really is a dirty word to me. The minute I start to think I have control over anything, except my own reactions, is the minute I've fooled myself into a false sense of calm.

I think the anxiety started affecting me again daily during the disciplinary process I went through in 2016 with one of my staff members. That whole situation brought to the surface my fears of being unacceptable if I'm not successful at what I'm doing. Having a staff member that was so resistant to the help I offered, the changes I suggested, and my hopes of building a cohesive team, just forced the message of "You're not doing this right" down my throat. Their failure to not change behaviors became my failure as a supervisor. At least, that's what I thought. I didn't realize it at the time, but the experience I had dealing with that situation triggered things in my trauma center that I didn't know were there. They were buried so deeply and had been with me for so long, that I wasn't able to move past it without some serious help. This is especially true because I hadn't been keeping up with my mental and emotional self-care. My armor was off. I was unprepared and blindsided by the onslaught of emotions this brought up for me.

During this difficult time, I whined to my therapist that I thought I had dealt with all my issues. What more could there be?! She used an analogy to explain it to me. One that I refer to often. She said that all the unresolved emotions and trauma throughout our lives, ones that we repress and stuff deep down inside of us are like garbage in a can. The can is you. It's clean and shiny when you're born. As life goes on and we are taught not to talk about our feelings or experiences, we just open the lid on that can and stuff them inside. You can imagine that, as time goes on, the stuff at the bottom starts to get stinky and decomposed. It's slimy, and soupy, and dark. It's almost undistinguishable from what it was when it first went into the can. I had my breakdown when I had so much "stuff" in my can, that it was overflowing, and I couldn't fit the lid on it anymore. My breakdown forced me to start emptying my can.

When I first started therapy, the "stuff" on top was newer and easier to address. It was still no fun to deal with, but at least I could figure out what it was and it wasn't too stinky yet. As I worked on healing, I was able to take the pressure off the lid, close it, and feel good about emptying it about half way. The problem is that the can wasn't empty. One little lift of the lid and all the stink of what was in there would come wafting out. This is exactly what happened when I tried to disregard what I was feeling while dealing with my staff member.

I could no longer ignore what was left in my garbage can. I had to work at cleaning it out. I started digging deeper into my long-standing hurts and false beliefs. When I looked at the coping mechanisms I learned in childhood, and that they don't serve me anymore, it was extremely uncomfortable. I had this voice in my head saying:

How cliché; blaming your childhood for your current issues.

Don't you dare go there! Everything in your childhood was great. What do you have to complain about?

That was all in the past. You shouldn't live in the past. You can't change it.

What I learned as I worked through my childhood emotional traumas, were these very important things:
- All the situations, words, and trauma you didn't deal with at the time will stay with you until you process them. It's not dwelling on them, or dredging up the past. It is pulling it out of the garbage can, looking at it from the perspective of the adult you are now,

working through the unexpressed emotions and residual feelings, then not putting it back in the garbage can.
- You cannot just "let it go" – whatever it is, until you've dealt with it. It will always come back to haunt you if you don't.
- You are not to blame for any of the trauma you experienced as a child. You were a child!!!
- Likely, your parents or other adults in your life that caused any traumas were working in the realm of their own traumas. Since they never worked through their own hurts and issues, they perpetuated the history of trauma. They were likely doing the best they could at the time and weren't emotionally healthy within themselves to be emotionally healthy in their relationship with you.
- You must do the work. The hard work. It's painful, unsettling, and will change you in ways that aren't comfortable at first – for you or the people around you. Don't give up! The reward is so much greater than the struggle.
- It's a constant process. Gain the tools, learn how to do the work, then implement the tools repeatedly until the new behavior becomes the automatic response. Sometimes you'll get it right, and sometimes you'll flub up, but it doesn't matter because progress is still progress.
- In the end, very few people you know will be at the same level of emotional healing as you. It can be frustrating as you try to communicate and deal with them, but give them grace. You used to be exactly where they are.

Around this time, I found another tool, by accident really, that helped me immensely. In fact, it's the reason I'm writing this book.

Due to me constantly trying to pull my shoulders up into my ears and hunch in on myself when I'm anxious, I get a massage about every two weeks. The massage therapist I had been seeing moved out of state, so I started seeing someone else. My new massage therapist, Brian, and his family ended up moving close to where we were living in our RV, so Ray and I became friends with them. Brian is an excellent massage therapist, but no matter how often I went, I was still having horrible back spasms and other problems.

Right before one massage session, I was face down on the table saying my usual pray for anointing, when the thought came to me that maybe my muscle issues were tied to my emotions. I had that thought because I noticed that the muscle spasms would be very intense one day and then sometimes gone the next without me doing anything to alleviate them except for applying Biofreeze and going to sleep. Nothing I did physically seemed to contribute to the muscle spasms or relieved them. I'd had a few experiences with emotional muscle release (my term...not sure if that's what it's called), but had never asked Brian about it.

When he came in the room and started working on my back, I asked him if he felt any emotional energy in the area of my muscle spasms. He hesitated for a second then said, "Yes. I feel that there is something there." I asked if he was comfortable doing some emotional release work with me. He said he was, so we said a prayer and asked God to work through Brian and guide him and for me to allow my body to release what it needed to.

Once I gave myself that permission, it was like a flood gate opening. I started crying once Brian concentrated on the areas of my back that I would get the horrible muscle spasms. We had about two or three sessions like this, where I would have the crying release – which did make the muscle spasms better for a few days. Then, something unusual happened.

After the first bit of crying, I started to hear from God. It would come in either the method of hearing Him speak to my spirit, not in the form of an audible sound but like a conversation you have with yourself; or He would talk to me with images. At first, I thought, *Oh, that's just my subconscious letting things go*, but it became evident to me that that wasn't the case.

I remember one time; I was praying silently as Brian worked on my back. I was praying about what I thought was bothering me, but my mind kept wandering to a certain word that made no sense to me. I kept trying to bring my thoughts back to what I thought I needed to deal with, but the word, and now an image, kept popping up. I finally quit fighting it and just relaxed into that word and image. It ended up making me deal with a long-buried hurt from my childhood that I was completely not expecting.

Over the course of the next couple of years, I had 32 emotional release sessions that resulted in a message from God. One of these messages was that God wanted me to write this book. That was in late 2016. God first brought this up to me through my husband. I was telling Ray about my sessions with Brian, and he said, "Sounds like you need to write a book." I scoffed at the idea and thought, *Who am I to write a book? Nobody would want to read about my life.* I let the idea go and forgot about it. That is until God kept bringing it up in my sessions with Brian. The more I put it off, the more He pestered me about it. I remember mentioning it to my good friend, Laurie. When she asked why I didn't just do it, I said, "God hasn't given me anointing for that yet," to which she replied, "Well, based on what you just told me, are you not anointed or have you not allowed yourself to be anointed?" Mind blown!!! Duh…what was I waiting for, a sign from God? He had been giving me signs, I just wasn't letting myself believe that He wanted ME to do this.

After that conversation with Laurie, I prayed and was reminded of the fact I had promised God that I would do whatever He asked me to do. Having absolutely no idea where to start, I decided to go back to what I learned in school and began putting together an outline. I even attempted to write the first few chapters. I worked on it haphazardly, but not seriously. Then, it was completely put aside in the spring of 2018 when my grandmother was hospitalized.

My parents had left for a month-long road trip in their RV. They'd been planning it for over a year, and my mom's cousin and her husband were taking their RV and going too. My grandmother was 95 and lived on her own, but my parents did all her grocery shopping, paid her bills, and would stop by once a week, or more, to check on her. A few months before my parents left, we set up a system where we would take turns (my parents, my siblings, and my cousins) calling her every night to see how she was doing. I had some in depth, funny, and sweet conversations with Grandma each week when I called. Obviously, I felt a strong connection to Grandma because I had lived with her and Grandpa my last few years of high school and when Ray was away at boot camp. After Grandpa died, Grandma lived with my parents, and especially when they lived next door, I saw her often. When she moved into her apartment in a city south of where I live, and I started working in the city north of where I live, I saw her only once every month or so. About the last five years of her life, she liked the idea of going and doing things, but the reality is that she rarely wanted to venture out; and even if she did, it would completely tire her out. For this reason, the phone calls were a nice way to connect with her.

The weekend after my parents left on their trip, my sister and I stopped by to check on Grandma. I hadn't been to her apartment for well over a year. Every time I'd seen her was at a family function or at my parents' house for dinner. I don't think my sister had been there for a long time either. I walked in, gave Grandma a big hug, then looked about the tiny one-bedroom apartment. I couldn't believe how dirty it was! Grandma had always kept an immaculate house, but after Grandpa died and as she got older, she didn't go at her housecleaning as vigorously as she had in the past. What I didn't expect was for it to be this dirty and cluttered. I looked over at my sister and we both raised our eyebrows and gave each other the "What the hell?!" face. My sister and I sat Grandma down and told her we would clean up a bit for her.

I felt some anger towards my parents, because I couldn't understand why they allowed the place to go uncleaned. Mom had asked me at least a year or more prior to this to come and help her clean the apartment, but I got sick with a horrible flu so we didn't do it. When I asked about rescheduling after I got better, Mom said that she was just going to investigate having someone come in and clean it once or twice a month. I said that I would chip in some money to help pay for it. Months later, when I asked Mom about it, she said she still hadn't found anyone, and I never pushed the issue because I thought it was being taken care of. I think I shoulder some of the blame because I hadn't been to the apartment for so long and therefore, had no idea how much the cleaning service was needed. I assumed that my parents were at least doing some of the basic cleaning when they stopped to visit with her, and maybe they were, but it was just too much for them to do since it was around this time that my mom was experiencing some health issues of her own.

As my sister and I were throwing in a load of sheets and towels to wash, we asked Grandma if she had taken her medication yet that day. She said she hadn't because she just didn't have the gumption to fix herself something to eat to take with the pill. When we looked in the fridge, it was clear it needed to be cleaned out. It was a jumble of vegetables, leftovers wrapped up in foil or put in mix matched containers with lids, and condiments that had seen better days. We were able to quickly put together some crackers and cheese so that she could at least take her medication.

We spent over two hours cleaning out the fridge, emptying cupboards of old food and food containers. We washed the dirty dishes in her sink and rewashed the dishes and utensils in the cupboard and drawers. They just didn't look thoroughly cleaned. We decided we needed some cleaning supplies and to get Grandma some food that didn't need much preparation.

It was apparent that she didn't have the energy to spend time cooking, and she confirmed to us that she wasn't eating much in a day.

When my sister and I got in the car to head to the grocery store, we lamented to each other how worried we were about Grandma's physical decline and the state of her and her apartment. It was a somber drive to the store, as we were both worried about Grandma and feeling incredulous about the care my parents had been giving her. Based on what we felt we knew about our parents, it didn't seem possible that they had been doing just the bare minimum for her; yet, that's what it seemed to us based on what we were seeing. This was hard for us to believe since my parents had done so much for Grandma as she aged. They really did take good care of her, but I think that it had become too much and that they were starting to realize that. They investigated assisted living facilities for her, but couldn't find anything with vacancy that was affordable. Elder care is a serious problem, and support for the people providing support to the elderly just isn't as readily available as it should be in my opinion.

We sped through the store, picking up cleaning supplies, a rotisserie chicken that was ready to eat, frozen meals she could easily microwave, snack packs of crackers, already sliced cheese, and any other food we thought she might eat that would be easy for her to prepare. We also got her some flowers to liven up the place and give her something cheerful to look at. I remember it was a sunny warm day, not unheard of in western Washington, but not exactly common either.

At this point in my life, I was taking 0.50 mg of lorazepam as needed for anxiety. Starting about six months prior, I had been taking at least one dose of the medication about 15 days out of a month. Most of the time I was taking it first thing in the morning as I was waking up with anxiety symptoms, most notably a tight nervous stomach. This day, May 6, 2018, Ray left, in the morning, for a week-long mountain biking trip to Utah, which meant I would be dealing with an increase of anxious episodes while he was gone. Add the stress of that with my added anxiety about warm weather, and my worry about Grandma, and the result is me not handling life very well. I was also gearing up for a two-day training class starting Monday and a presentation I had to do on Wednesday. To top it off, I also had work travel planned for the first three days of the week after that and would only see Ray for a little over a week before he left for a ten-day trip to Ireland. It was already in the books to be a challenging month for managing the anxiety.

When we got back to Grandma's apartment, we unloaded the groceries and showed her all the "easy to fix" food we bought for her. We wanted to make sure she knew what she had and hoped it would encourage her to eat more consistently. The whole exchange with her made me think of the "grocery getting" process my parents had been using with her for years. Each week, they would call and ask for her grocery list, then they would go get the items, then deliver them to her. Sometimes, if she needed something, Grandma would call them with a "need it now" list. Mom had mentioned months prior that she thought Grandma was just recycling the same list over and over because she kept asking for the same things. I remember Mom saying, "How many potatoes and pounds of butter does one person need?" We laughed about it at the time, but looking back, I think it was a sign that Grandma wasn't up to the task of taking care of herself anymore.

As I put some of the rotisserie chicken on a plate and gave it to Grandma, she looked down at the plate in her hand and said in a dejected tone "I'm so weary." It just about broke my heart to see Grandma like this and to hear her say something like that. I gave her a hug and tried to hide the tears on my face and the emotion in my voice when I told her that I loved her.

My sister finished cleaning the bathroom and then we hauled five large trash bags to the dumpster. Most of it was stuff out of her fridge, kitchen cupboards, and bathroom cabinets. Grandma had become a little bit of a hoarder. Probably a holdover from growing up during the depression and

Grandpa not being there to keep it in check. During the first few years after she moved into her apartment, she would go to "yard" sales at other apartments in the building and buy all kinds of knick- knacks and pretty things. Grandpa was always very strict and controlling about money, and while he was alive, Grandma was never allowed to spend money on things that she wanted for no other reason than that she liked them. After he died, and she got to that age where you just say, "Screw it! I'm going to do what I want to do." she went as crazy with yard sale spending as she could on her limited income.

My observation is that my grandparents had a good and loving relationship, but I saw an imbalance in it. I saw Grandma suppress her own needs, wants, and desires if they didn't fall in line with Grandpa's. She suppressed emotions, especially hurt and anger, and therefore, joy. She told me once that it's better to not express anger because it does no good except to upset the other person, and it doesn't change anything. For her, it was embarrassing and showed a lack of control if you expressed anger. Unfortunately, it's a lesson I learned well from her and my dad. I still have trouble showing anger when it's fitting and in an appropriate way. I just don't have any practice doing it and didn't grow up witnessing any good examples of it. Even though I know, based on many books and articles I've read on the subject, that it's terribly unhealthy, both physically and mentally, to not express anger, it's still a struggle for me. I think it's because I'm surrounded by people in my family, my husband, and some friends that get extremely uncomfortable and upset if someone around them expresses anger, whether it is directed towards them or not. Their reactions have taught me not to do it. I end up having to write letters I never send (and instead burn), or figure out some other way to release it out of my body. I'm still trying to figure out anger and how to handle that emotion – especially because anger is a secondary emotion and is caused by other feelings such as hurt, embarrassment, etc.

Getting back to Grandma. When my sister and I finally left Grandma's that day, we got in the car, looked at each other and said "Did you see she barely ate a few bites of the chicken?" and "Do you think she's going to be okay until we see her next weekend?" and "Do you think we should take her to the hospital? Something just doesn't seem right with her." After some discussion, we decided that she was doing okay; we didn't want to overreact, and we would just make sure to call her each night and see if our cousin, who lived in the same city, could stop by and check on her before the next weekend. In fact, the next weekend was Mother's Day, and we told her we would take her to lunch or bring her lunch, whatever she wanted to do.

We left her apartment that late afternoon physically and emotionally tired. I thank God that my sister was there with me and that we were able to help Grandma together. My cousin did stop by the early the following week and reported to us that Grandma appeared to be fine. Fast forward to the next Friday, May 11. I got a call that night from my sister, saying that Grandma had collapsed and was being taken to the hospital via ambulance.

Earlier in the evening, Grandma didn't answer when my dad called multiple times. He got worried and contacted my sister to see if she could stop by Grandma's apartment and make sure she was okay. My sister's oldest and youngest sons happened to be with her at the time. When they go there, they knocked on Grandma's door, and they heard her feebly answer that she had fallen in the doorway area, which is the passthrough between the bathroom and the kitchen. Having no key to get in, my nephews continued to talk to Grandma as my sister called emergency services. Thankfully, the EMTs had a master key and were able to get into the apartment without having to break the door down. Grandma was lying within a foot of the door.

Four EMTs showed up, two females and two males. Grandma only had a shirt on, so the female EMTs went in first, got her up, wrapped her in a towel, and sat her on the couch before everyone else went in. Grandma immediately asked someone to get her teeth for her, and once she had them in, kept saying to my sister "Don't tell your dad," over and over. She didn't want my parents' vacation ruined because of this "little" incident. That was nonsense, of course, so my sister called my parents right away.

I got the phone call as my sister was headed to the hospital. Thankfully her youngest son was able to go with her, as the oldest son had to go back to her place and check on the dogs. They had left in a hurry and both my nephews had puppies that needed care. My sister gets very edgy when she's under emotional pressure. She gathers all her feelings up around her and keeps a tight rein on them. When she called me, she wasn't crying but her speech pattern was very clipped and constricted, so I knew something was wrong. She calmly gave me the basic information about Grandma's condition, then proceeded to tell me that Grandma asked them to bring her some underwear.

My sister stopped by Walmart which was on route to the hospital. Her and her son, who was about 26 at the time, where standing in front of the women's undergarments frantically searching for the "grannie panties" because what else would a 95-year-old woman wear? Once they found them, they then proceeded to the checkout stand where she railroaded in front of a guy as she frantically told him why she needed to quickly check out with just one package of ladies' undergarments. I wanted to laugh because the situation was so ridiculous, and I could just picture my sister running crazily around Walmart with her mortified 26-year old son trailing behind her. My sister is a force of nature; never ever get in her way when she's on a mission to protect someone she cares about.

We cut off our conversation when they pulled up to the hospital, and she said she would call me once they got Grandma settled and let me know if I needed to head in right away. She finally called me back around ten o'clock and said that Grandma was settled in a room and resting. She was dehydrated, her organs were struggling, but she wasn't in any immediate danger. We decided that I would go in and be with her first thing in the morning, then my sister, brother and cousins would get there when they could.

I didn't sleep well that night, as you can imagine. I kept replaying in my head when I had seen her the week before and how I should have realized that she needed to go to the hospital. I know better than to dismiss my intuition. My sister and I both felt it that day, but we let our better judgement get overshadowed by our ingrained habit of making sure we never overreacted to a situation or made a big fuss about anything. Plus, it's difficult to switch on the reverse relationship of "parent and child" that you must do as your grandparents and parents age. It's not a natural transition. It's wrought with mistakes, frustrations, and hurt feelings.

My grandmother may have been a reserved person when I was growing up, but as she got older, she became much more demanding and sassier. It's almost like all the sass she didn't use for decades was being stored up to be unleashed once she hit a certain age. I hope that I keep getting sassier as I get older. It may be all we have left, once our bodies break down. When we would try to tell Grandma what to do, she would give us a direct look and would fire back with "Don't forget who used to paddle your bottom and can still do it if necessary!" It would always make us laugh, but it also made us not want to push her too hard.

Early the next morning, I headed out the door, wanting to get to Grandma as soon as they allowed visitors. The anxiety symptoms had been at an extremely high level ever since my sister's phone call the night before. Ray was still out of town. Thankfully Isabel, our dog, was snuggled up to me all night which gave me some comfort. I took 0.5 mg of lorazepam when I got out of bed which steadied me and kept a panic attack at bay as I drove to the hospital.

I talked to God as I was driving, and prayed that Grandma would be alright, and that she wouldn't hurt or suffer. I also prayed for the doctors, nurses, and all hospital staff that would be caring for her. I kept telling myself that I needed to take this one day at a time and not think of all that could happen in the days or weeks to come. I pulled out some of my dusty "dealing with anxiety" tools and sharpened them up because I knew I would need them if I was going to be there for Grandma.

I had seen Grandma in a hospital bed once or twice before, but never like this. She was in the Critical Care Unit, which means some serious issues were happening with her body. I wanted to cry when I walked in the room, partly from relief at getting to see her, and because I felt it in my bones, as I looked at her lying there, that she wasn't going to come back from this. She looked over at me as I walked in and said in a cheerful tone, "Hi, Grandma!", then smiled and reached out her arms for a hug. I kept myself together in that moment, but I can't say it was easy. Years of stuffing down my emotions and not dealing with them tended to come in handy sometimes.

My sister arrived shortly after I did. Only a few people were allowed in her room at one time, so as my cousins and their families showed up, we took turns hanging out in the waiting room to give everyone a chance to be with Grandma for a while. Fortunately, Grandma's functions had improved some overnight, and I think just being properly hydrated helped pep her up a bit. It didn't hurt that she loved all the attention she was getting. I left mid-afternoon as I needed to get home and take care of Isabel. Since I had work travel the first three days of the coming week, I said that I would stay with Grandma most of the next day which happened to be Mother's Day. My brother and I are the only grandchildren without kids of our own, and since our mom was out of town, I had no plans for the day. Ray would be getting home from his trip sometime early afternoon, so I knew Isabel would be taken care of.

When I got home Saturday afternoon, I made sure I was packed up and ready for my work trip so that I wouldn't have to worry about it on Sunday. I could focus all my energy on being there for Grandma. The doctor said she was holding steady, so I felt comfortable going out of town, knowing that one of the family members would be with her every day. We had figured out a schedule for the week since we knew it's always in the best interest of the patient if an advocate is there as much as possible. Doctors and nurses (especially, nurses!!) do an amazing job of caring for people, but their attention is pulled in many different directions, and we knew Grandma was in no shape to comprehend what the doctors were telling her.

I was wiped out from the emotional overload and being at such a high level of anxiety all day. I crashed hard that night and woke up feeling rested but with a tight nervous stomach and high anxiety. Once again, I took 0.5 mg of lorazepam right after getting up. After walking around outside with Isabel while she took care of her business, then eating breakfast, showering, packing up snacks, and my Kindle, the meds had kicked in enough for me to get the anxiety to a medium intensity level before I left the house.

When I arrived at the hospital, Grandma greeted me with a weak smile and a gesture of her hand for me to come stand next to her bed. I grabbed her hand, bent down, and kissed her paper-thin cheek, and quietly asked how her night had been. From the way she was restlessly moving around in the bed, I could tell she was in a state of discomfort. Her hand squeezed tightly against mine and she said, "Oh...I'm alright. I just can't get my back comfortable." If she was complaining, then I knew it was worse that she was telling me.

Grandma was raised by a cold and selfish mother who was part of the Christian Science Church (I use that term loosely). My great-grandmother believed that you would be healed through faith and didn't need to take her children to the doctor. Grandma was asthmatic when she was a child and suffered horribly with no professional care. If she complained, or allowed the symptoms to be visible around her mother, she was reprimanded and yelled at. Grandma learned at a very young age that if you were hurt or suffering, you had to deal with it on your own and to not expect any comfort or caregiving.

I observed widespread results of this childhood trauma in many of Grandma's behaviors. One of them being that she rarely voiced physical pain. So, when she complained to me that morning about "a little back pain," I knew it had to be much more than that. It was confirmed when the nurse came and in and, when I asked, told me that she'd had a difficult night. I looked over at Grandma for confirmation and all I could see was the pinch of her mouth and the tightness in her face. She was in pain. I reminded Grandma that the doctors couldn't help her if she wasn't honest with them about what she was feeling in her body. When she didn't sass back at me after that comment, I knew she definitely wasn't doing well.

As I sat with her throughout that day, she rested on and off, but whether she was awake or dozing she shifted around in the bed continuously and moaned in pain. I had never seen my grandmother like this, and it was ripping my guts out. As bad as it was making me feel, I knew it was a hundred times worse for her, so I did what she would have done for me; I sat by her bed and comforted her as best I could. It always amazes me how emotionally and mentally fatiguing it is to just sit with someone who is hurting. Give me physical exhaustion any day!

I took a few short videos of Grandma when her discomfort was at its worst, in case I needed to show it to a doctor. Even though I've never watched them, I can't get myself to delete them off my phone. When they pop up as I'm scrolling through my photos, I feel a pang in my gut and quickly avert my eyes. I'm sure there's some therapy homework headed my way about this, but up until this book is published, they're my sad little secret. Oh, I have a clue as to why I keep them; I'm just not ready to deal with it yet.

Towards the end of the day, the doctor came in to give me an update on Grandma's condition. He had arrived earlier in the day to exam her, then did another quick check while I was there. He explained to me that she was in pain because her kidneys were in trouble. They needed to give her fluids, but her kidneys weren't working properly enough to process the fluid. As a result, the retained fluid was putting pressure on her heart due to her congestive heart failure. They were giving her some medication to help the kidney function, and it was working some but not to the degree they needed it to. Knowing I would be out of town for the next three days, I was relieved to hear that they didn't see an imminent threat to her life since the kidney mediation was starting to work. Even so, before leaving that evening, I prayed with her and hugged her a little longer and tighter before telling her I'd be back to spend the day with her on Thursday.

I heard the words the doctor didn't speak to me. The ones telling me that this was the beginning of the end for Grandma. That she was 95 years old and her body was starting to shut down. I could read it in the doctor's eyes, but I especially saw it in Grandma's eyes. She knew. It's not something you voice aloud, but the eyes and body language say it. I heard it loud and clear.

I called my parents on my way home, so I could give them an update. I felt for sure that once they heard what I had to say, they would stop their trip and head home. Unfortunately, that was not the case. They decided to wait and see how she did in the next few days, talk to the doctors again, and then decide. Over the course of the next week, my siblings and I had several conversations with my parents. I was shocked and disappointed by their handling of the situation. It hurt, and I was angry about it. Some of their comments to us were:

"You father just doesn't want to see his mother that way." (Uh...like we do?!)

"She may die on our way home, then we would have missed the rest of our trip for no reason."

"Us being there isn't going to change the situation or make her better."

"You kids are handling this so well. We really appreciate all that you're doing."

"We'll have to pay another month's rent on her apartment if it's not cleaned out in a few weeks. You kids will have to take care of that for us."

It got to the point that I didn't even want to talk to my parents at all. It was too disappointing and upsetting. Finally, after

Grandma was in the hospital for over a week, my parents decided to come home. We had reached a point where Grandma needed to be moved to a care facility across from the hospital, and my parents were the powers of attorney. Nothing could be done until they arrived. When my sister told me that they were headed home, but that it would take a few days, I was relieved but also not ready to see them. My focus was on Grandma and being there for her. I did not want to deal with the emotional baggage of my parents.

The Thursday after Grandma was admitted to the hospital, I again spent the day with her. My cousins and siblings were coming and going too, and I teased Grandma that she would do just about anything to get all her grandkids together with her. When the doctor came in that day, I was the only family member there. I had observed the nurses coming in checking her vitals and how much that disturbed Grandma each time they had to do it. They'd also had problems with her IV line, and after unsuccessfully finding viable veins, had to give her a pic-line. All the poking and prodding was wearing on her. She let out a loud heavy sigh each time the blood pressure cuff automatically inflated, because it hurt.

The doctor was being very kind and sensitive as she worked around the subject of Grandma's health. I finally stopped the doctor and asked her point blank if she was trying to tell me that there was nothing more they could do for Grandma, except to make her comfortable. The doctor's eyebrows raised in surprise, then lowered in relief. I was grateful she was truthful and direct in answering my question with a "yes". I told her that since that was the case, then they needed to stop all the tests and treatments, and just let her be. The doctor agreed that was the best course of action going forward for the sake of Grandma's comfort. The doctor turned to Grandma and explained to her what was going to happen and if that was what she wanted. Grandma said, "Oh, yes. I hate when they come in and take my blood" then promptly turned to her side and took a nap.

I had to work the next day, which was Friday, but planned to be at the hospital Saturday, May 19. My sister, brother, and I happened to be together on Saturday morning before my brother had to head back to his home in Seattle. Even though the news of stopping all active treatment for Grandma had filtered from me, to my parents, my siblings, and my cousins, no one had clearly explained to Grandma what was happening. I pulled my siblings aside that morning, and we agreed that it would be a good time to talk to her about it.

I stood on one side of the bed holding Grandma's hand, my sister and brother were on the other side of the bed touching her on the shoulder, and holding her other hand. I decided that I probably had the most experience with these types of conversations, so I said a quick internal prayer and took the initiative. I explained to Grandma that there was nothing more the doctors could do, that she would be kept as comfortable as possible in her last days, using whatever medications necessary. It was purely by the grace of God that I got through that without having a massive panic attack or crying so hard I couldn't talk. I think the worst part is when she asked when she would be able to go home. I had to tell her that she wouldn't be going home to her apartment again, ever; she would be moved to a care facility across the street as soon as my parents arrived to take care of the paperwork. There we were, standing around her bed telling her she wasn't going home and that she would be dead soon, and she didn't shed a tear. I looked at my brother and sister. They were crying, and I had tears starting to run down my face, but she just looked at us and said, "Okay. Whatever you kids think is best."

After going through the dying process with Ray's mom, Jessica, and with my grandmother, I firmly believe that God gives us a "knowing" as we approach death – whether that be seconds, minutes, days, or weeks. An understanding and acceptance happens, and with it, a type of peace. I don't know if this is something that happens for everyone, or just those close to God. As awful as it is to watch someone you love die, it's also oddly comforting to experience that part of living that only happens at the end of life.

My parents arrived home two weeks after Grandma was first admitted to the hospital. We were then able to move her to the care facility, and we all set about caring for Grandma in her final days. I chose to stay with Grandma while my parents and others cleaned out her apartment. There was visible tension between me and my parents, and I decided that I needed to let them know how I felt, so that it wouldn't fester inside of me and affect our last bit of time together with Grandma. Keep in mind that in my family, the preferred method of handling these types of situations is to not talk about it, but instead to bury any unpleasant feelings, and not burden anyone else with them. This way, everyone can proceed as if everything is okay and no unpleasant conversations have to happen that make people uncomfortable.

Since I knew my sister and brother felt the same way I did about our parents not heading home as soon as Grandma was admitted to the hospital, I asked if they were okay if I set up a dinner on May 29, with all of us, so that I could bring it up and let my parents know how I felt. It would also give them a chance to talk about it too and for all of us to come up with a plan to make sure someone was with Grandma every day. I prepped for days before the dinner, practicing what I needed to say since I usually get emotional or forget what to say in the middle of a confrontational conversation. I experienced horrible and frequent anxiety symptoms the day before, and the day of, the dinner. At this point, I was still taking only one 0.5 mg dose of lorazepam a day, but it was now almost every day. Ray had left on a trip to England and Ireland a few days prior and would be gone for 10 days, so I didn't have him there to bolster me through this.

I ended up driving the few miles to my sister's house and riding to my parent's house with her and my youngest nephew. Because no one, except my siblings, knew what I would be bringing up to our parents, my sister's oldest and youngest sons were at the dinner too. Why wouldn't they be? Of course, they were grown men so it didn't deter me from what I needed to do. I was more concerned about my parents feeling more uncomfortable with the conversation because their grandsons were there.

I don't even remember getting through dinner, except that I didn't eat much – my stomach was in knots – and that idle talk felt forced and everyone seemed weary. I probably talked myself out of this confrontation 43 times during dinner. I desperately did not want to have this conversation; partly because it's so uncomfortable for me and partly because I didn't have very high expectations of my parents reacting favorably to it. Their traumas run deep, and I knew that this was going to be painful for them, which is not exactly something I looked forward to. I don't like hurting anyone, but of course putting the needs and feelings of others always before my own is what got me into so much trouble with anxiety in the first place. So, I girded my loins, pulled up my big girl panties, took a deep shaky breath and dove in.

I blurted out, "Dad and Mom, I want to ask you something. Help me understand why you had a hard time deciding to come home after Grandma was admitted to the hospital." Dead silence. Eyes were darting around the room, and there was nervous shifting about in chairs. What followed was a stilted conversation mostly between me and my mother with an uncomfortable outburst from my father where he essentially said, "We've worked hard our whole lives, and this was our one chance at a trip like this that we've been planning for over a year. I didn't want to disappoint your mother, and we didn't feel there was anything we could do here."

You must understand that my dad isn't exactly a talker, especially when it comes to talking about his emotions or feelings. Things tend to burst out of him when forced or is put in a position where he can't get away. Mom's contribution to the conversation was to try and placate me and downplay the severity of the hurt I was feeling. Unfortunately, but not surprisingly, my siblings didn't back me up. Instead, they tried to smooth it over by providing possible excuses for my parents' behavior and that we probably just didn't understand their point of view or what they were going through. After I kept asking, "Help me understand....," and they kept deflecting, I gave up and said, "Yes" when my mom asked if I had gotten the answers I needed. At that point, I knew I would never get the answers I needed or wanted because they weren't capable of giving them to me.

I don't fault them for that, or carry around anger towards them because of it. I understand that they, like most of us, are just doing the best they can with the lot they were given in life. If they had worked on their trauma, through therapy or some other means, then I would expect different from them; but they never have, so I don't. I've learned through my own "self" work to love people where they're at. This is something the Bible teaches again and again. I believe that it not only makes you less frustrated with people, but it allows you to shine the light of your love on others in a way that makes a profound impact on their lives. I mean, come on! We all just want to be loved and accepted as we are. Of course, God is perfect at that, but we have to work at it a bit harder. Some days I fail at is miserably, but I keep trying because I know it helps me manage the anxiety better if I'm not constantly being disappointed in people because they can't meet my expectations.

After I made the evening super awkward with the gall to bring up my feelings about the situation surrounding Grandma, we suffered through a short conversation about our schedules so that we could make sure someone was with Grandma most of each day. As we gathered our things to leave, I gave my parents each a hug goodbye. Mom hugging me back with an "Everything is fine." smile on her face. Dad, on the other hand, didn't hug me back and then turned away and wouldn't even look at me. I understand that he was hurting and working at sorting out his feelings about the whole situation – after all, it was his mother that was dying – but I'm not going to say that it didn't sting a little. It was though, a clear example of the message I received often in my life of "You're not lovable if you behave in a way we don't like."

My sister, nephew and I silently walked out to her car, got in, and just sat there for a second. I then took a deep breath and expelled it with a woosh and a sigh, then said, "That was rough. I think I need some ice cream." I was feeling shaky and tired, as I usually do when I come down from an anxiety high. My sister suggested a burger place that was on our way home, and off we went. I didn't say anything else for a few minutes, then said to my nephew, "I'm so sorry you had to be there for that. I know it was probably uncomfortable, but I needed to say what I did." He totally surprised me by agreeing and saying that he was proud of me for talking about how I felt and not just sweeping it under the rug. He said that we do that way too much in our family. Uh….DUH…although I thought it was very enlightened of him to recognize that.

The next few weeks were a blur of time spent at the care facility with Grandma, dealing with work issues while going into the office when I could, and the usual things you must do to keep life going, such as: grocery shopping, a teeth cleaning appointment, laundry, and the like. I wasn't practicing good self-care, and as a result, my blood pressure was high (for me) when it was checked at my dentist appointment. I'd never had higher blood pressure reading before, not even when the anxiety and panic were at their worst. It freaked me out! I started to obsessively worry about it. It reminded me of when I would obsess about my heart health, and any little twinge or odd feeling I would get in my body would set off intense anxiety. I instantly thought it was something fatal and went into an anxiety spiral. Of course, most of the stuff I was feeling in my body that wasn't "normal" were bodily symptoms because of the anxiety. I also know that I was obsessing over my blood pressures as a way to distract from the fact that my grandmother was dying.

I made an appointment with a doctor for June 12. When she started asking me what was going on that might have caused the elevated blood pressure readings, I started crying. After telling her about Grandma, she thought it was likely a physical reaction to an emotional issue. She prescribed an increase in my daily lorazepam dosage, which was 0.5 mg two or three times a day, or as needed, with no more than 2.0 mg/day. That day, I went from taking one 0.5 mg dose a day to three doses. I was consistently taking two or three doses a day for the days following. It didn't help that we were told by the hospice nurse that afternoon that Grandma was showing the signs of being close to death.

I always knew, and understood, the intimate connection between the mind, emotions, and body because I had experienced it for most of my life. I also did research into it after my breakdown. Mostly, I saw the immediate physical response when the feeling of anxiety and panic started; as well as the immediate impact to my thoughts and emotions if my body was out of balance or had something wrong with it. These were things, physically and mentally, that I could pinpoint right away. The elevated blood pressure was something I didn't feel or see coming. What other unfelt or unseen impacts were there to my body because of my lifelong high stress, anxiety, and panic levels? I didn't even want to think about it.

I spent all of June 13 with Grandma. Most of the immediate family was there. A few close friends of Grandma's and the family's stopped by to pay their last respects. I felt uncomfortable in my body. All my muscles were tight, and I wanted to scream but couldn't. I wanted to cry uncontrollably, but couldn't. It was as if I was in the same unsettling limbo that Grandma was in. She was, thankfully, made comfortable with the help of medication and was sleeping most of the time. I couldn't stop touching her hands, her leg, her hair, her face, I wanted to remember the feel of her and that physical connection that is shared energy. I felt terrible and so tired in body and spirit. Everything around me was like in a fog. I know it was partly the disassociation that happens so often when the anxiety is high, and I'm not capable, or able to, deal with all my emotions at the same time. I laser focused in on Grandma and being with her. I kept at bay all the emotions and feelings that were gnawing at me, until I had the time and space to deal with them.

Before I left that night, I asked to have a few minutes alone with Grandma. The rest of the family went out into the hallway, and I pulled a chair close to her bedside and leaned it towards her. She was resting, but I know that she could hear me. I prayed over her and then thanked her for being my grandmother. In that moment, I couldn't find all the words I wanted to say to her, knowing they might be the last. I was trying not to cry as I hugged her but failed miserably when she reached up and grabbed onto my arm as I circled mine around her. No more words needed to be said. She knew how I felt about her. As I walked towards the door, I turned, paused, and said, "Goodbye Grandma. I love you so much, and if you leave before tomorrow, be sure to tell Grandpa hello for me."

I stepped out into the hugs of my family, said that I would see them tomorrow, then wearily walked the fluorescent lit halls to the exit door and fresh air. I drove home with the window down and a warm breeze drying the tears on my hot face. I woke up the next morning with horrible flu symptoms. There was no way I could go to the care facility until I was better. I stayed home the next two days, and early on the morning of Saturday, June 16, I received a phone call from my mom letting me know that Grandma had passed away the hour before. She was alone, and I think that's how she wanted it. She didn't want any of us to witness her final breath, to have that in our memories of her. One of the caregivers at the facility said that was quite common. That people don't want witnesses to their death.

I was feeling better, just some residual congestion, so I met up with my sister and cousins at my parents' house later that morning. I know Grandma would have liked us being together, crying over our loss, rejoicing in her being released from her earthly body and being back with God, telling stories and laughing about our times together; supporting each other as we mourned.

I was disappointed when my parents said the funeral wouldn't be until sometime in July because of their schedule. I knew that the longer the time between her death and funeral, the harder it would be to get closure and move along in the mourning process. The anticipation of the funeral caused me to experience multiple panic attacks in the four weeks I waited with my grief. I tried not to think about it, but that never works well.

The week of the funeral, I was sick to my stomach every morning and had to use the panic attack help app, D.A.R.E., that I have on my phone the whole drive to work. The two or three doses of lorazepam that I was taking every day was barely keeping me functioning. I was scared I wouldn't get through the funeral without having a massive panic attack. Even though I knew worrying about having one can cause one, I couldn't seem to get a grip on my out of control thoughts. With much prayer, and consciously and purposely implementing positive self-talk and affirmations, I was able to get into a steadier mindset the morning of the funeral, July 14. I ended up taking a 0.5 mg of lorazepam at six o'clock a.m. and again at eight-thirty a.m.

When we got to the church, my sister pulled me into the nursery so she could practice her eulogy with me. As I was listening, then giving her feedback, I was blowing air through my nose so fast that I felt like a steam strain. My sister was as wound up and I was, so I grabbed her hands and we prayed, which helped slow down my breathing, and I was able to take a minute to be in the moment.

I sat between Ray and my sister in the front pew. As the funeral started and progressed through the reading of scripture, singing, and the eulogy, I thought to myself, *I'm doing okay. I'm anxious, but it's not too bad. I've got this.* Then, at the very end, the pastor asked us to stand up and sing "How Great Thou Art", and I couldn't do it. My legs wouldn't move, I was frozen in my seat. I immediately had such a clear memory of standing between my grandparents in church, as a child, looking up at them as we sang this song. My grandfather had a wonderful singing voice, and I swear I heard his voice just then.

That was the crack that split the dam open. I cried. I cried hard. I was doubled over crying. I felt my cousin's hand on my back and my sister reach down and grip my shoulder for a second. I couldn't stop crying.

The singing stopped, the service was concluded, and people were directed to the adjacent building to where food was set up. I was still crying. I was the only one crying. As I was doubled over, looking at the ground, I saw the shoes of my family. They were standing around me, awkwardly talking. They didn't know what to do. I felt like an alien. I wanted to laugh at the hilarity of the situation. After a few minutes, I was able to talk and said, "Go. Go. I'll be fine. I just need a minute." My brother said he would stay with me, and thankfully shooed everyone else away. He and Ray sat with me and let me finish crying while they talked over my bent back. I finally sat up, blew my nose, and gave my brother a wry smile as he gave me a side hug.

I felt spacey and thought I might be on the verge of a panic attack after that outpouring of emotions, so I took a 1.0 mg dose of lorazepam. I then stood up, said that I was going into the bathroom to get cleaned up and would meet them in the other building in a few minutes. By the time I got a plate of food and found a place to sit down, I was feeling very detached from the events. The lorazepam had kicked in, big time. Between that and the drain of all the crying, I thought I was going to fall, face first, into my plate of veggies and dip. I barely remember talking to a few people, before finding Ray and saying, "We need to leave before I fall asleep."

I ran into my cousin on the way to the truck, and it was all I could do to not slur my words. Ray had to help me into the truck, and on the way home, I finally felt relaxed. Obviously, it was due to too much lorazepam, but oh, did it feel like a relief. Once we got home, I barely got my dress off and my pj's on before I drifted off to sleep. Ray was wonderful and went to work so I could rest undisturbed. I think I finally woke up four hours later. My head felt like a cotton ball from all the crying, and I was starving. I had made it through the day without a panic attack, which I was glad for, even though I felt embarrassed by my show of emotions at the end of the service.

Beginning at the time surrounding Grandma's death, the frequency of days that I experienced a tight nervous stomach and other anxiety bodily symptoms upon waking increased. I was relying more and more on the lorazepam to get me through the day, but eventually it wasn't working at keeping the panic at bay. I realized that there were issues deeper than the death of my grandmother that were contributing to the rise in anxiety that I was going through.

Thankfully, I was seeing my therapist weekly during this whole ordeal. Being able to talk to someone – a professional someone – helped me get through it without spiraling into the deep end of the anxiety and depression pit. When I told Jeanette about how embarrassed I was about my uncontrollable crying at the funeral, she said that my reaction was healthy and that everyone else's reaction seemed unhealthy. I know that this story about my grandmother's death was a bit long and drawn out, but I needed to give a clear picture of the situation that became a catalyst for a key breakthrough in my healing process – forgiveness.

In the month between Grandma's death and the funeral, Jeanette told me that there was a book about forgiveness we were going to work through. Ugh…. forgiveness. I didn't have high hopes for this, since the other books I had read about it, even devotionals and praying about it, hadn't spurred any real connection about forgiveness for me. It felt like any forgiveness I did was just on the surface. Plus, holding onto righteous anger felt so good. It feeds that part of me that likes to feel superior. Why would I want to give that up?

So, I bought the book *Forgiveness…How to Make Peace With Your Past and Get On With Your Life* by Dr. Sidney Simon and Suzanne Simon. When I grudgingly sat down to read the introduction and first chapter before my next therapy appointment, I was already set against the whole process. Can anyone say "resistance"?!

To my surprise, the introduction hooked me. By the time I got through the first chapter I had underlined numerous sections and put stars next to most of the paragraphs. Once again, Jeanette was right on track with what I needed, even if I didn't know what that was. We worked through the book slowly and methodically. I was given homework every week that elicited such intense emotions in me or dredged up ones that I had buried. There were a few times that I cried so hard from what felt like the bottom depths of my soul that I threw up. It was as if I was expelling all the hurt and pain. Cathartic, yes, but also extremely exhausting and anxiety eliciting.

During the nine months that it took me to work through the forgiveness book (July 2018 through March 2019) – that's right, nine months! – I went through some painful realizations about myself, some of my behaviors, and why I adopted those survival behaviors. Working on yourself, growing as a person, and trying to learn and implement new ways of "being" is not enjoyable. In fact, it's horrible to go through, but it's necessary if you want to become the best (or better) version of yourself. Every week, at the end of the therapy session I would say in an exasperated voice, "What is the homework this week?" and then give a deep sigh. Even though I knew the outcome of all this work was going to be rewarding, I did not look forward to the anxiety and panic hell it might trigger. Sometimes it would take me days, after doing the homework, to come out of my disassociation fog. It was a struggle to not have tremendously high anxiety all the time. I have to say, one of the most difficult parts of this work was trying to learn to forgive myself. That's something I continue to struggle with. It's not easy forgiving your "child self" for not doing what your "adult self" would have done. I don't know how many times Jeanette said to me, "You were a child. That wasn't your responsibility. You didn't do anything wrong." So many of my problems developed when I carried those childhood protective, or learned, reactions into adulthood.

I don't ever want to discourage you from doing the work, whether it's working with a professional or doing it on your own. I do want you to be aware that it's going to be difficult at times, and you may experience, like me, an increase in anxiety and panic symptoms. I know though that if you stick with it, and push through the painful parts, you'll come out much improved in the end. Keep in mind, this is an ongoing process and not something you do for a year and then "Ta-da! I'm magically cured of all my problems." That's not how it works.

I think back to all the levels of healing I've done in the last nine years, and just when I think I've hit a long plateau and can rest on my laurels, something happens that tells me otherwise. It does get easier. I did find that, at each level, I carried with me the knowledge from the previous levels. It's never a bad thing to have a variety of tools in your toolbox. (Hey, my dad is a carpenter and my husband a mechanic, of course I'm going to gravitate towards the toolbox analogy.)

As I was working through the forgiveness book in therapy, a few monumental things happened in my life.

Yet again, just as I was getting comfortable and feeling confident in my job, God said "Guess what? I have somewhere new I want you to go." My reaction? "NOOOOOOOOO!!!!" I just knew I wasn't going to win this fight, but believe me when I tell you that I tried. There was a job opening for City Surveyor at a local municipality. The job announcement had been floating around for about six months. I had seen the advertisement and thought, *Wow!*, and not in a good way. It included a lot of varying job duties within our profession, plus a few I had never seen before for a land surveyor. I thought, *I would never want that job!* People kept mentioning the job to me and was getting thrown into my face all the time, to the point that I couldn't ignore that God was trying to get my attention. The last straw was when the city reached out to me in an email and asked if I would apply for the job. *Okay! I get it! I'm supposed to apply for this job! Get off my back already, God!* I dutifully, but grudgingly applied for the job.

I got an interview and was called back for a second informal interview. I was so terrified that I would get offered the job.

What would I do?! I wanted to obey God, but I also didn't want to leave my current job. I had finally gotten my team to a good place and enjoyed my work there. Again, I knew that if God wanted it to happen then it would happen. Darn it!

Right around this time, our beloved pug Isabel's health was rapidly declining due to a medical condition. We were struggling with the decision whether to have her euthanized or not. The last thing I wanted to do was wrestle with two big decisions at the same time. I got a phone message from the hiring manager the day before we were to take Isabel to the vet, where she wouldn't be coming home with us. I just couldn't deal with it all, so I called her back and left a message explaining the situation and I would call her back after the weekend.

The most important thing to me at that moment was spending my last bit of time with a soul that had comforted me and been with me through some dark times. She was my heart. Out of the four pugs we'd had, she was the one I was most connected to, which is saying a lot since I was deeply attached to all my dogs. Ray and I had a good last day with Isabel and gave her all the love we could. When we left the vet's office, we both cried so hard I got nauseous, and I thought Ray was going to black out. When Monday rolled around the last thing I wanted to do was deal with the possibility of a new job. I was still grieving and was sinking into a bit of a funk.

I was finally able to touch base with the hiring manager the following Thursday and was offered the job. After spending a weekend of praying and arguing with God about it, which caused me untold amounts of anxiety by the way, I finally got on my knees. I put my Bible on the floor, opened it up, prostrated myself with my face in the Bible and just surrendered the decision to God. I mean, who was I kidding? The only place that fighting God has ever gotten me is a place I never wanted to be again. Sometimes it just takes me awhile to get to that place of surrender, which really is a place of peace. When I was done praying, I lifted my head and looked at the pages of the Bible that were in front of me. The scripture that my eye turned to was Jeremiah 17:7-8.

7 Blessed is the man who trusts in the Lord. And whose hope is in the Lord.

8 For he shall be like a tree planted by the waters, which spreads out its roots by the river, and will not fear when heat comes; but her leaf will be green, and will not be anxious in the year of drought, nor will cease from yielding fruit.

So that's what I did. I trusted in the Lord and let Him plant me where he wanted me. I accepted the job. I must tell you that in between the interviews and the job offer, there were quite a few negotiation emails between myself and the hiring manager. I kept trying to put up roadblocks so that I wouldn't be offered the job. I told her about the anxiety and that it may affect my ability to do the job sometimes. I told her I would need to give two-months of notice at my current job. I asked for all kinds of stuff that I was sure would deter her from wanting to hire me. Every time, she came back with, "Okay. No problem."

Looking back, it's so clear that God was going to make this happen no matter what, and I just caused myself a whole lot of stress and anxiety fighting it. Again, and again, God has shown me that if I just trust him, then it all works out. So much easier to know than to do. Trusting is difficult for me, even with God. I'm so thankful that He never gives up on me! Now, I am over two years into my new job. I can't say it's been easy, but I keep reminding myself that God will give me grace, and whatever else I might need, to accomplish whatever He asks of me. I often wonder, as I navigate through the challenges of my new job, *Why did God put me here? What is the purpose?* It's so exciting to me when, little by little, He reveals the purposes. It gives me hope and strengthens my bond with Him.

One of the purposes of me having the new job was revealed to me about the fifth month in. I was talking to a coworker that swung by my desk to drop off some paperwork. We had chatted a few times, but I didn't know her well. Somehow, we got onto the subject of being busy, and she shared with me that her life had been hectic the last year because she was writing a book and it was close to being published. As an avid reader, I was of course interested and asked her about the book and how she came to write it.

As she shared the story of her book with me, she mentioned that she wouldn't have been able to do it without the help of her author's coach. Ding. Ding. Ding! I had never heard of such a thing, but I instantly knew that's what I needed to investigate for getting started on my book. I reached out to her writing coach, Sage Adderly-Knox, to set up a time to chat and find out more information on the process and the cost. Within the first few minutes of talking with Sage, I felt a comfortable connection with her. Everything she said, and how she said it, indicated to me that she would be supportive, motivating, kind, and not afraid to hold me accountable. She said she had an opening for her 6-month one-on-one coaching program, told me the cost, and then gave me a few days to think about it.

After the phone call, I felt an excitement surge through me about writing the book. Once again, God brought me to the right person at the right time. I wasn't making any progress on writing this book, so He created the situation that would bring Sage into my life and help me through the process. Even though the cost wasn't ridiculously high, it was still a substantial amount to plunk down when you don't know if you'll recoup the funds. I was trusting God in this, so I knew He would make the financial part work out if this was the direction that He wanted me to take. I prayed on it all afternoon, and enthusiastically talked to Ray about it that night. We agreed that some extra funds we had in savings could go towards the coaching. After months of mourning my old job, and Isabel, I was renewed with a sense of joy. It was marvelous!

Once again, I was in the middle of multiple stressful endeavors at the same time. I was still learning my new job, starting the book writing process, and we were planning a trip to the England and Scotland in four months. All these things alone are anxiety triggers for me and, I imagine, most people. To add all three onto my plate meant I needed to come up with a game plan for managing the unrealistic expectations I usually put on myself in any situation that presents new challenges.

Adding to the *Holy Crap! What am I doing?* moments, was a trip I had to take in July for work. A trip to San Diego. For a week. By myself. I was going to a conference where there are tens of thousands of people attending. For the first time in over 15 years, I had to fly without Ray. I had to be in the airport – a place that historically has triggered panic attacks – on my own for hours before my flight. I was going to a city I had never been to before and to a conference I had never attended. This was the unknown, which is another major anxiety and panic trigger. When I said "yes" to the trip, I knew it would really push me into scary places in my brain, but I also knew that I needed to get over this hurdle and take the opportunity for new successes in my healing expedition.

There were three other people, from different departments at work, that were going too. We all made our own travel and hotel accommodations. In fact, the conference is so large and busy that I didn't see them at all during my week in San Diego. Another reason I didn't see them is that I didn't want to. I didn't want them to see how much of a struggle this trip was for me. I didn't want to be vulnerable in that way with people I didn't really know. It takes a long time for me to trust that someone won't be dismissive or hurtful – sometimes without them even knowing they're doing it – when I share the anxious part of myself, that I keep so hidden. Whether people are aware of it, or not, my experience is that they do treat me differently when they find out I have anxiety and panic attacks; I struggle coping with situations that they find mundane or common. It's mostly because they don't understand what it's like and so they don't know what to say to me about it.

The week leading up to the trip, I tried to get myself ready for it. I made sure all my meals were healthy, got plenty of sleep, prayed about it, upped my positive self-talk, and journaled about all my thoughts and feeling. Even with all that preparation, I still woke up the morning of my flight with a tight stomach and scattered thoughts. I ended up taking twice my usual dose of 0.5 mg of lorazepam that day just to get me through it without a panic attack. My anxiety was at such a high level all day, that I barely felt the effects of the medication. I was dog-tired by the time I got to my hotel room. I kept myself distracted in the airport by eating some lunch, walked around to burn up some of the anxious energy, and played solitaire on my phone. During the flight, I kept my brain distracted with an audio book while I created masterpieces in my adult coloring book. This strategy worked on my flight there and back.

Once I was in my hotel room, safe from the prying eyes of others, I called Ray to let him know I had arrived safely. The second I heard his voice I started crying, mostly from relief that I had gotten through the day okay. After we hung up, I cried in bits and spurts for like 15 minutes. Releasing all those emotions I had held in my body all day – and probably the whole week prior – was so relieving.

My hotel, situated a few blocks from the convention center, was right on the water and I had a gorgeous view of it from my window. The weather was a beautiful upper 70s with a breeze. I should have been excited. Instead, I was uneasy and a bit terrified. I didn't venture any further than a few blocks to the north and south of my hotel. I only had one meal at a restaurant, otherwise I picked up a quick lunch at one of the vendors at the conference, ate what I brought with me, or had room service. Navigating through the throngs of people at the conference was overwhelming. I found myself getting into my "tunnel vision" mode. This is where I block out everything and everyone around me except for what is directly in my walking path or directly in a tight circle of where I am sitting or standing. It's a trick I picked up at a very young age to cope with highly uncomfortable surroundings. I know this isn't exactly a healthy coping mechanism, but it does work for me. I was able to attend classes/presentations and go into the huge exhibit hall, which was packed full of people with so many visual things vying for my attention.

It was one of the most challenging weeks that I'd had in a long time. The trip was chalk full of all the experiences and components that trigger high level anxiety and panic attacks for me. Sadly, it did not disappoint. I was trying so hard to just keep myself together and manage the anxiety responses in my body and behaviors that I was ready to come home on day three of the trip. I was also beating myself up for not doing better at keeping the anxiety at bay and for not getting out and about more. I was also upset with myself for not being more social – or at all, and for not retaining most of the information I received during the classes because my thoughts were like a tornado in my head.

Once I got home, I realized that I may not have experienced the trip the way I was hoping, but I still did it. I still stepped out of my comfort zone, pushed myself to new successes, and survived once again. I did it!!! I did it in the weird, awkward way that I seem to do most things, but I did it. After letting the anxiety and panic rule most of my decisions, I'm thankful that I'm now able to just "Do it afraid!" Well…most of the time.

After that trip, I was confident that even though I had experienced in the last three years, more struggles with anxiety than I had in the previous four or five, I would be able to go and enjoy our trip to England, Wales, and Scotland in the fall. At least I hoped and prayed that's how it would be. You never know. Even though I had been to England in 2015, I was in a better place then, in regards to handling the anxiety, than I was at this point. I was worried that I would struggle most of time and ruin the trip for Ray.

I know that I'm not always pleasant to be around when I experience high levels of anxiety or have frequent panic attacks. I'm edgy because I'm trying to manage the bodily symptoms and get a handle on what my thoughts and feelings are doing. Stress can be contagious, so I know that the people around me feel my discomfort, whether they realize it or not. Even after all these years, my husband has a hard time knowing what to do when I'm dealing with an episode of anxiety and panic. He's told me that he's convinced that if he comforts me during a panic or anxiety attack, or accommodates me, then it will tell my subconscious that if it behaves badly then it will get rewarded with affection.

I've tried to convey to him that a hug lowers stress responses and blood pressure. That affection, empathy, and understanding, in either word or physical form, would help me, but he's not convinced. I understand why he feels that way. He's seen and experienced how strong my mind is; how it can take over and do underhanded and sneaky bad things to me. I get that. I've come to realize, and accept, that people can only be how they are comfortable being, can only do what they feel comfortable doing, and can only give what they have received. It certainly stings when my needs aren't fulfilled in the crucial moments of feeling like I'm breaking from the inside out, but I know that sometimes that's an unreasonable expectation for me to have about others.

Something happened recently that is a great example of this. I was in a car with three people who I know love me. We were on our way to lunch, and I was feeling very anxious. It kept building and building as we got closer to town. I took 0.25 mg of Lorazepam hoping my bodily symptoms would subside so I could enjoy my time at lunch. Unfortunately, I didn't catch it quickly enough and a mild panic attack set in. I was sitting in the back seat with a few tears running down my face, but I had sunglasses on so no one could see. Of course, I was hoping that if I just let some of the tears out then it would take some of the panic pressure off until the medication kicked in. The person in the passenger seat had the driver pull over and said, "I know Kris gets carsick in the back seat so pull over and I'll have her switch with me. *Oh boy! If I move to the front seat then I won't be able to hide my panic attack.* The thought of that just added fuel to the panic fire. I said, "No. I'm fine. We're almost to town." When the person insisted, I said "I'm having a panic attack and need to just stay where I'm at." Then I started really crying. Someone gave me some tissues and a cold bottle of water. That was it. The driver never said a word.

The other two passengers commenced to talk about me and what is probably causing my anxiety issues, as if I wasn't even sitting there. I was so mad! Which really means that I was offended by their behaviors. Not one of these people that know me, know my struggles, and do love me, offered me any empathy. No hug. No "Hey, I'm here if you need me. What can I do to help you?" I felt invisible. They either wanted to ignore "it" and me with "it", or try to fix me. I cannot even tell you how frustrating it is to me that I can't express my thoughts and needs in those moments. Remember, my thoughts and feelings at these times are like the chaotic scribblings of a two-year-old, all jumbled together. I know that none of the people I was with would intentionally hurt me. Perhaps they just didn't know what to do, or it's not upsetting to them because it's old news, "Oh, it's just Kris having another panic episode. Ho-Hum."; or they are super uncomfortable being around me when it happens. What I do know is that a little bit of empathy goes a long way in helping disperse the anxiety and panic. Even though I was surrounded by people who love me, I felt so utterly and horribly alone as I was going through that panic attack. Sadly, that is not a new feeling for me.

There is a great video on "Sympathy vs. Empathy" by Brene Brown. I think it illustrates the difference beautifully. When I share my struggles with people, or they witness me going through an anxiety or panic attack, I generally get hit with sympathy statements. Rarely do they exhibit empathy.

Sympathy makes me feel worse because it points out the obvious and gives empty platitudes. Empathy exhibited is: acceptance, not trying to fix you, and just being there in the pit with you however you need them to be. Sadly, that's a skill our society has lost. I absolutely adore Brene Brown for bringing the words "vulnerability", "empathy", and "courage" back into our conversations. If you haven't read any of her books, or seen her talks online, I highly suggest it. If you too suffer from anxiety and panic disorder(s), then I think you will find her wisdom invaluable, as I do.

But I digress. Back to the trip to the U.K. The interesting thing about that trip is that my anxiety was minimal. I had a few small panic episodes and moments of high anxiety, but for the most part felt such relief to not be doing my daily grind. One of my favorite movies, because I can relate, is "What About Bob?" with Bill Murray. In the movie, there's a line where Murray's character says, "I'm taking a vacation from my problems!" That's how I felt on this trip. I didn't wake up with a nervous stomach every day, even though I didn't know what the day would bring. I felt an easing in my body that I hadn't felt for years. I even got a horrible flu our last week there, yet didn't panic about it. That's very unusual for me. Usually I tend to obsess and worry about bodily symptoms, especially when I don't feel well. It wasn't until we were a few days from heading home that the anxiousness started cropping up in my body. On a scale of 1 – 10, my anxiety level went from a 2 to a 10 overnight. I was so discouraged that all the anxiety symptoms that were gone during the trip were right back to the same intensity as soon as we got home.

Reflecting on this, it tells me that there is much in my day to day life that contributes to the challenges in my mental health. This is no surprise to me. Working towards changes and figuring out which ones to make takes time. Plus, I must consider that any choices I make will have a direct impact on my husband and many other people in my life. Not to mention that I no longer make big decisions without first being directed by God, and praying about it. That's what works for me since I've experienced the alternative, and it just never ends well.

CHAPTER SEVEN

Conclusion

As I'm trying to finish up the first draft of this book, the COVID-19 pandemic is happening. We've been under a "Stay Home, Stay Healthy" order almost a year. I'm extremely thankful that my job allows me to continue working from home; although, I never thought I would say that I'm looking forward to being back in the office, even if it's just a day or two a week.

During this foreign and strange time in history, I've taken certain steps to help with my mental health. I do not watch the news. I get my information by doing my own research online and visiting reputable sites. I've been writing in my journal more, sometimes twice a day, to process my thoughts and feelings. I've been digging into devotionals, reading the Bible, and praying. I've taken advantage of some extra time (No commute!!! Yay!) to either get on my treadmill, do yoga, or some other form of exercise. If the weather is not a torrential downpour, I'll ride my 1960's Collegiate Schwinn bicycle up and down the driveway. There's a bit of a hill, so I'm working on building up my leg strength. Basically, I'm practicing some high-level self-care. I've faltered in staying consistent with it, but overall, I've been able to support myself through these strange times.

One thing I did not anticipate happening during this pandemic was the relatively low amount of stress I'm feeling about contracting the virus. The logical thought would be that someone with an anxiety disorder, especially health anxiety, would have heightened anxiety and panic because of what's going on in the world. Surprisingly, I do not. At first, my lack of response

was freaking me out. I kept waiting for the panic to suddenly kick in. Worrying about not worrying was making me anxious. Once I observed my reactions – or lack thereof - about what was going on and in regards to how I was dealing with the situations, I realized a few things:
1. I run at such a high level of anxiety most days, just dealing with normal life, that a pandemic was no match for the horrible "What if?" scenarios I had in my head all the time. *A pandemic you say? Oh...(yawn)...that's such a bore. I've already imagined much worse circumstances, just last week.* I'm not trying to make light of the horrible things many people have had to endure during this time, but you must understand that my thoughts conjure up all kinds of horrible outcomes constantly. My mind is kind of battle-hardened to things like this.
2. I have a multitude of coping skills in my handy "toolbox", and I know how to use them. Without even being aware of it, I take out and use what I need at any given time, for any given situation. I understand that many people who have never experienced anxiety before are unraveling into puddles of fear and worry during this. They have no experience with this sort of behavior by their minds and bodies, and that they are ill equipped to deal with it.
3. I have my faith in God. I know that no matter what happens in this world, He is the one in control. If I die, I'll be with God, and that doesn't sound too shabby.
4. I have the goal of finishing this book, and I'm about four months behind my original timeline. That's a great motivator and a way to focus my energy and thoughts on something positive.

I do have to say that only leaving the house a couple of times, in the first few weeks of the "stay home" order caused the agoraphobia to kick back in. I'm such a homebody introvert, that forcibly being housebound was like a wonderful unicorn dream to me. I noticed that my subconscious was starting to say, *We don't want to leave the house...ever. It's nice here, and there are scary situations and horrible people out there. See? You're not waking up with a nervous stomach every day. If you leave the house, the anxiety and panic will come back.* I knew I had to push myself to leave at least every few days. Even if it was just to drive around, go to the business to work for a bit, or go to the Post Office and get the mail. I had to make myself drive and stay involved in life outside my house and property.

The first few times I ventured out, I had strong anxiety and panic symptoms. Driving is still challenging for me, most days anyway. This was especially true after having the agoraphobia pop up; it was not a fun exercise. One thing that I do to distract my mind from wandering to obsessive, scary thoughts while I drive is to listen to an audio book or a podcast. It's been working well and has been extra helpful while I got past the agoraphobia hump. Thankfully, this part of the agoraphobia has minimized, and I'm back to my normal level.

One positive thing that has happened during this "stay home" order is that I was able to completely wean off the lorazepam. Even though I was only taking 0.25 mg/day, just in the morning when I first got up, stopping the meds completely was brutal. I had a straight week of intense anxiety and panic attacks with long periods of feeling spacey and disassociated from the world around me. It's what I've experienced each time I've dropped a dose, so I was prepared for it, but it was still rough. The second week was better, and now it's been months since I weaned off the meds. I'll share in Part II of the book, The Toolbox, what I used to assist me each time I lowered my dosage.

I hope you feel you know me a little by now and that despite my lifelong struggles with anxiety, I have had a good life. I never want to give the impression that even though I deal with anxiety, to some degree almost every day, it is not who I am. It does not define me. It does not make me a victim or my life a tragedy that needs to be sympathized over. I'm just a person, like you, that has days of normalcy, of happiness, of sadness and darkness, and extraordinary days that shine a light into my soul and give me hope.

Thank you for allowing me to share my story. I pray that it touched your heart, made you laugh, and gave you an opportunity to either have a better understanding of someone struggling with an anxiety disorder, or that it touched a chord in your own story that is likely similar to mine in many aspects.

Please continue to Part II of the book, which I'm calling "The Toolbox". It provides insights and information on what has helped me as I move along on the path of my healing expedition.

| FAR FROM PERFECT

My first birthday, 1971

My sister and I dressed for dance rehearsal in our home-made costumes Mom made.

Age seven. Always smiling to hide my discomfort.

Ten-years-old at my cousin's birthday party. It was held at Chuck-e-Cheese's, and I hated the noise and chaos in the place.

Being 13-years-old in the 1980's was hard with all that hair.

Grandma, me, Grandpa, Mom holding Aaron (brother), Dad, Katie (sister). Around 1984

Summer of 1985. Ray and I at his house after I finished cheerleading camp.

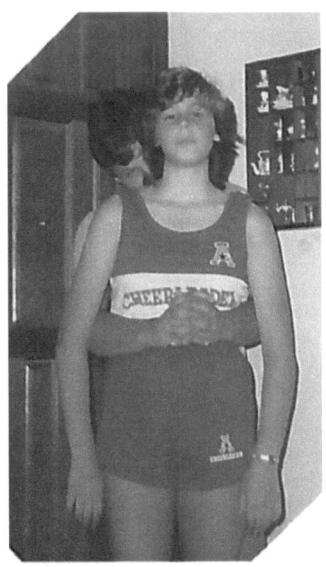

Homecoming 1985. What you don't see are the pink faux alligator skin heals I'm rocking with that sweater dress.

High School Graduation in 1989. Lots on my mind. I was getting married the next day.

Our wedding, June 1989.
Ceremony and reception outside at Ray's mom's house.
From left to right: Dad, Mom, me, Ray, Jessica, and Ray's dad.
I only have a few memories of that day.

| FAR FROM PERFECT

Pugsey, Nook, and I in the motorhome. Circa mid-1990's.

Working in Alaska, March 1994. Wearing so many layers.

At work in Alaska, October 1995, removing construction signs.

Me and my sister-in-law, New Year's 2000 in Las Vegas with Ray's family.

My college graduation, June 2001, with my mom and dad. Happy day!

Ray and I visiting his mom (Jessica) in the hospital while she was getting treatment for leukemia.
Circa 2007.

Me, Grandma, and my sister.
Fall 2009

Ray and I with his siblings and their spouses at Jessica's Celebration of Life, November 2010. I was already spiraling towards my emotional breakdown.

Pastoral views near Oxford, England during my first trip to the UK and Ireland in September 2015. I never dreamed I would be able to make a trip like this.

Conwy, Wales during my second trip to the UK in September 2019.

PART II

The Toolbox

CHAPTER EIGHT

Am I Broken?

Until recently, I've had this thought that I need to be fixed, healed, cured, and that I needed to get over this problem that I have. My inner voice said things like:
- You're so weird. Why do you get scared about doing normal things?
- You can't let people see how weak you are.
- Hide your thoughts and feelings at all costs because no one will understand. They may use them against you later.
- You're such a stupid girl! Why do you let them push your buttons like that? Now you've reacted badly and look like a bitch.
- You're such a burden to your family/husband/friends. You better suck it up and try to be normal so they'll keep loving you.
- You can't be honest with anyone about how you feel because your truth might hurt them, and their feelings are more important than yours. You're probably just overacting anyway.
- If you can just find the "thing" that is causing the anxiety and panic then you'll know what to do to fix yourself.
- I'm praying, reading my Bible and trying to let my faith be bigger than my fear. Why hasn't God rewarded me by taking away the anxiety and panic?
- Ok. You got this! Suck it up and be stronger than the anxiety! It's just mind over matter. Other peo-

ple have been cured. You can be too if you'll just do the work.

- *I have caused all of this by having bad and negative thinking. All I must do is think positively about everything, not have unreasonable expectations about people and events, and basically change everything about myself. Yeah...I can do that....*

These are damaging thoughts. Some I've had for as long as I can remember. What I despise the most is that there is so much information out there now that reinforces the thought that anyone dealing with anxiety and panic can be cured and must be cured. There are multiple programs and books available that tell you that if you just do "this" and "that" then you can be fixed. I've tried a few of the programs and have read many of the books that purport to help you break free from this albatross around your neck. It's extremely alluring, this concept that my life can be void of all the thoughts, bodily symptoms, and worry that come with anxiety and panic. Just think of all the things I could do and accomplish! Every time, I would feel hopeful and excited about finding the key to unlock my cure. Think of how proud and happy my husband and family would be! It would be glorious!

Sadly, each time I would go through the program, or read the book, and implement the steps necessary to finally be "fixed", I never was. Oh, sure, I would find a few "tools" that would help sometimes, but I was still broken. Many times, I would have stretches of days, weeks, months where I would experience less anxiety and panic symptoms. I would think *This is finally it. It's what's going to work. I'll never have a panic attack again!* Then, like a fog that silently sneaks up on you at twilight in the fall, you feel that clenching of the stomach, the pulse beating under your jaw, the quickening of your breath, and the tingling in your fingertips. *Oh no, a panic attack! Why?! I was doing everything right, wasn't I? It's all my fault. I didn't do the steps perfectly, or I didn't use the "tool" properly.*

Once the "cure" doesn't work, then my feeling of self-hatred and disgust are back even stronger. As a result, the anxiety worsens, and I'm more miserable than ever. It gets even worse when people say things like, "I don't understand. That worked for me/my friend/other people." I've had someone close to me tell me they had a massive panic attack and it was so awful, but then also mention that just a few hours later they were at a crowded pub celebrating a friend's birthday. Hearing things like that used to make me feel like such a loser because after I have a massive panic attack, I'm barely able to get out of bed and function. It saps all my energy, I stay anxiety sensitive, and I certainly can't be around large noisy groups of people. This *"anxiety hangover"* can last a few days, or even a week, after a massive panic attack.

It wasn't until recently that I realized the terms "anxiety" and "panic attack" are getting incorrectly used in many instances. Anxiety has become the trendy "off the cuff" term to use for any feelings of fear in a situation. On one hand, I'm glad that anxiety is finally being talked about, but on the other hand, the flippant way it's used so often just ends up minimizing the impact is has on someone who truly suffers from an anxiety or panic disorder. We've all done this sort of thing with many health terms. How many times have you said, "Oh my gosh! You almost gave me a heart attack/stroke/epileptic fit!" when reacting to being taken by surprise? Now you can add the terms "anxiety attack/panic attack" to the end of that sentence. I hear it more and more.

I was in a meeting not too long ago and a woman said, in response to problematic project that she finished years ago, "It gives me anxiety just thinking about that project! Hahahaha!" I understand that she was trying to make the dramatic point that the project was a nightmare and she was glad it was over, but her statement struck a chord with me. Everyone else laughed, but I felt some anger about it, then felt ashamed for feeling the anger, then had an anxiety attack the rest of the day because her words flashed me back to feelings of anxiety. My strong reaction surprised me, but it also made me analyze why it triggered me towards anger and then anxiety. I realized that someone making light of feelings of anxiety brought up the feeling I had growing up, when my anxiety symptoms weren't taken seriously or addressed in a healthy way. The whole situation made me feel broken again, and it took me a few days to work through it.

I had to work through it because what I've learned is that I'm not broken. If you suffer from anxiety and panic you aren't broken either. Say that to yourself. *I. Am. Not. Broken.* Now say it again with conviction. *I. Am. Not. Broken.* I know you won't suddenly feel unbroken just because you said so out loud. It's taken me years of intense work on myself to even start to believe that I'm not broken. As the situation in the last paragraph shows, it's a thought I'm constantly mindful of. I have Bible verses and affirmations handy that I use to counter that false thought with the truth. The truth being that God doesn't make mistakes. That He made me this way for a purpose. That if I let Him, He will use it for good. That none of us are perfect, and that we are, in fact, far from perfect. We're all doing the best we can.

The truth is that you are not alone in your suffering. Others experience and feel what you do, and there is nothing wrong with you. The truth is that you are loved beyond measure, even if you have a day that didn't go as you planned or as you hoped it would. You. Are. Not. Broken. You are human. You are a work in progress. You are amazing with all your imperfection. You are unique and special. The truth is that it's okay to make mistakes and not do everything perfectly. It's okay to not be okay all the time.

Struggling with the very real circumstance of what dealing with anxiety and panic disorders do to you and your life does not make you weak. It makes you stronger than most people will even know. Working at your job while feeling severe anxiety symptoms, and not running away, makes you strong. Doing simple tasks at home while being exhausted after getting through a day, or a week, where you deal with the aftermath of constant adrenaline spikes, makes you strong. Even if you don't feel strong in body, you're strong in spirit. Being strong in spirit is what gets you through and moves you forward in your healing expedition.

I want to be clear that, when I say "healing" I don't mean "fixing". I mean that you're taking steps in the direction of setting yourself up to better handle the struggles. I mean that you deal with traumas, past and present. I mean that you take good care of your body by exercising and eating a clean diet. It means that you find tasks that give you some joy and satisfaction, whether that's painting, gardening, listening to or creating music, woodworking, reading, cleaning the house (hey… don't knock having a uncluttered environment), or the myriad of other things that bring people joy. It also means learning to accept yourself as you are and to remove the expectation that you, or someone else, put on you to be free of anxiety and panic forever. I'm not saying it can't happen, I'm saying to remove the expectation.

CHAPTER NINE

Why Am I This Way?

For most of my life, I would ask myself *Why am I like this? What is wrong with me?!* I kept blaming myself because I couldn't control my body or my thoughts. As a child, especially, I didn't understand that I wasn't to blame for creating coping mechanisms to get through situations that were stressful for me. Then, I carried those coping mechanisms into my adult life even though I didn't necessarily need them anymore. It wasn't until I started the "Attacking Anxiety" program that I learned about some of the ways that past emotional traumas were affecting me.

My therapist, Jeanette, explained it to me this way. As children we're brand-new computers with clean, clutter and virus free, hard drives. The hard drive is our soul, who God made us to be. As life goes on, people in our lives input their own data, their own programs, and infect our hard drives with their viruses (their thoughts, feelings, traumas, etc.). When that happens, our computer (us) starts to malfunction (in my case, have anxiety and panic attacks). The work we do on ourselves, whether through therapy or some other means of processing our traumas, is us attempting to remove the data, programs, and viruses we don't want or need.

Our nuclear and extended families, school mates, teachers, people in our church, childhood friends, neighbors, and other influential people in our lives growing up, unwittingly infect our "hard drives". Parents say things they heard their parents say, behave in the same way or directly opposite of their parents; siblings are cruel to each other because they're reacting to things around them and you're just collateral damage; school mates tease you because they're insecure therefore making you insecure; other adults in your life project their fears, values, and outlooks onto you; and childhood friends that hurt your feelings, because they're trying to navigate through life as well, causes you to be distrustful of others .

The comments below, that seem normal and perfectly acceptable to say, make you feel shameful about who you are. God does not want us to feel shame – which tells us that we are bad. Conviction is what God wants us to feel – which tells us that our sin (action) is bad. Shame is an attack on our identity and tells us that we've messed up too much to ever be redeemed and fulfill our potential.

"I can't believe you behaved that way. What are people going to think?"

"You need to dress better."

"Why are you always playing in the mud?! You're a bad girl. Now you've gotten your shoes dirty; those were expensive!"

"Good girls/boys don't behave that way."

"Sit still and quit asking so many questions! Why do you insist on pestering me all the time!?"

In other words, statements that say, "You're unacceptable as you are." make a lasting impact on how we see ourselves. We start changing to conform to what those around us expect from us, regarding behaviors, looks, and performance. We start to realize that if we don't "toe the line" then we won't be loved. I don't know one person that has not been a victim of this. None of us get through childhood unscathed. The degrees of trauma are different, but we're all affected on some level. Very few of us get help cleaning up our "hard drives" early in adulthood. Most of us end up going through painful experiences that finally force us to deal with our issues, otherwise we could never do it. I'm no different. It took a massive emotional and physical breakdown at age 40 for me to finally start cleaning up my "hard drive". Some of us, even after going through a painful experience, choose to not ever deal with our issues. They go through life constantly hitting "Ctrl+Alt+Del", or the "Esc" button because their "hard drive" never quite works right and is always freezing up on them.

I've also found that, often, anxiety issues are hereditary. What I haven't been able to figure out, from my research on it, is if it's more of a "nature" or a "nurture" type of hereditary reaction. For instance, my mother has had one panic attack in her life and is nervous is some social situations, and I think my father deals with anxiety on some level and so did his mother. My two siblings also deal with types of anxiety and panic issues, but is it because of our physical makeup, or is it because we grew up in the same household? I'm not aware of any of my cousins on my mother's side having anxiety or panic issues; but the two cousins on my father's side do. That could be because they grew up in an abusive household which caused or contributed to their anxiety issues. It all gets a bit confusing the more you delve into it. My conclusion is that it's likely a bit of both in most people, with perhaps "nature" being stronger in some, and "nurture" being a stronger influence in others. Just know that whichever way you think contributed to you having to deal with anxiety and panic symptoms, it's not your fault or something you did. It just is what it is; we need to proceed from there and not spend time blaming or wallowing in "poor me" thoughts or behaviors. You can have a pity party, but don't book a cruise.

The good news is that if you deal with anxiety and panic attacks, you are likely intelligent, empathetic, sensitive, creative, driven, and imaginative. A May 11, 2020 article titled "The Characteristics of High Functioning Anxiety" by Arlin Cuncic[6]; lists some of the positive characteristics as:

Outgoing Personality
Punctual
Proactive
High-achieving
Detail-oriented

---
6   verywellmind.com

Helpful
Passionate
Loyal in relationships

I think we can all agree that these are great traits to have. Many people have them, not just people with anxiety. The difference is what drives these traits in those of us with anxiety. Most of the time it's because we're people pleasers, which is born out of a fear of not being acceptable or lovable as we are. Are you seeing a pattern here?

That same article notes that according to the National Institute on Mental Health (NIMH), around 19% of adults in the United States have an anxiety disorder (approximately 40 million). I'm sure that percentage is much higher since many people suffering with an anxiety disorder don't talk about it or get help for it. According to the Centers for Disease Control and Prevention website, 7.1% of children aged 3-17 years (approximately 4.4 million) have been diagnosed with anxiety, with the percentage having increased from 5.4% in 2003. Although it makes me sad that so many people, children included, suffer with these disorders, it certainly makes me feel less alone in my struggles. I'm sure that these numbers have increased dramatically during the pandemic, especially those relating to children.

Recently, I was attending a leadership training through my work. Part of the training was to complete the questionnaire for determining your Meyers-Briggs Type Indicator (MBTI), which indicates your psychological preferences for perceiving the world and making decisions. The results of the questionnaire were evaluated by someone trained and certified to do so. The results indicated that I am a type INFJ (Introvert, Intuition, Feeling, Judging). When I did some research into this personality type, I found out some interesting things. Only about 1-3% of the population is this type, making it the rarest of types. Because an INJ is a "feeler" and a "thinker", they're often at odds with themselves. No surprise there! As I read more and more about this MBTI type of personality, I could see that people that are INFJs are likely prone to anxiety. This knowledge was just another tool I could put in my toolbox. The more I can discover and learn about myself, the more I understand some of the root causes of what contributes to the anxiety issues. It helps explain why I reacted so differently to situations when compared to others. If you even have the chance to learn about your MBTI, then I encourage you to do so.

Have you ever pondered over what it is that anxiety might be trying to tell you? I have. When I pay attention to my body's reactions during certain situation, I can later analyze what it might be about the situation that triggered a trauma response in me. This is where journaling is especially helpful. Breaking down situations and discovering if they reveal any unhealed traumas in your past (or present) can help you prepare for the next similar situation. Being prepared will help modify, and hopefully reduce, the anxiety reaction to the situation. Pay attention to how you react to people, thoughts, and situations. Do you see a pattern? Perhaps the anxiety is trying to keep you safe around the types of people or situations that you've been hurt by in the past. If you always feel highly anxious before meeting with a family member or friend, then what is the reason? If you can figure that out, then you can decide what to do. Maybe taking a break from them, until you can be around them in a way that's healthy for you, is what you'll need to do. Of all the things we're afraid of, taking care of ourselves shouldn't be one of them.

CHAPTER TEN

Don't Tell Me To Relax!

One of the worst things you can say to someone suffering from an anxiety or panic attack is "Just relax." Please do not tell me to relax, calm down, to just breathe (as if I forgot how to!), or to ask, "What's causing it?". I understand that the person saying these things is probably trying to be helpful, and that they don't know what to say or do. I get that. Truly, I do; but for me, the best thing you can say is, "I'm here for you in whatever way you need to me be." Then, just be there.

Since my body, senses, thoughts, and emotions are heightened during an attack, I tend to stiffen up and shut down externally. That may give the appearance of not wanting to be touched or comforted, so just ask if it's okay to hold my hand, hug me, put your arm around me, or sit next to me. Often, just that connection to another person makes me feel less lonely during a very frightening time.

According to an April 10, 2018 article by Erica Cirino[7], titled "What are the Benefits of Hugging?", hugs can make you happier. It states that when we hug, touch, or sit close to someone else, the chemical oxytocin is released in our bodies. Oxytocin is associated with happiness and less stress; it causes a reduction in blood pressure and the stress hormone norepinephrine. The article also states that touch can reduce anxiety in people with low self-esteem. I'll take a hug, please!

The article quotes family therapist Virginia Satire as once saying "We need four hugs a day for survival. We need 8 hugs a day for maintenance. We need 12 hugs a day for growth."

---

7   healthline.com

That's a lot of hugs! Even though several articles I found online state that hugs should be 20-seconds long to get real health benefits from it, a January 28, 2011 article by Rebecca Kessler[8], called "Hugs Follow a 3-Second Rule", says that most hugs last no more than (you guessed it) 3-seconds. Take some time today to hug someone you're close with (husband, parent, sibling, significant other, good friend) for 20 seconds. Take note of how you feel before, during, and after the hug. I tried this with my husband a few months ago. About 10-seconds in, it started to feel awkward, and my brain was telling me to let go. I'm glad I didn't because right about the 20-second mark I could feel the muscles in my neck and upper back (where I generally hold a lot of tension) start to loosen; my thoughts slowed down; and when we broke apart, I felt....good. So good in fact, that I pestered my husband for another long hug later that day. Luckily, he's a hugger!

It's wonderful when the people around me offer me comfort while I'm going through an anxiety or panic episode. My problem is that I am uncomfortable asking for what I need during those times. If someone doesn't offer, then I won't ask. The thought of being rejected, scrutinized, judged, or having additional unwanted "Look at her!" attention, stops me from reaching out. It's a horrible feeling to have a need, but not know how to, or be too afraid to, ask for help in fulfilling that need. I absolutely abhor thinking (or feeling) that I'm bothering someone. If I approach you and your response indicates to me, whether true or not, that you're annoyed with me for approaching you, then I will never do it again. It's difficult enough asking for help when you're at your most vulnerable; but when that person responds with "You'll be fine. Just relax," or something of that nature, then my trust in that person is broken.

The dismissive response tells me that I'm weak, unreasonable, and unacceptable when I'm in a state of panic or anxiety. A good friend of mine recently shared with me a conversation she had with her temporary supervisor. A situation came up that caused a co-worker to experience heightened anxiety. My friend was discussing the situation with the supervisor, as they worked at resolving the issue that caused the situation. The supervisor said, "I just don't understand why that person would have anxiety. I guess if you had a super stressful job like CEO of a company, or something like that, then I could see someone experiencing some anxiety, but not someone who just works a regular job. I just don't get it. What's the big deal?" Unfortunately, this is a reaction I have heard many times from people who've never experienced anxiety or panic attacks. They just don't "get it".

Please do not judge what you don't understand and can't experience. Anxiety disorders aren't about not being able to handle normal stressors. I don't get a panic attack from going into Wal-Mart because I'm stressed about my job. There's deeper, more complex reasonings at hand. It's a warped sense of self, it's past (or recent) traumas that are unprocessed. It's a glitch in the fight-or-flight response; it's a myriad of things that result in the issue. As much as I would like people to know how it feels for me to have an anxiety or panic attack, I would not wish one on anyone. Ever. My husband, Ray, thought he understood what I went through because I had described it to him often enough, and he had seen firsthand the effects it has on me. He would get impatient with me sometimes, and I could hardly blame him. It even frustrates me. Then, one day, something happened that enabled him to get a glimpse into my everyday struggles.

It was about a year before my emotional and physical breakdown. Ray had gone to the doctor for a yearly checkup. He went to a clinic that has multiple doctors, so he saw a doctor that he had never had an appointment with before. He'd been in a bit of a funk for several months, as he was trying to deal with his mother's declining health. He also hadn't been taking good care of himself. The doctor was very stern and said he needed to make some significant changes in his eating, exercise, and stress management. She also gave him a sample of time released Lexapro, which is a medication used to treat anxiety disorders. I was puzzled as to why she was having him try it, but if she felt that's what he needed then I wasn't going to discourage it. Not knowing how his body would react to it, and the fact that Ray is extremely cautious about anything new he ingests, he took his first dose on a Sunday morning when he knew he would be at home all day. It's a good thing he was thoughtful about this since he ended up having a terrible reaction to the drug. The result was Ray having waves of panic attacks over a 48-hour period – which is the amount of time it takes for the mediation to clear out of the body. Every six hours, the medication would release a new dose which put Ray into either a heightened anxiety attack, or a full-on panic attack, that would last hours. Just as his body would start to calm down another wave would hit. He didn't sleep but maybe 2 hours over a two-day period, generally just 30-minutes at a time.

After doing some research online about Lexapro, I called Ray's doctor to see what could be done. She said, of course, to not take any more of the medication. She also suggested that he take a dose of my lorazepam to help offset the anxiety affects. I couldn't get Ray to take any lorazepam. At this point, he was fearful of taking anything. I couldn't even get him to eat more than a few crackers and take small sips of water occasionally. He was pacing the house like a caged animal, wouldn't let me touch him but then would suddenly ask me to stoke his forehead or rub his back. He kept tell me that he was dying and I needed to take this more seriously. I, knowing exactly what was going on with him, stayed calm and was surprisingly unaffected by his ordeal. I wasn't alarmed because I knew what was going on. I had complete empathy, but also felt a bit vindicated when he said "I finally understand what you go through. How do you do this? How do you function every day like this?"

We can look back now and laugh about the role reversals. We both gained new perspectives and understanding. I feel awful that Ray ever had a panic attack, but he thinks that God wanted him to really know what it's like to go through a panic attack and to have some compassion about it. Although Ray had a very adverse reaction to Lexapro, I don't want this to discourage anyone else from trying medications if that's what they need. His reaction was not typical, as I know several people that have taken that medication for years without any adverse effects.

Most people have good intentions, and think they are helping, when they make suggestions about what you can do to "... fix your anxiety problem", as one person said to me. Sometimes I laugh to myself when they make suggestions. I mean, do they really think I've just been sitting around having panic and anxiety attacks and not looking for tools to put in my toolbox? You can be sure that if someone, who has never experienced anxiety, has heard about something to help, then certainly those of us that do experience it are aware of it. I always listen though because you never know when you might hear something new. It would be nice if people didn't come at it like a puzzle to solve or as if we're victims that need to be saved. Yes, we do need help, but we don't need to be treated as if we're fragile and don't know how to take charge of our own health. Please be considerate and ask before offering a suggestion. You don't know where someone is in their healing expedition, and your suggestions may come across as condescending.

Here's a list of some of the things people have said to me about how to deal with anxiety (some helpful, some not):

- Be aware of your thoughts – replace negative (untruths) with positive (truth) thoughts.
- Be in the moment.
- Take slow, deep breaths through your nose only. (This can be helpful if you're hyperventilating during a panic attack.)
- Ignore your body sensations and focus your mind on something else. (Really hard to do in the middle of a massive panic attack.)
- Count to 90 the second you feel fear in the body.

(Didn't work for me.)
- Snap a rubber band on your wrist when you start to feel anxious. (All I got was a bruised wrist.)
- Meditate for an hour every day. (Would be nice, but I can fit in maybe 10-15 minutes.)
- Just let it happen. (Easy for you to say...)
- Move and burn up the adrenaline. (Sometimes this works...sometimes it makes the panic worse.)
- Run towards the panic attack. (Not instinctual, but can work to just let it happen and not fight it if you're in a place to do that – not easy when you're in a room full of people.)
- Relax all the muscles in your body.
- Take a magnesium supplement – lots of it. (FYI.... magnesium has a laxative effect on some people!)
- Spend time every day in nature. (I would love to! Not always feasible though.)
- Do cardio every day. (Does a heart rate of 113 during a panic attack count? Asking for a friend...)
- Do yoga every day. (I absolutely love yoga, and get lots of benefit from it. Don't get to it every day though.)
- Only use medication. (Definitely a good band aid, but not suggested for long term total care.)
- Find a creative hobby. (I love being creative, so for me this is a good one.)
- Just think differently – think positive. (The struggle is real!)
- Do brain teaser games. (Not sure how this helps, but they are fun.)
- Eat or take certain foods, teas, marijuana plant derivatives. (No marijuana anything for me, thanks.)
- Stay away from certain foods, teas, marijuana plant derivatives.
- Practice mindfulness. (Definitely takes practice. Good for harnessing those thoughts of the scary future.)

- Practice gratitude – make a list every day of at least three things. (I did this for months; it's helpful, but not going to "cure" my anxiety.)
- Take various supplements. (I work with a nutritionist and naturopath. More on this later in the book.)
- Use essential oils. (I find certain combinations to be very helpful with stress.)
- Take a time out…. (From my life? Not sure what this meant.)
- Limit alcohol and caffeine. (NO CAFFEINE for me. <sigh> I do partake of an occasional Guinness.)
- Count to 10 slowly. (Did not find this helpful…at all.)
- Drink more water. (This is just a good practice for everyone.)
- Find a mantra to use. (I have a few scriptures and mantras I use when I start to feel anxious.)
- Write it out. (Journaling is essential for me.)
- Talk to someone you trust. (Hhhmmm…. not easy to do. That's why I have a therapist.)

Most of these are helpful suggestions for everyone, not just those that suffer with anxiety. While many are handy tools for your toolbox, they alone won't completely rid most people of anxiety. Plus, if I did everything that I was suggested to do "every day", I wouldn't have time to go to work, and that's not an option for me. I kind of like to eat and have a roof over my head.

I recently read an article about toxic positivity. The examples of it made me think about what I've learned about the power of empathy, and what the lack of it looks like.

Here are some examples of toxic positivity statements:
- You'll get over it.
- Just be positive!
- Think happy thoughts.
- Just be happy!

- See the good in everything.
- Stop being so negative.

I've had people say these exact statements to me when I was experiencing a panic or anxiety attack. They're horribly dismissive of what I'm feeling and going through. They're hurtful and usually make me feel considerably worse, not better.

The power of empathy is expressed in statements like these:
- I'm in it with you.
- I'm not here to fix you.
- I'm not here to feel it for you.
- I'm here to feel with you and to let you know you're not alone.

Never underestimate the power of showing empathy to someone else. There's an excellent video on YouTube of a presentation and video that Brene Brown does about empathy. She's doing some cutting-edge work concerning behaviors.

What is great about someone truly showing me empathy, is that they are conveying to me that I'm not a nuisance, a bother, an inconvenience, or someone they see as needing to be fixed. They're saying, "I accept you as you are, and you are loved." I don't know about you, but I certainly want to get that message from someone else, especially when I'm in the throes of a massive panic attack or have had a day full of anxiety. I'm already doing a superb job of mentally beating myself up, I don't need help doing that! To the few people who have shown me true empathy during my difficult times, I say, "Thank you!"

CHAPTER ELEVEN

Down The Rabbit Hole

If you type "How to stop anxiety" into your browser search bar, the results will be thousands of articles, books, blogs, products, social media pages, and programs that promise to rid you of anxiety or at least help you cope better. Reading through all that information is itself anxiety-producing. The amount of information is overwhelming. I've gone down that rabbit hole more times than I care to admit. It always leaves me feeling worse, not better. For years, in a desperate attempt to "cure" my anxiety, I would try almost anything I thought might work.

To save you the trouble of ending up down those same rabbit holes, I've compiled a list of some things I've tried and the results I've had. Please keep in mind that what has worked/works for me might not work for you. One person's anxiety issues and symptoms are not the same as another's. We all have different backgrounds, bodies, traumas, and environments. Also, remember that as you change (physically, mentally, emotionally, spiritually) your needs will change, and therefore, what works at one point in your life probably won't work forever. I understand this is frustrating. I've gone through so many things that worked for a while, then I had to find the next thing that worked. It's an ongoing and lifelong process. Do not get discouraged by this. Needing new things means you're not staying stuck in the same place, and that's great.

Natural Remedies
I grew up in a household that used and embraced natural remedies, supplements/vitamins, and alternative medicine. Going in this direction was automatic for me. Before my breakdown in

2010, I was taking supplements to support my adrenal glands, liver, brain function, digestion, and others as needed. I also regularly took vitamin B and D, and minerals (such as calcium, magnesium, and trace minerals). I was doing everything right but getting no relief.

As I found out, after seeing a naturopath and having extensive bloodwork done, all I was doing was barely keeping my head above water. The constant anxiety and panic attacks were depleting my body of what I needed, faster than my body could take it in. The naturopath explained to me that high stress symptoms in the body, such as anxiety and panic attacks, burn up vitamins B and D in the body, along with other nutrients. I was shocked when my bloodwork came back with results of my vitamin B and D being so below normal that it was critical. I was prescribed vitamin B shots for three months (shots every 2-3 days), and a high dosage of easily absorbable vitamin D supplement. It took six months of me getting what I needed, in the amount I needed, along with the work I was doing to lower the amount of anxiety and panic attacks, to get my bloodwork results in the low to mid-range of "normal". I knew, based on how I felt, that my body was suffering as a result of the anxiety and panic attacks, but it really scared me when I saw those first bloodwork results.

I also felt justified in the fact that it wasn't "all in my head". It may have started there, but it did take a toll on my physical health. I also can't stress enough the need to support your adrenal glands. Long term high stress reactions can create adrenal fatigue. Seek a professional (I suggest a naturopathic doctor) to help decide what would work best for you. There are plenty of good, high quality, supplements specifically for adrenal support.

Since the breakdown, I've tried many natural remedies. Some that have helped me (long term and short term), and some that have not. Here's my list:

- **Homeopathic Remedies/Drops:** Specific blends to deal with stress, anxiety, calming the brain, and others. I used these only under the care of a professional practitioner of nutrition approved by the company to sell the products. The company that made the products I use(d) is Professional Formulas out of Lake Oswego, Oregon. These worked for me on and off for several years. I used some daily for maintenance, and some for use at acute times (such as high anxiety or the onset of a panic attack).

- **Homeopathic Pellets**: I use the brand BOIRON, which has numerous formulas for all kinds of body symptoms and ailments. These can be purchased at most high-end health food/supplement stores, or online. Again, I used these on and off for years to treat my anxiety and symptoms, but still use them today for other issues (such as headaches, colds, etc.). What I love about homeopathic supplements is that they do not interact negatively with medications, cannot be overdosed on, and are tolerated well by most bodies.
- **Seed/Flower Essences**: These are available through a naturopath or nutritionist (recommended) or online from Bach. Certain formulas pertain to certain emotions that have not been dealt with or emotional traumas. Such as: Regal Lily is used for people who feel mildly detached or disassociated from their true selves. They usually feel as if they have been victimized and controlled by the work of others. These come in liquid form and are taken sublingually (via a dropper).
- **L-Theanine**: This is an amino acid, found most commonly, in tea leaves. I took this one on and off for several years to help ease stress effects on my body and to unwind my mind. According to WebMd.com, it has a chemical structure similar to glutamate, an amino acid that occurs naturally in the body and helps transmit nerve impulses in the brain. It has no

known side effects, and does not cause drowsiness like many anxiety relieving supplements and medications. Per WebMD.com, it does interact with some medications, particularly certain ones that treat high blood pressure, and stimulants (such as epinephrine and pseudoephedrine).

- **St. John's Wort and 5-HTP:** Both are said to increase serotonin production. They just didn't work for me at all. The few times I tried them, because everyone said they were "so great", there was no change in my anxiety levels, and I had terrible side effects such as dizziness and nightmares.
- **Inositol:** I used a powder form mixed in water. This was prescribed by a naturopath and should not be self-administered. This can have an adverse effect on some digestive systems, but I had no issues. I took this on and off for about a year or so, but quit taking it because it can lower testosterone levels. Since I was in the middle of perimenopause, my bloodwork showed a drop in my testosterone levels and I didn't want to make it worse.
- **GABA** (Gamma-aminobutyric acid): According to the United Kingdom's National Health Service website (www.nhs.uk), lorazepam works by increasing the levels of GABA (a calming chemical), in your brain. When I first started weaning off my 2mg/day dose of lorazepam, I used a GABA supplement to help my brain deal with the withdrawal of it. Once I got down to a 1 mg/day dose I was able to stop taking the GABA supplement, as I just needed it to get down off the higher daily dose with minimal effects of withdrawal. Of course, I engaged with my therapist and nutritional practitioner before using GABA and lowering my dose of lorazepam.
- **Adaptogens for Stress:** Ashwagandha/Rhodiola/ American Ginseng. The only one of these that I've

tried it ashwagandha. A nutritionist recommended I try it, as she has several clients (and herself) that got stress relief when using it. The ashwagandha did not work for me. It caused my anxiety to amp up. My body is generally sensitive to nightshades (tomatoes, eggplant, etc.) so once I found out ashwagandha is a nightshade it explained why I had a bad reaction to it. If you don't have an issue with nightshades then it might work for you. Rhodiola, which is derived from a perennial flowering plant, should only be used for short term (6-12 weeks at a time, with a break in between) according to WebMD. Also, according to WebMD, it stimulates the immune system, so anyone with an autoimmune disease may experience worsening symptoms; it also lowers blood sugar levels and blood pressure, so be sure to monitor both when using Rhodiola to avoid either getting too low. The website verywellhealth.com states that while American ginseng has great benefits for fighting fatigue, diabetes, and increasing mental function, possible side effects include anxiety, insomnia, restlessness and other. All of which would NOT be helpful to someone suffering from anxiety disorders. Like any herb or supplement, do your research and consult a professional before using; and even then, be sure to pay attention to what your body is telling you.

- **Clinical Grade Lavender**: Comes in capsule form. My naturopath recommended Integrative Therapeutics Lavela (Clinically Studied Lavender Oil), but I ended up buying Nature's Way CalmAid (Clinically Studied Lavender Oil). The CalmAid was slightly less expensive and I found out they have the same parent company. Both can be purchased online. I have found this to be extremely helpful with my day-to-day anxiety. I take one capsule daily and

another one later in the day if needed but find that's only under very stressful conditions.
- **Valerian Glycerite:** This is a liquid extract of valerian. I take this for immediate help of a panic attack. I initially got this from my naturopath, but found two other brands I like that I can get online. I just take one to two droppers full and put it directly into my mouth. For me, this is powerful stuff. The first time I used it, I was driving to town with mom and was feeling highly anxious. I decided to take my truck through the carwash, and knowing how those can trigger a panic attack for me, I took just one dropper full of the Valerian. I didn't have a panic attack, and my anxiety level went from extra high to low in about 15 minutes. I also take it at night if my mind won't shut down enough for me to get to sleep. By using the Valerian Glycerite and the clinical grade lavender, I was able to completely wean off the last daily dose (0.25 mg) of lorazepam. Be cautious taking this with anxiety medications. If combined they can make you drowsy.

Other Resources

Aside from remedies for the body, I've found many resources that helped me with my emotional and mental challenges. My experience is that the mind, emotions, and body are so intricately connected that if there is dysfunction in one, there is dysfunction in all. This is not new information.

There are some excellent books about the mind-body connection, healing traumas, healing the body, finding help from God/in the Bible, ways to manage anxiety symptoms, and recognizing and replacing negative thoughts; some that I've read, and recommend, are:
- Three books by John E. Sarno, MD; *Healing Back Pain the Mind Body Connection*; *The Mindbody Prescription, Healing the Body, Healing the Pain*;

and *The Divided Mind, The Epidemic of Mindbody Disorders*
- *The Body Keeps Score: Brain, Mind, and Body in the Healing of Trauma*, by Bessel Van Der Kolk, M.D.
- *The Healing Code*, by Alexander Loyd, PhD, ND, with Ben Johnson, MD, DO, NMD
- *The Heart's Code, Tapping Into the Wisdom and Power of Our Heart Energy*, by Paul Pearsall, PhD.
- *The Dark Side of the Light Chasers*, by Debbie Ford
- *When the Body Says No, Understanding the Stress-Disease Connection*, by Gabor Mate, M.D.
- *D A R E: The New Way to End Anxiety and Stop Panic Attacks*, by Barry McDonagh
- *From Panic To Power*, by Lucinda Bassett
- *Life Without Limits*, by Lucinda Bassett
- *Running Scared: Fear, Worry and the God of Rest*, by Edward T. Welch
- *When I am Afraid*, by Edward T. Welch
- *Goliath Must Fall, Winning the Battle Against Your Giants*, by Louie Giglio
  - There's an excellent study guide available for this book
- *The Search For Significance Devotional Journal*, by Robert S. McGee
  - This is based on the book of the same name, which I did not read.
- *I Declare, 31 Promises to Speak Over Your Life*, by Joel Osteen
- Two books by Masaru Emoto; *The Miracle of Water; and The Hidden Messages in Water*
- Three books by Joyce Meyer; *Battlefield of the Mind; Be Anxious for Nothing; and Power Thoughts*
- I also have numerous small books of quotations, prayers, and sayings that help me replace negative thoughts with the truth, boost my confidence, calm my mind when anxious thoughts start to run ram-

pant, and are a great way to start the day or for anytime I need a new perspective. Some of my favorites are:
- *The Secret Power of Speaking God's Word*, by Joyce Meyer
- *The Daily Book of Positive Quotations*, by Linda Picone
- *The Quiet Mind: Sayings of White Eagle*
- *Blessings, Prayers and Declarations for a Heartful Life*, by Julia Cameron
- *Prayers for an Anxious Heart*, Barbour Books (multiple contributors)

Body Work

Since there is such a connection between the body and the brain, I've found that treating the mind alone doesn't work for me. I also need to treat the body. Emotions are stored in the cells of our body. According to the book I previously noted, *The Hidden Messages in Water* by Masaru Emoto, which says in the prologue "Modern researches have shown that the condition of the mind has a direct impact on the condition of the body. When you are living a full and enjoyable life, you feel better physically, and when your life is filled with struggles and sorrow, your body knows it."

I think we've all felt those emotional effects in our body. Whether it's boundless energy because you feel happy and joyful, exhausted, and tired because you're depressed, or have tight muscles in your shoulders, back and stomach from anxiety. We've all felt the connection between our emotions, what we're thinking, and our bodies.

I hold a lot of my emotions and stress in my middle and upper back, my neck, my stomach, and my hands. If I don't regularly see a chiropractor and massage therapist, the next thing I know my shoulders are up into my ears, and I'm hunched over because my stomach is so tight (not washboard abs tight, dang it!). About ten years ago, just prior to my breakdown, I found an amazing chiropractor. I had gone to several talented chiropractors over the years and they all contributed greatly to my overall health, but this guy was different. He treated me as a whole person; he looked at everything that was going on with me. He took the time to sit down and listen to my story, concerns, and then provided some insight and information about what else I could do to help in my total health. Even when I knew I would have a massive panic attack trying to drive the 30 plus minutes from my work to his office, I rarely missed an appointment because I knew I felt better afterwards; I felt less anxious, and I felt I could breathe. It's important to find partners in your healthcare that never criticize, really listen to you, are patient with you, and truly have your best interest in all they do.

Even though I've had some less than positive interactions and outcomes with various people working in the healthcare field, I trust that God will follow through on His promise to lead me to the right people if I trust Him. The good news is that He has. Besides my amazing chiropractor, I've had the pleasure of being helped by some truly gifted massage therapists. One of my staff members, when I worked for the state agency, is a massage therapist. Obviously, when I was her supervisor, I didn't think it was ethical to be one of her massage clients. What she did do (Bless her!) was direct me to someone she knew that did Bowenwork. I had never heard of Bowenwork, but looked it up online and was intrigued by the process and the results people were getting. I made an appointment with the practitioner and was excited to experience it for myself.

Because I was raised in a household that embraced alternative medicine and natural medicine, I am cautious but open to "out of the box" healing methods that do not directly conflict with my beliefs as a Christian and what the Word of God says. I know, in my Spirit, if it's something I should or should not be pursuing, or opening myself up to. Every person's beliefs are different, and I'm not here to tell you that something you try is "wrong" or "sinful" or that something I try is "right" or "holy". It's not my job to make those decisions or judgements. Just know that I love and care about you even if our beliefs are different. To me, we are all children of God and connected by something far more important than "religion".

The best way to describe Bowenwork is that it's a bit like a cross between acupressure, energy work, and EFT (Emotional Freedom Technique). According to the American Bowen Academy website[9] "Bowenwork is a system of touch that initiates a series of responses through stimulation of the nervous, musculoskeletal, and fascial systems and the energetic pathways. Practitioners perform a sequence of small movements on specific points on the body, interspersed with rest periods." The practitioner asked what health issues I wanted her to work on. For me, it was the spasms in my mid-back, my sinuses, anxiety, and some tightness in my hips. After the first round of sessions, I saw small changes but nothing major. She explained to me that the results vary with each person. She's had some patients with immediate relief of symptoms, and some who experience little to no relief. I went back to see her for another round of sessions – although, you can go once, multiple instances in a short period of time, or just when needed – and had much better results. I think it was because I had progressed in some of my therapy work, and I wasn't so "clogged", energy wise.

It was interesting because I would get these odd involuntary muscle twitches and jerking in between the sequence of movements the practitioner would perform. I never had any dramatic outcomes from the Bowenwork, an instance where I could pinpoint and say, "Ah-ha! I felt complete relief of____because of this." Instead, it was something that allowed other treatments to work more effectively and was one more thing that propelled me forward in my healing expedition.

I believe that for someone dealing with the body effects of anxiety attacks and panic attacks, massage is a must have tool in your toolbox. I know many people that just won't go to a

---

9   americanbowen.academy

massage therapist because it makes them uncomfortable; they feel too vulnerable. My mother is one of those people. A massage to her is stressful and certainly only something she's done when absolutely necessary, and even then, only with someone she knows and feels safe with. I also have a friend with some severe past traumas and a horrible body image who also avoids massages like the plague. When her migraines got so frequent and severe that she was desperate for relief, she went to see a female massage therapist that worked out of her chiropractor's office. Even then, she kept all her clothes on and only allowed the massage therapist to work on her head, neck, and shoulders. What I'm trying to convey is that I get it, massage is not for everyone. Me, on the other hand, gleefully looks forward to all my massage appointments.

I've had times where I'm experiencing a high level of anxiety or am on the verge of a panic attack when I arrive for my appointment. I learned to let my massage therapist know that I'm struggling, which takes some of the anxiety pressure off me, plus it helps them know to focus on getting my body to relax before continuing with any of the therapeutic work. Don't be surprised if you start to cry during or after a massage, or start feeling strong emotions when a "hot" emotional spot is being worked on. I've found that the best massage therapists are the one who do it because they feel it's their calling, their purpose, and that they get joy from helping others. These are the massage therapists that can feel those "hot spots" of emotions you're holding in your body. Over the last 15 years, I've been blessed to have at least six of these truly gifted body workers help me and go along in my health expedition with me.

All of them understood the connection between the mind and the body. All of them cared enough and were brave enough to explore methods of releasing debilitating emotions I had stored in my body. Many of them had been trained in various techniques and methods that go beyond the usual relaxation or therapeutic massage. Through my experience, I've learned that our bodies and minds have infinite ways to repair and heal. It's truly quite amazing to me. I never expected the bursts of emotional release that happened to me while being worked on by these gifted individuals. The intensity of them and the reactions of my body scared me sometimes. It's a powerful thing to finally pull out the cork of bottled up emotions, to lift the lid and sift around in your emotional garbage can. I had no idea that I had all of that inside of me, for years and years. It's no wonder that I've experienced anxiety all my life. I truly believe that if you don't deal with your emotions and issues when they come up, they eventually deal with you…and not in a pleasant way.

Another great way to release emotions from the body is exercise (Groan!). Find what works for you. If you're angry or frustrated then maybe boxing, kickboxing, or a high intensity workout will help you express those emotions. If you're stressed, anxious, feeling like a bound-up rubber band, then maybe yoga, Pilates, or a stretching workout would be helpful. I have a co-worker that loves exercise dance classes or videos. Moving her body rhythmically helps her feel more connected to herself and allows for self-expression with no judgement. Whatever it is, for whatever emotion(s) you are feeling, just be sure to move your body. Walking is wonderful exercise and sometimes all that you can manage when experiencing high anxiety. That was the case, with me, for a long time.

I recently read an entry in my journal from late summer of 2011, where I was so proud of myself for walking up and down our driveway (it was a long driveway) three times that day. That was a big step forward for me. For a long time, I struggled with thoughts of *I'm going to have a heart attack if I exercise, especially if I'm too far away from my safe place (home).* I never wanted to walk too far away from my home, my office, my car – anyplace I felt was safe - because *What if I did have a heart attack, or a panic attack, and I was stuck somewhere having this terrible problem!* It took years for me to understand that *I* am my safe place. Don't get me wrong, I still have fleeting thoughts of, *It's not safe to walk more than a few blocks or a quarter-mile from my house, car, or office.* Those "what if..." thoughts are so sneaky! Just be sure to start slowly with the exercise, don't push yourself. Work up to what is comfortable for you physically, and mentally. I started to make great strides when I worked with a personal trainer that helped me move past some of my exercise fears. Find someone who will encourage you, will be understanding, and will work with you, at your pace.

I've Also Tried...
About a year after my breakdown, I was expressing to my mother some of the stressful things going on at work. She suggested that I try "scream therapy". Uh...what?! She explained that I should do it on my way home, alone in my car, to help release stress. I was like, "So, I just start screaming? That seems weird." Apparently, it's a thing. I don't know about you, but it's so difficult for me to release emotions verbally, especially in the manner of yelling or screaming. When I was growing up, we did not yell or scream in our house. I always feel stupid and embarrassed the few times I've done it. It takes a lot to get me to that point. It's just not a comfortable thing for me to do, but I thought I'd give it a try next time I left work frustrated or upset.

Fast forward a few weeks, it's a warm sunny day, and as I got in my car to leave work and head for home, I opened the panoramic sunroof in my car. It had been a stressful day at work, and I decided to give the "scream therapy" a try. So, here I am, driving 25 mph down the main street of the small town I worked in, people are walking by on sidewalks shopping and enjoying the rare sunny weather. Me, having totally forgotten about the open sunroof, started screaming like a banshee on the prowl in medieval Ireland. I didn't realize at first that I was scaring people until an elderly couple in an adjacent crosswalk stopped, as if startled, and looked around in surprise as I passed through the intersection. It took me a minute to catch on to what had happened; at that point, I discovered laughter therapy. I recommend it over "scream therapy" any day.

There's a proposed method of snapping yourself out of an anxiety or panic attack that I keep seeing explained on different social media and online platforms. It's called grounding. The idea is to use mindfulness to connect to the "now". When you start to feel anxious or are having a panic attack then tap into your senses and name one to three things that you see, hear, feel, etc. I believe that the idea is to get yourself out of your head and not so focused on what is happening in your body. I've tried this multiple times. For me, it doesn't work. When I start to panic or am in a high level of anxiety mode, my thoughts are already so disjointed and electrified that my brain is beyond the point of giving a rat's ass about what I'm smelling or seeing. This might work for someone with lower levels of anxiety or if you can catch the panic attack way before the first symptoms. I have tried it when in a stressful environment, such as when I'm around a large group of noisy people and implement it as I'm first introduced into the situation. Doing so does work to stop my thoughts from moving too far forward in the "What's going to happen in 10 minutes?" scenarios; but I find that I must keep doing it to get long lasting results.

A couple of things I've tried recently that work quite well for me, is an acupressure pad and weighted blankets. The acupressure pad is helpful in relieving some of the tension in my body, especially at the end of the day. There are several available online for a reasonable price. I find it useful as a good fill in for the time between my chiropractic and massage appointments. It seems to help my body communicate with itself properly.

Weighted blankets are the best thing since sliced bread. Oh. My. Gosh! I have a small, lap sized, one that I keep at work. I have a mid-size, but heavier weighted one, that I snuggle under in the living room while watching TV or reading a book. And I have a large, mid-weight, one that I keep on my bed. As you can see, I really, *really*, really like them. The science behind weighted blankets, according to my therapist, is that they simulate a hug or the touch of another. I've talked to people that don't experience anxiety, and they love them. We all have stress in our lives, why would you not want a weighted blanket?!

CHAPTER TWELVE

Practicing Self Care
WHAT DOES THAT LOOK LIKE?

We know that it's important to take care of ourselves. We see and hear other people reminding us to practice self-care, but what is that, really? My marvelous writing coach, Sage, often says that self-care is whatever you need it to be. I think that's brilliant! Certainly, get ideas from people and information around you, but pay attention to what makes you feel joy, peace, energized, strong, and ready to take on the world. Admittedly, I was horrible at practicing self-care until I was forced to. Having a complete mental and physical breakdown tends to make a person inclined to reexamine their lives. As Dr. Phil McGraw often says "How's that working for you?" I can honestly declare that what I had been doing to myself, and not doing for myself, the first 40-years of my life was not working for me.

I want you to get this truth statement so deep into your head that it becomes a "knowing" in your soul. Ready? TAKING CARE OF YOURSELF IS NOT SELFISH. Read that out loud a few times. If it makes you feel uncomfortable when you do that, then likely, you desperately need to practice self-care.

It was extremely difficult for me to get comfortable with making myself a priority. I don't mean in a selfish way but in a healthy way. I remember the first time I heard explained the example of pouring from an empty pitcher. You start out in life with a full pitcher. As you go on, you pour out of your pitcher as you give to others. That's a good thing. When we get ourselves into trouble is when we forget to fill up our pitcher. Pretty soon, there is nothing left to give. Our pitcher is empty. When you practice self-care, you are replenishing the contents of your pitcher. You cannot give what you do not have.

If we don't take the time and effort to fill ourselves with peace, kindness to ourselves, joy, understanding, or to create a healthy body, then we do not have those things to give or contribute to those around us. It's certainly not easy. Many of us suffering from anxiety disorders and depression do not feel worthy of taking care of ourselves. We feel worthless, damaged, hopeless, ugly, and misunderstood. The tasks associated with self-care seem daunting and unfamiliar. I continue to struggle with this. I'm exceedingly better at it than I've ever been, but I can promise you that when you do it, the resultant feelings boil down to self-love. That's something I rarely feel, and is not easily achieved for me, so when I do get it, it is amazing.

To get started on a regular practice of self-care, I'll share ways that I practice self-care – either currently or have tried in the past. I hope that you find some of these helpful.

Journaling

It seems so simple, right? Get a notepad or journal, a nice pen or pencil and start jotting down your thoughts and feelings, and you're on your way to finally understanding yourself. Wrong! Anyone who's tried journaling can attest to the momentary feeling of panic and fear that comes over you when you get ready to pour out your soul in written word. It's terrifying. Completely, and utterly terrifying.

Once it's down on paper, then someone might read it. Someone might see all the crazy going on in your head. If you don't understand it, why would anyone else; especially someone in your family or your significant other?! All these thoughts are enough to petrify your hand as it's poised over the paper with pen gripped between your fingers. I would love to be able to say that all those fears are unfounded, but sadly, they are not.

About 10 years after we were married, my husband and I were having a minor argument about, what I'm sure was something insignificant, when he happened to throw into the conversation, "That's not what you said in our journal." Suddenly, he realized what he'd just said because I had frozen in my tracks and was giving him the wild eyed "You better run!" look. I instantly burst into tears because I felt so betrayed. I said, very quietly, "You read my journal?" Since I was still a steadfast people pleaser back then, I felt the need to explain that what I write in my journal is just random thoughts and feelings and are written to process the information in my brain and really doesn't mean anything. What I wrote was not bad, or wrong, or even an untruth. What I realize now is that it was tapping into some of my husband's insecurities about his place in my nuclear family. Basically, I didn't handle it well, and stormed into the bedroom, grabbed my journal, and threw it into the roaring wood burning fireplace, as I proceed to yell, "Fine! I'll never write in a journal again!"

After that whole debacle, to my own detriment, I didn't write in a journal again for about six years. That trust was broken, and it took a long time for that to be built back up. Now, I have all my journals from 2011 to now. Unfortunately, in a now regrettable moment of disgust with myself, I threw away all my journals prior to 2011. At the time, I could not stand to read my entries from the years leading up to my breakdown. I was terrified of becoming that person again; that downtrodden and victimized person. I did not see the value in her then, but I do now.

I hope you decided to take up journaling in whatever form that is for you. If it's difficult and scary at first, just write a few lines about an event in your day. Don't put pressure on yourself to conform to what you think you must write about or how you must write it. There are days when all I can get out are single words. I have entries that are just these words: cried, laughed, tired, anxious, and ahhhhh…comfy sheets. The point is to get it out of your head in a way that helps you process it. I also find it cathartic to write a letter to someone that hurt me, and then burn it. I've also done this with thoughts and feelings that I want to get rid of and not hold onto anymore.

For a few years after my breakdown, I wrote in my journal every night, even if it was just a word or two. I have to say, it's nice to have a confidant that doesn't try to fix you, make you feel better, or judge you. Often, my journal entries start as a letter to God. They become written prayers, and I find comfort in linking myself to Him in that way. For me, there is something magical that happens when pen meets paper. It's a tangible connection to diverse parts of myself.

Being Artistic
I'm not great at it, but I love to paint, draw, create collages, color in adult coloring books, take photographs, or use color to create by using many different mediums. When I get to be creative, I'm in a world of my own, and it's the only time, besides maybe reading and writing, that my mind and body take a break from anxious thoughts and feelings. When I was a child, I would run off into the woods on our property with a sketch book and charcoal pencils to draw. The first time I got to create using oil paint, my heart sang with joy. The feeling of that brush gliding over the stark white canvas was addictive. I was only 11 years old, but I knew this was something I would want to do for the rest of my life.

Unfortunately, by the time I was 14, I got caught up in being a teenager and set aside what I so dearly loved. I denied that part of myself because I was afraid to be judged about it. It's an intimate thing to create art, and I was too scared to expose myself to ridicule and rejection. I packed my art supplies around for 20 years before I started painting again. I have a hard time forgiving myself for not creating space in my life for something I loved, for something that should have always been a part of my self-care. I didn't though, because I was trying so hard to fit into the mold of what I thought I was supposed to be and what everyone else expected me to be for them, that I forgot about myself. The real me. The me that sadly, never was. If you're young, please do not ever toss aside what gives you joy;

and if you're in the middle or later part of your life, then find it again. I have, and I can testify that making that space, whatever changes you must do in your life for it, is well worth it. It's something I continue to work on, but I know that I'll get there, and so will you.

Relaxation in the Form of…
What relaxes you? Is it a bubble bath? Time with close friends? Lying quietly listening to your favorite music? Meditation? Is it watching a movie or TV show that makes you laugh deeply? Is it aromatherapy? Playing with your children, or your pets?

Take a few minutes and write out a list of what you know is relaxing to you, or what you would like to do to relax. It doesn't matter if the list is long or short. Put a check mark next to the items that you do daily or weekly. Put an X next to the ones you rarely, or never, get to do. If you have more X's than you do check marks then you may need to reevaluate what realistically works with your life and schedule. If your ultimate relaxation technique is an hour-long quiet bubble bath, but you work full time and have two small children, then it might not be plausible for you to do that every week. Instead, you may be able to take 10-minutes in your car, before you drive home, to do a guided meditation. I have a great meditation app on my phone (there a many available) that has a daily 10-minute guided meditation. At first, it was hard for me to do just anywhere, but I found that the more I consistently did it and found a semi-quiet and private place to do it in, the easier it became. I started to crave the meditation. What I'm trying to convey is to find what works for you, and your life.

Diet and Exercise
Of course, a key part of self-care is a healthy diet, and exercise. There is a plethora of information out there about the connection between gut health and mental health, but I'm not going to get into it in this book. I do encourage you to do some research on it, read some books about it, and consult

a naturopath or nutritionist. In the meantime, a good first step is to stay away from: sugary drinks (such as soda, most mainstream sports drinks, energy drinks, and blended coffee); caffeine (such as coffee, black tea, energy drinks, and an excess of chocolate); processed foods (eat food as close to its original form as possible); and white food (flour, sugar, rice, potatoes). I know it sounds like you won't have anything to eat, but just try it for two weeks or a month and see if you feel any different.

What I will say is that if a diet, a pill, or a type of exercise promises to completely rid you of anxiety and depression, be cautious. Many companies and people prey on those of us that are desperate for relief. Do your homework first, and don't be disappointed if you do try a reputable diet or exercise program and don't see the results you expected or were promised. It just means it wasn't meant for you.

CHAPTER THIRTEEN
I love Me

Those are difficult words to say, aren't they? I love me. How dare I be so conceited?! Some of us (ah-hum) were raised in an emotional environment that didn't encourage us to put ourselves before others. It was selfish and unseemly. This made it impossible for me to be okay with feeling good about myself. What I should have been told, and shown, was that I can't truly love someone else unless I love myself; and I can't truly love myself until I know the love that God has for me. Once I figured that out, then I started to feel less guilty about taking care of myself and prioritizing my needs first. Don't forget; this goes along with the empty pitcher scenario that I wrote about earlier.

Before I get into this part, I wanted to go over a few things that I think are important to understand. You are not to blame for having anxiety or depression. You did not go looking for it. Likely, it's an uninvited guest that's taken up residence in your body, mind, and soul. You're not choosing to stay in the pit of despair and hopelessness; someone just hasn't handed you a ladder yet (I hope this book is that ladder for you!). I know this. I understand some of what you've been going through – I say "some" because none of us can truly have the same experiences as another person. But you are not alone. You are lovable. You are not a loser for having these conditions. If anything, you are ridiculously stronger than people who don't have to fight day, after day to function in a world that is not kind to us. You are amazing. Now, having said that...

Take Charge of Your Own Healing.
The only person who can help you, is you. The only person who has the power to change your thoughts, your patterns of destructive behaviors, and your reactions to what goes on around you, is you. There is tremendous control in that! This is a good thing. Since most of us that deal with anxiety and panic disorder are all about having control, let's use it in a positive way. Instead of trying to control people, situations, and outcomes; let's practice some self-control.

When this was first presented to me, I was dumbfounded. I was so immersed in being the victim of my suffering, that I didn't see that I had the power to step out of that role. But I had to make a choice. Did I want to continue in my suffering? Come on now.... we all know how cozy and familiar that suffering is. If we're honest with ourselves, at least a small part of us likes it – not like "This is so much fun!", but like "I know what to expect, even though it's scary," sort of way. I liken it to the saying "The devil you know is better than the one you don't."

I get that it's horribly terrifying to step out of that comfort zone of dealing with what you've been dealing with forever (if you've had anxiety all or most of your life, like me). Just remember, you don't have to take giant steps into scary territory. Just take small steps. I call them baby steps. It sounds corny, I know, but we are like babies taking our little steps forward into an unknown universe of our own healing.

Celebrate your Successes!
Many times, I've lamented to my therapist that it feels like I take three steps forward, then two steps back. It's horribly frustrating. One time, she had me list out all the forward steps I had taken in my healing expedition. What were my accomplishments? Once I listed them out, I realized that I had taken infinitely more steps forward than I ever realized. I encourage you to do the same. Make a list of all the times you were able to do something that was a struggle for you: a modification

that you made to bring about positive changes in your life; a realization that you made that cleaned up some of your emotional garbage can.

For an example, here are over 20 things that are on my list (in no particular order):

1. Surrendering to God
2. Buying the "Attacking Anxiety and Depression" program.
3. Doing the program work – listening to the tapes, going through the workbook, and actively putting into practice what I was learning.
4. Realizing that I do have control over my thoughts and words.
5. Finding a therapist then actually going to see her.
6. Grocery shopping and not having a panic attack.
7. Driving on the freeway.
8. Eating in a restaurant.
9. Doing anything while feeling afraid.
10. Forgiving myself if I have a panic attack.
11. Realizing confrontation is not a bad thing; then practicing it by having those hard conversations with people.
12. Taking care of myself is not selfish.
13. Not putting an expectation on myself to be "cured".
14. Trusting God in all things.
15. Starting a new job – twice.
16. Public speaking.
17. Staying in a hotel by myself/traveling by myself.
18. Being in an airport and flying on a plane.
19. Making new friends.
20. Exercising.
21. Going to a doctor's appointment by myself.
22. Waiting in a line, any line, and not having a panic attack – or at least not running out if I feel one coming on.
23. Talking about having anxiety issues/sharing my story.
24. Writing this book.

This is not a comprehensive list, but you can see that I was able to come up with a varied list of positive outcomes. I imagine you can come up with more than a few things right now and then get excited about what you can add to the list in the coming years. Remember, those forward steps take time. It's an unrealistic expectation (something those of us with anxiety disorder are good at setting up) to think that issues building up for 10, 25, 50+ years aren't going to be processed and healed overnight. It takes time, so be patient with yourself. Also, don't be hurt when someone close to you doesn't get why you're so excited about being able do something that they don't think twice about doing. Not everyone will understand (in fact, most won't) how those victories over normal daily life "stuff" is so important. That's okay. You celebrate you!

Whatever you do, keep moving forward. It's so imperative to not let anything or anyone distract or divert you from choices you've made to move forward in your healing expedition. Even if you do take a few steps back as you go along, just take a moment to enjoy the familiar scenery then look up towards your goal and move towards it again. I've stumbled plenty over the last nine years. I think I've even fallen over the edge of the trail a few times, but eventually I get back on my way with new scars on my hands and my knees, but they just remind me of all that I've overcome. Sometimes I feel as if I'm crawling instead of taking steps, and that's okay too. Whatever keeps you moving forward. The bonus is that you can't unlearn something. The knowledge that you pick up about yourself, the people in your life, and the world around you cannot be forgotten. The modifications you make in your life, attitude, mind, body, and whatever else, changes you. You no longer react to situations and people the same. Therefore, the outcome is different. You are different.

For a long time, I had this fear that I would have another breakdown. Every time I was challenged once again with a period of intense anxiety and panic attacks, this voice in my head would mock, *You're going right back to where you started.*

Loser! My therapist reminded me that I never will. I know too much now. I will never be that same version of myself. Once I really understood that, I was able to be more accepting of myself, and not just when I thought I was "anxiety free". I still have times when I'm disappointed in myself for having anxiety or panic attacks. I try to see myself as God sees me: as His child and someone He loves unconditionally. God knows me – really knows me – and accepts me as I am. I'm not a surprise to Him, and the fact that He has chosen to use my imperfections to glorify Him and to help other people is humbling to me. It keeps me going and lifts my spirit when I catch myself talking negatively to myself. I'm adding some of my favorite scriptures at the end of the book. I hope you find as much comfort, encouragement, and joy in them as I do.

Be Vigilant!
You may, or may not, ever fully rid yourself of anxiety attacks and panic attacks. I hope you do. I hope you find all the tools that work well together for you that give you continuous peace. I've had periods in my life, some of them years long, where I was barely troubled with intense anxiety attacks or panic attacks. It's a nice respite from the ongoing turmoil, but I find that I must be vigilant and watchful about habits and old patterns that don't set me up for success. When I get lazy about doing so, is when I start to see the anxiety sneak back up.

Here are some things I must be aware of in order to manage the anxiety:
- I cannot relax my guard about what I'm thinking about – as Joyce Meyers says "No stinkin' thinkin'!".
- Letting my mind wander to negative thinking. I make a conscious effort to stop the negative thought and replace it with a positive one.
- Be aware of what you say. You hear the words that come out of your mouth, and your body reacts to them.

- Exposure to toxic or negative people must be limited. Remember, sarcasm is negativity disguised as humor.
- Seek out people that speak and live positively.
- Surround yourself with uplifting music, books, television/movies, people, and activities. I keep different positive quotes, saying, and scriptures around my house and in my workspace at the office.
- Focus on you. Clean up your emotional garbage can.
- Work at bringing myself back to a place of peace, and not settle into a state of anxiety. This is especially true after a few days of extended anxiety attacks, or after experiencing a panic attack. If you fear the next one, then you start the cycle. A bad day doesn't have to be a bad week, etc.

Unfortunately, I don't have the luxury of being complacent about my mental health. There was a time, about five years ago, that I seemed to have the anxiety well under control. It had been several months since I'd even had a minor panic attack. I thought I would be at this "free from anxiety" level for the rest of my life. Thinking I had the anxiety under control, I focused on my physical health. For the four years previous I had focused solely on my mental health and though I did change my diet and lose weight I was still physically out of shape. This is when I started working out at the gym three to four times a week. I'm not saying that exercise and taking care of your body is a bad thing. It's a good thing; but for me, I had just gone from one extreme to another. I forgot that life is about balance.

I was digging into some of the stuff at the bottom of my garbage can in my therapy sessions and doing the homework but not really paying attention to how it had residual effects on me emotionally and mentally. I started to get high anxiety or short panic attacks at the gym. Then it started at work, then at other times. I felt myself backsliding and then I really started to panic. It was manageable, but was starting to affect my quality of life again.

My experience is that when you push yourself out of balance, then the body, mind, and soul find a way to bring you back into balance. Instead of listening to what my body, mind, and spirit were trying to tell me; I kept pushing too hard one way when I found myself too far the other way. I was either being forced to focus on my mental and emotional health or on my physical health. When that happened, the one I wasn't focused on would suffer. It all came to a head when my grandmother fell ill and passed away. After dealing with that, I was a mess in all ways possible. It certainly didn't help that peri-menopause was causing all kinds of third level hell on my total wellbeing.

Over the last few years, I've painfully started to find the middle ground. I spend time on, and put effort towards, my complete health. Giving myself some grace, and being patient with myself as I find a balance that works, does not come naturally to me. I don't think it does for most people. I take comfort in the fact that I can now recognize when I find that sweet spot in my life and celebrate it when I do, but don't get discouraged (too much!) when I fall out of whack again. Life will continue to have ups and downs, but I've survived all my worst times and have seen hope and joy on the other side. I hang onto that hope when I'm in the midst of difficulties. One of my favorite mantras is *This too shall pass*. This is especially helpful when I felt weary from an ongoing anxiety attack or when I felt a panic attack coming on. I also use one from Joyce Meyer's teaching that is *Something good is going to happen to me today!* Another one is *God will not leave me, nor forsake me*. I have dozens more that I use when I need to support myself during times of struggle. I encourage you find ones you like and see if repeating them over and over help you through a difficult time.

Let Other People Help You.
I'm sure that sounds like a weird way to show yourself some love. Practicing self-care is not about being an island all the time. Sometimes, it's about taking a chance and trusting the people in your life. I know…SCARY!!!! Believe me, I've been

heart hurt plenty by people who professed to be my friend, or care about me. It hurts. I get that, but realize that if they reject you, by not being supportive or understanding, it isn't about you, it's about them. Don't cut yourself off from the possibility of amazing experiences and connections with other people because of previous hurtful experiences.

I'm not saying to vomit talk about all your issues to everyone you meet, but to listen to your instincts and share or accept help when it's appropriate and when you feel comfortable or compelled to do so. I mean, I wasn't exactly thrilled about writing a book about my life, and sharing my closely guarded secret of dealing with anxiety and panic attacks. It's only been the last few years that I've told a few people I work with about it. I'm certainly feeling some pangs of panic whenever I think about this book being out in the world for all to see. I'm showing my soft underbelly, and I don't like it. Not one bit; but I trust that by doing so I can help someone else. If it's just one person, then it's worth it for me.

Many times, over the last nine years, I've felt compelled to share my story with someone, often someone I don't know well. Each time, the person shares that they have similar issues and thanked me for helping them feel not so alone in their struggle. Each time the reward of helping someone else far outweighed my fear of vulnerability. I am glad that I didn't ignore the Holy Spirit's urging for me to step out in faith.

How many times have you been in a state of high anxiety or trying to stave off a panic attack when someone asks "Are you okay?" and you say "Yeah...I'm fine," then give a small smile and silently yell at them to go away and leave you to suffer by yourself? I do that. ALL. THE. TIME. Before I even think about a reply, that's what comes out of my mouth. What I really want to say, but never do is, "No. I'm not okay. I'm dealing with the onset of a panic attack and am feeling extremely scared and helpless. Can you sit with me for a while so I don't feel so alone?" I never say this because I assume that most people would give me a weird look, make up an excuse to leave and then hurry away; or worse, they would say "Uh…okay," then sit down next to me and say all those things we talked about earlier that are more hurtful than helpful. It would become awkward, which would make the anxiety and panic worse. Right?! I want to avoid the whole experience, along with the subsequent pity look that would ensue every time I saw that person thereafter. No, thank you. Been there, done that, and I would like to avoid it at all costs.

That's how I feel, but that's not what I try to practice anymore. The reason I try not to shut down and hide away is that someone else's reaction to you is more about them than it is you. I now have an understanding and can accept when someone doesn't behave or react in the way I would expect an emotionally healthy person to react. I used to take all of that on myself. If someone raised their voice at me, or was condescending or mean in their words or tone, I thought it was because of some mysterious thing I had done to upset them. Not true, or rather, rarely true. I was commiserating just this thing to my therapist during a session about three years ago. She said "You do know, that it's not all about you, right?" I questioned "What?" She explained, by using examples of situations I had told her about, that the other person's behaviors were because of their issues and unhealed traumas, and not about me.

It's not all about me? I'm not the cause of all bad words or behaviors directed to me? What kind of mad sorcery is this?! I was dumbfounded. My whole life, I thought anything negatively directed towards me was my fault. I never let that childhood coping mechanism go once I reached adulthood. It was liberating to finally take off those blinders. To finally see that everyone has issues and that I only had to take responsibility for problems I created or contributed to, and not all of them. This may be a revelation to some of you, as it was for me. I know my therapist tried to get me to understand this in the past, but I never "got it" until then. I believe that we see what we need to, when we're ready to see it. It can't be forced, as we all go at our own pace in our healing expedition.

CHAPTER FOURTEEN

Recognizing Anxiety

Sometimes it's hard to know if you, or someone you know, is dealing with anxiety attacks. The symptoms of anxiety attacks are so varied and vast that it's easy to excuse them away as being unimportant. That may be true if it was one or two symptoms that happened occasionally. If you can identify with a few of the ones listed below, and they happen often, then you may want to reach out to a mental health care professional for evaluation and diagnosis.

Here are a few, certainly not all, common symptoms for anxiety:

- Restlessness
- Feeling disconnected from the world
- Muscle tension
- Rapid heartbeat
- Trouble breathing
- Lack of patience
- Procrastination
- Overthinking
- Avoidance
- Needing reassurance
- Headaches
- Memory Issues
- Insomnia
- Constant worrying
- Being a perfectionist
- Hate making decisions
- Criticizing self-talk

- Catastrophizing
- Cancel plans at the last minute
- Always have an excuse to leave an event early
- Get overstimulated in crowded or busy environments
- Be very particular about their environment and who they will be around
- Difficulty concentrating
- Dizziness
- Irritability
- Fatigue
- Increased startle response
- Believing everyone is judging them
- Being hard on themselves if they perceive they have failed
- Having unreasonably high expectations for themselves, others, and situations
- Being hyper sensitive to touch and sound
- Shakiness in the limbs/weak limbs
- Feeling of impending doom
- Having a tight/nervous (butterflies)/upset or nauseous, stomach
- Feeling spikes in adrenaline repeatedly in a short period of time
- Feel like you can't turn off your brain
- Nervous sweating
- Worrying about future event(s)
- "What if…?" thinking
- Can't relax body or brain
- Worrying and ruminating on past events or conversations
- Over-planning
- Sensitivity to heat and/or hot weather
- Crying and/or difficulty managing emotions
- Intolerance of uncertainty/doesn't like surprises or spontaneity

I can identify with all these symptoms. How many do you recognize in yourself or someone you know? Once you check them off, or highlight them, you may be surprised by the number. Keep in mind also that there are levels of anxiety.

Nightly, I use a weekly calendar notebook to track my physical and mental health. I put notes or symbols for the exercise I did, if I had to use any of the supplements that help with managing anxiety, and what level of anxiety I experienced that day. I tend to use Low, Medium, and High to indicate my anxiety level; but I recently saw a wonderful "Anxiety Chart" that lists anxiety as level 1 through level 9, with the different symptoms typically experienced during each level.[10] I think this chart would be helpful to communicate to others what you're experiencing, especially for children. If you don't think the chart matches what you feel, then you can make your own.

Children

If we, as adults, have a difficult time expressing how we feel during an anxiety attack or panic attack, think about how problematic it is for a child. Children don't have the vocabulary or experience to describe their bodily symptoms. They may just say that their stomach hurts, that they have a headache, or they're scared. If anxiety is "normal" to them, then they may think everyone goes through it, so it's no use saying anything. This is especially true if, when they voice their feelings (mental, emotional, or physical), the adults in their life minimize or disregard what they are saying. It's easy to assume an upset tummy is because of something they ate or a headache is due to dehydration or something else.

From my experience as a child with anxiety, I would rarely even say that something wasn't right, or that I didn't feel good. I didn't want to bother anyone or be embarrassed about my complaints. I didn't know that constant thoughts of impending doom or imaginations of terrible things happening to me

---

10   themighty.com.

or loved ones wasn't healthy or so called normal. Initially, I thought everyone had those kinds of feelings and thoughts. I believed that everyone constantly worried about everything, like I did. It wasn't until I was in elementary and middle school that I realized I was different. That just made me worry more.

I recommend that you pay attention to the things the child doesn't say. Watch their body language for signs of being uncomfortable around groups of people, when they are being pushed out of their comfort zone, when they are criticized, or around people that are aggressive or extroverts. Do they shrink in on themselves by sitting away from others? Do they tense up their shoulders and hunch over their stomach? Do they tap their legs, feet, or fingers to expel excess adrenaline? Do they stick to their safe adult like glue when out in public? Do they choose not to engage with other children, or have a nervous facial tic like I did as a child? Do they have trouble sleeping or getting to sleep because of a mind that won't quiet down? Do they react unreasonably to situation that seem normal to you – such as going to the dentist, meeting new people, going to school, being in social situations? If so, you may want to evaluate the situation and see if they are suffering from more than the usual/normal amount of anxiety we all experience in childhood.

Please do not ignore the signs that a child in your life may be suffering with anxiety or panic attacks. In this current day of having a magnitude of information available at our fingertips, and the stigma of mental illness being addressed, there is no excuse to not get help for a child with these issues. Alternately, do not label or let the child be labeled as being "broken". Be sure and get a diagnosis from a qualified professional and learn how to help the child manage their thoughts and feelings. Do not assume they have an anxiety disorder because if they don't and you told them they did, then you just created a trauma for them that may lead to other issues later in life.

Teenagers may feel the need to try and self-medicate for anxiety with alcohol and drugs or even promiscuity. It's hard to decipher anxiety symptoms in teenagers because so much is changing with them daily. Besides trying to figure out who they are/who they want to be, navigating the social aspects of high school, and the physical changes that happen, it's no wonder that according to the National Institutes of Health, nearly 1 in 3 of all adolescents, ages 13 to 18, will experience an anxiety disorder.

Some of this is attributed to the fact that children and adolescents are being pressured to succeed, the world right now feels scary and threatening, and social media puts an outrageous amount of high expectations on teens to be/look/feel a certain way. That's not even adding in the bullying – physical, verbal, or cyber. Not surprisingly, the statistics indicate the number of teens with anxiety disorders has risen drastically since 2007.[11] Since this correlates with the rise in teenage suicides and attempts, parents need to feel the urgency in being educated about indications that their child is struggling. At the very least, the earlier they can get help, the better chance they have to live a joyful and productive life.

---

11   healthychildren.org

CHAPTER FIFTEEN
The Positive Aspects

A few years ago, a friend asked me that if I could wave a magic wand and never have anxiety again, or if it could erase all the anxiety and panic attacks I've ever had, would I do it. Of course, the obvious answer from most of us would be, "Yes, yes, oh for goodness sakes yes!", but I was intrigued by this question. Once I quieted down the knee jerk reaction of saying, "Yes!", I told her that I wasn't sure. She was surprised by this answer, as was I.

I went home that day and really thought about her question. A few days later, I was writing in my journal and decided to make a list of all the positive aspects and outcomes I've experienced because of my struggles with anxiety and my triumphs over it. Were there any? It seemed like such an odd thing to even ponder, but as I prayed about it first then put pen to paper, I was astounded at what came out.

My list looked something like this:
1. I've learned that I'm full of fortitude and strength.
2. I've learned to confront situations in a healthy way.
3. I've learned to self soothe.
4. I've learned to adapt to uncomfortable situations.
5. I'm organized and driven.
6. I have, and express, empathy for others.
7. I deeply appreciate and am grateful for the love others show me.
8. I have a significantly better and more meaningful relationship with my mother.
9. I can love others as they are, where they are, for who they are – and not judge them based on their actions alone.

10. I have grown closer to, and have developed an unbreakable deeply personal relationship with God.
11. I take better care of myself: physical, mentally, and emotionally.
12. I realize what is most important in life (and it isn't things or money!).
13. If you don't have your health, you have nothing.
14. I enjoy (mostly, ha-ha!) exercising and discovered the bliss of yoga.
15. I'm continuing to grow and learn as a person.
16. I can recognize the struggle of anxiety disorders in others, and can help them through telling my story and experiences.
17. I have high emotional intelligence.
18. I can happily spend time alone – something many people struggle with. (This has come in handy during the COVID-19 pandemic!)
19. And the list goes on...

If you had asked me ten years ago if I was glad that I struggled with anxiety and panic attacks, I probably would have given you a sinister look, laughed in your face, and asked you to leave my presence. My answer would have been an emphatic "NO!" After all the miles I've covered in my healing expedition, I can honestly say that I'm glad I've lived the life I have. Without going through all my experiences and struggles, I wouldn't be writing this book. That would be sad because writing this book has given me the opportunity to help others, and that is the greatest gift I could get out of all I've gone through. I am far from perfect. Now, finally, I am perfectly fine with that.

Our Greatest Fear

Our deepest fear is not that we are inadequate.
Our deepest fear is that we are powerful beyond measure.
It is our light not our darkness that most frightens us.
We ask ourselves, who am I to be brilliant, gorgeous, talented, and fabulous?
Actually, who are you not to be?
You are a child of God.
Your playing small does not serve the world.
There is nothing enlightened about shrinking so that other people will not feel insecure around you.
We are all meant to shines, as children do.
We were born to make manifest the glory of God that is within us.
It's not just in some of us; it's in everyone.
As we let our own light shine, we unconsciously give other people permission to do the same.
As we are liberated from our fear, our presence automatically liberates others.

—Marianne Williamson

HELPFUL SCRIPTURES
(Amplified Bible, Classic Edition - AMPC)

The Lord is my light and my salvation—
Whom shall I fear?
The Lord is the refuge *and* fortress of my life—
Whom shall I dread?
     Psalms 27:1

Keep *and* protect me, O God, for in You I have placed my trust *and* found refuge.
I said to the Lord, "You are my Lord;
I have no good besides You."
     Psalms 16: 1-2

"I love You [fervently and devotedly], O Lord, my strength."
The Lord is my rock, my fortress, and the One who rescues me;
My God, my rock *and* strength in whom I trust *and* take refuge;
My shield, and the horn of my salvation, my high tower—my stronghold.
     Psalms 18:1-2

Turn to me [Lord] and be gracious to me,
For I am alone and afflicted.
The troubles of my heart are multiplied;
Bring me out of my distresses.
Look upon my affliction and my trouble,
And forgive all my sins.
     Psalms 25:16-18

He who dwells in the shelter of the Most High
Will remain secure *and* rest in the shadow of the Almighty [whose power no enemy can withstand].
I will say of the Lord, "He is my refuge and my fortress, My God, in whom I trust [with great confidence, and on whom I rely]!"   *Psalms 91:1-2*

For He will command His angels in regard to you,
To protect *and* defend *and* guard you in all your ways [of obedience and service].
They will lift you up in their hands,
So that you do not [even] strike your foot against a stone.
    Psalms 91:11-12

When I am afraid,
I will put my trust *and* faith in You.
In God, whose word I praise;
In God I have put my trust;
I shall not fear.
What can mere man do to me?
    Psalms 56:3-4

Wait for *and* confidently expect the Lord;
Be strong and let your heart take courage;
Yes, wait for *and* confidently expect the Lord.
    Psalms 27:14

Wait for *and* confidently expect the Lord;
Be strong and let your heart take courage;
Yes, wait for *and* confidently expect the Lord.
    Psalms 27:14

Trust in *and* rely confidently on the Lord with all your heart
And do not rely on your own insight *or* understanding.
In all your ways know *and* acknowledge *and* recognize Him,
And He will make your paths straight *and* smooth [removing obstacles that block your way].
    Proverbs 3:5-6

A calm *and* peaceful *and* tranquil heart is life *and* health to the body,
But passion *and* envy are like rottenness to the bones.
    Proverbs 14:30

All the days of the afflicted are bad,
But a glad heart has a continual feast [regardless of the circumstances].
    Proverbs 15:15

For God did not give us a spirit of timidity *or* cowardice *or* fear, but [He has given us a spirit] of power and of love and of sound judgment *and* personal discipline [abilities that result in a calm, well-balanced mind and self-control].
    2 Timothy 1:7

There is no fear in love [dread does not exist].
But perfect (complete, full-grown) love drives out fear, because fear involves [the expectation of divine] punishment, so the one who is afraid [of God's judgment] is not perfected in love [has not grown into a sufficient understanding of God's love].
    1 John 4:18

We have come to know [by personal observation and experience], and have believed [with deep, consistent faith] the love which God has for us. God is love, and the one who abides in love abides in God, and God abides *continually* in him.
    1 John 4:16

The Lord bless you, and keep you [protect you, sustain you, and guard you];
The Lord make His face shine upon you [with favor],
And be gracious to you [surrounding you with lovingkindness];
The Lord lift up His countenance (face) upon you [with divine approval],
And give you peace [a tranquil heart and life].'
    Numbers 6:24-26

The thief comes only in order to steal and kill and destroy.
I came that they may have life, and have it in abundance [to the full, till it overflows].
John 10:10

May the God of hope fill you with all joy and peace in believing [through the experience of your faith] that by the power of the Holy Spirit you will abound in hope *and* overflow with confidence in His promises.
Romans 15:13

Peace I leave with you;
My [perfect] peace I give to you; not as the world gives do I give to you.
Do not let your heart be troubled, nor let it be afraid.
[Let My perfect peace calm you in every circumstance and give you courage and strength for every challenge.]
John 14:27

Therefore humble yourselves under the mighty hand of God [set aside self-righteous pride], so that He may exalt you [to a place of honor in His service] at the appropriate time, casting all your cares [all your anxieties, all your worries, and all your concerns, once and for all] on Him, for He cares about you [with deepest affection, and watches over you very carefully].
Be sober [well balanced and self-disciplined], be alert *and* cautious at all times.
That enemy of yours, the devil, prowls around like a roaring lion [fiercely hungry], seeking someone to devour.
But resist him, be firm in *your* faith [against his attack—rooted, established, immovable], knowing that the same experiences of suffering are being experienced by your brothers and sisters throughout the world. [You do not suffer alone.]
After you have suffered for a little while, the God of all grace [who imparts His blessing and favor], who called you to His *own* eternal glory in Christ,

will Himself complete, confirm, strengthen, and establish you [making you what you ought to be].
 1 Peter 5:6-10

For with God nothing [is or ever] shall be impossible.
 Luke 1:37

And which of you by worrying can add one hour to his life's span?
So if you are not even able to do a very little thing [such as that], why are you worried about the rest?
 Luke 12:25-26

The Lord your God is in your midst,
A Warrior who saves.
He will rejoice over you with joy;
He will be quiet in His love [making no mention of your past sins],
He will rejoice over you with shouts of joy.
 Zephaniah 3:17

Now faith is the assurance (title deed, confirmation) of things hoped for (divinely guaranteed), and the evidence of things not seen [the conviction of their reality—faith comprehends as fact what cannot be experienced by the physical senses].
 Hebrews 11:1

but He has said to me, "My grace is sufficient for you [My lovingkindness and My mercy are more than enough—always available—regardless of the situation];
for [My] power is being perfected [and is completed and shows itself most effectively] in [your] weakness." Therefore, I will all the more gladly boast in my weaknesses, so that the power of Christ [may completely enfold me and] may dwell in me.
So I am well pleased with weaknesses, with insults, with distresses, with persecutions, and with difficulties, for the sake of Christ;

for when I am weak [in human strength], then I am strong [truly able, truly powerful, truly drawing from God's strength].
    2 Corinthians 12:9-10

For though we walk in the flesh [as mortal men], we are not carrying on our [spiritual] warfare according to the flesh *and* using the weapons of man.
The weapons of our warfare are not physical [weapons of flesh and blood].
Our weapons are divinely powerful for the destruction of fortresses.
We are destroying sophisticated arguments and every exalted *and* proud thing that sets itself up against the [true] knowledge of God, and *we are* taking every thought *and* purpose captive to the obedience of Christ,
    2 Corinthians 10:3-5

"Come to Me, all who are weary and heavily burdened [by religious rituals that provide no peace], and I will give you rest [refreshing your souls with salvation].
Take My yoke upon you and learn from Me [following Me as My disciple], for I am gentle and humble in heart, and you will find rest (renewal, blessed quiet) for your souls.
For My yoke is easy [to bear] and My burden is light."
    Matthew 11:28-30

When you pass through the waters, I will be with you;
And through the rivers, they will not overwhelm you.
When you walk through fire, you will not be scorched,
Nor will the flame burn you.
    Isaiah 43:2

You will keep in perfect *and* constant peace *the one* whose mind is steadfast [that is, committed and focused on You—in both inclination and character],

Because he trusts *and* takes refuge in You [with hope and confident expectation].
Trust [confidently] in the Lord forever [He is your fortress, your shield, your banner],
    Isaiah 26:3-4

Do not fear [anything], for I am with you;
Do not be afraid, for I am your God.
I will strengthen you, be assured I will help you;
I will certainly take hold of you with My righteous right hand [a hand of justice, of power, of victory, of salvation].
    Isaiah 41:10

Do not be anxious *or* worried about anything, but in everything [every circumstance and situation] by prayer and petition with thanksgiving, continue to make your [specific] requests known to God.
And the peace of God [that peace which reassures the heart, that peace] which transcends all understanding, [that peace which] stands guard over your hearts and your minds in Christ Jesus [is yours].
    Philippians 4:6-7

I can do all things [which He has called me to do] through Him who strengthens *and* empowers me [to fulfill His purpose—I am self-sufficient in Christ's sufficiency; I am ready for anything and equal to anything through Him who infuses me with inner strength and confident peace.]
    Philippians 4:13

Have I not commanded you?
Be strong and courageous! Do not be terrified or dismayed (intimidated), for the Lord your God is with you wherever you go.
    Joshua 1:9

'For I know the plans *and* thoughts that I have for you,' says the Lord, 'plans for peace *and* well-being and not for disaster, to give you a future and a hope.'
Jeremiah 29:11

Set your mind *and* keep focused *habitually* on the things above [the heavenly things], not on things that are on the earth [which have only temporal value].
Colossians 3:2

The Light shines on in the darkness, and the darkness did not understand it *or* overpower it *or* appropriate it *or* absorb it [and is unreceptive to it].
John 1:5

In conclusion, be strong in the Lord [draw your strength from Him and be empowered through your union with Him] and in the power of His [boundless] might.
Put on the full armor of God [for His precepts are like the splendid armor of a heavily-armed soldier], so that you may be able to [successfully] stand up against all the schemes and the strategies and the deceits of the devil.
For our struggle is not against flesh and blood [contending only with physical opponents], but against the rulers, against the powers, against the world forces of this [present] darkness, against the spiritual forces of wickedness in the heavenly (supernatural) places.
Therefore, put on the complete armor of God, so that you will be able to [successfully] resist and stand your ground in the evil day [of danger], and having done everything [that the crisis demands], to stand firm [in your place, fully prepared, immovable, victorious].
So stand firm and hold your ground, having tightened the wide band of truth (personal integrity, moral courage) around your waist and having put on the breastplate of righteousness (an upright heart), and having strapped on your feet the gospel of

peace in preparation [to face the enemy with firm-footed stability and the readiness produced by the good news].
Above all, lift up the [protective] shield of faith with which you can extinguish all the flaming arrows of the evil one.
And take the helmet of salvation, and the sword of the Spirit, which is the Word of God.
With all prayer and petition pray [with specific requests] at all times [on every occasion and in every season] in the Spirit, and with this in view, stay alert with all perseverance and petition [interceding in prayer] for all God's people.
Ephesians 6:10-18

For additional information and resources, visit
www.KristinaHorton.com

Follow the author on social media at:
@kh_author (Instagram)
Kristina Horton (Facebook)
@HortonKris (Twitter)

Kristina Horton is a licensed professional land surveyor, currently working in the public sector. Being a native of the Pacific Northwest; she and her husband – together since high school - settled into their hometown after a decade in Alaska. She rarely passes up a chance to pet a dog, or share a laugh. She recently fell in love with traveling to historical sites in Ireland and the UK, with of course a few stops at local pubs along the way, for a pint of Guinness.

Far From Perfect, released in early 2021, is her debut book. It's the story of her journey living with anxiety and panic disorders since childhood, and the sharing of the wisdom and knowledge she picked up along the way.

www.ingramcontent.com/pod-product-compliance
Lightning Source LLC
Chambersburg PA
CBHW020902080526
44589CB00011B/403